To Yong-bom, Ki-won, Ch'ol-su, Chae-hon, Ch'un-sik,
Tak, Chin-ho, and Wun-hak, Eun-do, Dong-oh, and Doo-young for their
friendship

Contents

Foreword

A Legal History of Asian Americans, 1790–1990 presents a poignant
account of the history of racial intolerance that has permeated our legal
system since its inception. The sacrifices of hundreds of courageous Asian
Americans catalogued in this volume, affirm the work of those who continue to strive toward creating a system based upon principles of dignity,
equality, and compassion. The names of individuals who were brave
enough to step into the legal arena represent only a fraction of the countless numbers of sojourners who risked all they had in search of a place
where justice and freedom could be realized.

We are often disabled in confronting the reality of institutional racism
because its defining characteristics are often intangible, nonquantifiable,
and impalpable. This book overcomes that disability—partly because of
circumstance, partly because of *perspective.* The circumstance to which I
refer is the passage of time and the inevitable making of a historical
record. Sadly, that record is replete with examples of intellectual dishonesty, racial bigotry, cultural chauvinism, and greed. The perspective,
which is so valuable to our understanding and acceptance of the truth
about the evolution of our system of justice, comes from a first-generation
Korean American who has chosen to dedicate his skills to the writing of a
piece of *American* history. Professor Hyung-chan (Robert) Kim has presented a review and analysis of the experiences of Asian Americans who,
as newcomers, were destined to remain invisible, voiceless, and exploited
for at least three generations. The present volume recovers those lost
chapters in the history of America—accounts of the hopeful who continued, at all cost, to pursue the American dream.

A Legal History of Asian Americans also represents the challenge that
must be met by future generations of legal scholars, jurists, and prac-
titioners. Our generation undoubtedly is the beneficiary of invaluable

insights gained through the experience of those who have gone before us. Undaunted challengers such as Fong Yue Ting, Wong Quan, and Lee Joe lost all hope when they were rudely awakened to the fact that due process under the law was reserved for whites only. The courage of individuals such as Kaoru Yamataya revealed the callousness of our social policies through the response to her petition (documented only as "the Japanese Immigrant Case") in which her dreams were crushed because of "her misfortune" that she could not speak English well enough to refute the words of an immigrant official who deemed her unfit for entry into America. The fact that "racial undesirability" was the real basis for the alien land laws that prohibited Asian Americans to gain ownership of real property is no longer subject to serious debate. But more disturbing and troublesome is knowing how many times lawyers, government officials, and judges acted in complicity with such odious interpretations of the law.

In meeting the challenges ahead, advocates must recognize that achieving the ends of justice will be limited only by the bounds of one's creativity and ability to craft strategies inclusive of the experiences of a growing and diverse America. Members of the judiciary must appreciate the pivotal role they play in shaping the consciousness of the American people through their decisions in cases that call for a balance of legal, equitable, and ethical considerations. Legal scholars have the unenviable responsibility of expanding the dialogue and analyses to ensure that the hopes, dreams, and visions of all Americans stay alive.

We face a time in which social, political, and economic conditions pit marginal groups against one another, with disastrous consequences. We face a future in which cultural and ethnic diversity is inevitable and is, in fact, reality in most large urban centers across the nation. We face a world in which hope still rests upon the notion of a dream still to be found in America. Our legal system remains one of the principal arenas from which society expects to receive guidance, reason, and justice.

It is with faith in the strength of the human spirit, with hope in the voice of visionaries, and with compassion in the hearts of women and men who have gained some measure of understanding in how the law can create and destroy that we will move forward toward that dream that has eluded us for so long.

Angela Oh
Lawyer and Community Activist
Los Angeles, California
October 1993

Preface

It has been almost a quarter of a century since I joined the faculty of the now defunct College of Ethnic Studies, Western Washington University, to teach in the field of Asian American Studies. Ever since I began to teach this introductory course, the Asian American Experience, in 1971, I have been interested in the role of law in creating, maintaining, and perpetuating institutional racism in America. This interest has motivated me to investigate major decisions the Supreme Court of the United States has made over the last 150 years on the litigations brought by persons of Asian ancestry. My research resulted in publication of a book, *Asian Americans and the Supreme Court,* in 1992, by Greenwood Press. During the last three years, I have been examining the role of various laws Congress has passed between 1790 and 1990 to establish federal policies for immigration and naturalization. Most of them have adversely affected persons of Asian ancestry during the last 200 years. My study, when it is completed, will be published as a book, *Asian Americans and Congress,* by Greenwood Press. The present volume is the fruit of my labor to combine the most salient aspects of the two studies into a useful textbook for an undergraduate course in Asian American Studies. I sincerely hope that students and scholars in the field will find it useful.

Results of historical research, no matter how carefully they were obtained through a scientific method of investigation, tend to leave in the mind of the researcher a lingering doubt about their efficacy for providing the reader with accurate perspectives on the subject investigated. I am no exception to this self-doubt. In spite of my doubt, however, I am now inclined to extrapolate from my studies the following three conclusions. First, there has been a definite pattern of institutional discrimination practiced by the American judicial system against the Asian immigrant on the basis of her race. This practice of institutional racism was particularly pronounced in the decisions made by the courts in the areas of exclusion, expulsion, deportation, citizenship, and property and civil rights. Second, immigration and naturalization laws passed by Congress during the period under study have been discriminatory against the Asian immigrant on the basis of his race. This institutional racism practiced by Congress was inseparably related to the question of who should be admitted into the membership of the community called America. Of course, the answer was that only whites could become members of the community. Both politicians and the public entertained only this myopic concept of community membership at the beginning of this nation. This narrowly drawn concept had excluded all racial minorities from the community membership. Third, racism, be it personal or institutional, as it was practiced during the period under study, was grounded in the human psyche. Whether it was practiced by a judge, a member of Congress, a labor leader, or a sand-lot politician, they were all victimized by the fear of the unknown and unfamiliar. It took a courageous person to challenge his or her own culture's assumptions on race and transcend or fight against them. I hope there are more courageous people today than there have been in any period of our history. We need them because our society will be diversified increasingly. Diversity requires tolerance, as democracy does. We shall have both.

I would be remiss if I failed to acknowledge my debt to the following individuals for their support for this book: Ms. Michelle Slyke and Mrs. Arlene Belzer for their editorial assistance, Ms. Peggy Reynolds and Mrs. Anne Spring for their willingness to assist me with the computer and typing, and Professor Robert Lopresti for his willingness to go out of his way to provide me with the necessary government documents. My friend and colleague, Professor Philip Vander Velde, was willing to tolerate my absent-mindedness while I was working on this book. I am grateful to him for that. As usual, my wife, Kwang-oak, and my sons, Jerome and Justin, suffered my absence, from their presence, as I suffered from the pressure of research and writing. I thank them for that.

A LEGAL HISTORY OF
ASIAN AMERICANS,
1790–1990

—1—

Introduction

People of different racial and ethnic origins have lived in America ever since its very beginning, and they have left rich stories of their lives and accomplishments. History in America has been, however, the story of victors, not of victims. Stories told to Americans have been written by academic and establishment historians who have been blinded by their cultural conditioning to see what has been considered important by the dominant culture. Consequently, with the exception of the unusually perceptive and the avant-garde in their profession, historians have ignored minority people and their stories. Rich stories of Asian immigrants and their descendants in America have also been ignored, if not belittled. Thus, John King Fairbank bemoaned his colleagues' inability or unwillingness to tell the diverse experiences of Asian Americans when he characterized American academic historians as being parochial, myopic, and ahistorical. He argued that people in the profession have ignored the impact East Asia had on the internal development in the United States. He charged that when China, in particular, and East Asia, in general, were discussed among the circle of American professional historians, they were often viewed as being unique and different.[1] Although there might have been a few exceptions to his general charge, he is basically correct in his claim that East Asian contributions to American development, particularly to the development of the Pacific region, have been greatly ignored. This was particularly true within the context of trans-Pacific migration.

The migration of people from Asia to the United States is an important part of the history of people from around the world who have come to America to make it what it is today, but the trans-Pacific migration has been greatly ignored or neglected by American historians, who have treated the topic as if it had never existed or had never mattered. They have continuously treated the trans-Atlantic migration as if it were the only movement of people from one continent to another and as if it were the only migration that mattered in American history. When historians discussed the trans-Pacific migration, it was mentioned only as a footnote to strengthen their viewpoints or to distort its significance. Thus, Hubert Howe Bancroft stated, "We want the Asiatic for our low-grade work, and when it is finished, we want them to go home."[2] To him, Asians were fit to work for America, but they were not fit to live here. Frederick Jackson Turner, famous for his frontier hypothesis,[3] was successful in linking the spread of European institutions in Colonial America first, and subsequently in frontier America with the trans-Atlantic migration. But he was unable or unwilling to see the American West as being influenced by men, ideas, and institutions from East Asia in particular, and Asia in general, through the trans-Pacific migration.

EARLIER STUDIES ON ASIAN IMMIGRATION

Even after the "scientific studies" on migration came into vogue as a result of publication of Arthur M. Schlesinger's article, "The Significance of Immigration in American History,"[4] in 1921, professional historians continued to relate the development of American institutions to the trans-Atlantic migration, and the trans-Pacific migration was continuously ignored. The trans-Pacific migration was treated by people who had political or economic axes to grind in arguing either for or against exclusion or inclusion, but no serious scholarly works made their way into print. It was only after the beginning of the twentieth century when a few scholars began to pay attention to the general topic of trans-Pacific migration. These works, including Mary Roberts Coolidge's *Chinese Immigration*,[5] Bruno Lasker's *Filipino Immigration to the Continental U.S. and Hawaii*,[6] and Yamato Ichihashi's *Japanese in the United States*,[7] were, however, limited to the then prevailing theoretical perspective that was dominated by concerns with assimilation.

Particularly, the California thesis presented by Coolidge in her work deserves mentioning because it influenced subsequent scholarly works. According to Coolidge, anti-Chinese sentiment was confined to California, where labor leaders of Irish descent stirred up high emotion among Irish and other white ethnic workers, who perceived the Chinese as being unfair competitors. Her work was followed by *The Anti-Chinese Movement in California*,[8] by Elmer Sandmeyer, who argued in his book for the idea that Californians wanted to solve the "Chinese problem" by local means, but they had to put political pressure on Congress to pass the Chinese Exclusion Act of 1882, as the U.S. Supreme Court had consistently ruled California's anti-Chinese laws unconstitutional. This thesis was later challenged by Stuart Miller, author of *The Unwelcome Immigrant: The American Image of the Chinese, 1785–1882,*[9] in which Miller repudiated the California thesis. Miller stated that anti-Chinese sentiment was not confined to California, but that people in New England as well as in other parts of the country harbored deep-seated anti-Chinese feelings, and that the Chinese Exclusion Act of 1882 resulted from the generally diffused negative stereotypes and prejudices against the Chinese.

Ichihashi and Lasker came under the influence of Robert E. Park, who believed that immigrants, including Asians, will go through race relation cycles[10] and will be ultimately assimilated into American society. The former was concerned with assimilation of Japanese, while the latter investigated the extent to which Filipinos in Hawaii were acculturated into the local culture. Many of the scholarly studies that followed them examined various aspects of Asian American assimilation into American society. Represented among them were Rose Hum Lee's *The Chinese in the United States of America,*[11] Betty Lee Sung's *The Story of the Chinese in America,*[12] and Harry Kitano's *Japanese Americans: The Evolution of a Subculture.*[13] Besides the race relations cycle hypothesis, which was in vogue for many years in American studies on migration, Robert E. Park was responsible for the concept of marginal man.[14] According to Park, a civilization may advance as a result of the interaction of two cultures, but the individual undergoing cultural contact and conflict may go through rather dislocating experiences. Such a person, according to Park, is "condemned to live in two societies and in two not merely different, but antagonistic cultures."[15]

The concept of marginal man was further developed by Everett V. Stonequist[16] and was later applied to studies on Asian American identity and personality, although the concept was somewhat altered in the 1960s. Scholars who investigated changing characteristics of personality of Asians in America, particularly those of second-generation Asian Americans, were William Carlson Smith, Trinidad A. Rojo, Emory S. Bogardus, K. K. Louis, and George De Vos. Even some of the post-1960 literature on Asian American identity dealt with cultural conflict and its impact on personality development among Asian Americans. Representative among these scholars are Stanley Sue and Derald Sue, both of whom attempted to develop a typology of personality of Asian Americans in 1971. In their seminal work, "Chinese American Personality and Mental Health,"[17] they argued for the idea that a new Asian American personality type may emerge as a result of cultural contact and conflict between traditional Asian cultures and the white Anglo-Saxon middle-class culture. This person is different from the marginal man Robert Park hypothesized, in that she will have Asian American identity. The Sue brothers have not, however, articulated what personality traits this Asian American would have as the cultural and psychological content of his or her Asian American identity.

TWO-CATEGORY SYSTEM

While scholarly discourse on the proper method of studying minority experiences in America continued into the 1960s, three new theoretical perspectives emerged to challenge the assimilationist and pluralist interpretations of the trans-Pacific migration. They charged that assimilation and cultural pluralism are not adequate in explaining the power conflict that exits between minority groups and the dominant group in America. Arguing that racial minorities in America constitute internal colonies, a number of scholars began to focus their attention on both historical and sociological geneses of internal colonialism. They often applied the conventional Marxist class analysis to their works.[18] Lucie Cheng and Tamayo Lott are representative scholars among them. Another major theoretical perspective that has begun to receive increasing attention from scholars who study the Asian American experience is the "middleman minority hypothesis."[19] Edna Bonacich, who is mainly responsible for this perspective, believes that Asian Americans occupy an intermediate position between other racial minority groups and whites in America, where they face hostility and discrimination because of their community's solidarity. This group solidarity, however, enables them to create and develop their own economic niche, even in a hostile environment. Finally, the last perspective worthy of our attention is the idea of a two-category system.[20] Although there are different two-category systems developed by a number of scholars, they all seem to argue for the idea that there are superordinate and subordinate groups in American society, as whites who are superordinate wield power over the racial minorities who are subordinate.

Harry Kitano and Roger Daniels argue in their book, *American Racism*,[21] that there is a pervasive racist ideology in America that says all whites are superior to all nonwhites. This boundary of superiority-inferiority is sharply drawn, strictly in terms of color, and this boundary system is maintained and perpetuated by means of stereotypes that serve as the foundation for prejudice of whites against nonwhites. They further argue that when prejudice does not function well as a deterrent against nonwhites' intrusion into the boundary system, a harsher measure might be resorted to by the dominant group. Thus, prejudice may evolve into discrimination, and if the latter does not work well to keep nonwhites in their place, then it may lead to segregation. If these three ordinary measures do not prevent nonwhites from crossing over the boundary, then extraordinary measures may be used against them: apartheid, expulsion, and genocide, in the order of severity of measures to be taken against nonwhites.

Not too dissimilar from the two-category system is the notion that the boundary system that separates whites from nonwhites in America and elsewhere in the world often results from the desire for power to control limited social goods and services for unequal distribution. The dominant group has developed a rationale for including people of their kind and excluding people of different kinds. Donald Baker, who is responsible for this two-category system of inclusion versus exclusion, believes that the system is based on the somatic and cultural norms held by whites in America.[22]

Finally, Benjamin Ringer argues in his book, *"We the People" and Others*,[23] that America developed a two-category system of "People's Domain" and "Plural Domain" even as European immigrants began to settle in the Eastern seaboard region, and the Founding Fathers legalized this separation between whites and nonwhites in the form of the original Constitution. Ringer believes that nonwhites were excluded from the People's Domain, as they were considered unworthy of membership in the American community. His argument has empirical cogency supported by a long history of congressional legislative actions since 1790. Included among them is the Uniform Standard for Naturalization that Congress passed in 1790 that restricted American citizenship to only "a free white person." This restriction lasted until 1952 for the majority of Asian immigrants in America.

OTHER MODELS

All these theoretical models, with the exception of the internal colonial, attempted to explain what has happened to Asian immigrants upon their arrival in America. They do not account for why Asians decided to immigrate to the United States and to other parts of the world. The internal colonial perspective challenges the conventional scholarly method of studying immigration. For a long time scholars interested in international migration of people as a research topic examined the so-called push and pull factors that existed in sending and receiving countries, respectively. According to the push-pull model, there must have existed, in their own country, powerful natural, sociocultural, and politico-economic forces working together or separately to push people out of their native land. Equally important for consideration are forces of major magnitude that pulled foreign people to the receiving countries for a variety of reasons. This push-pull model is now being challenged by a number of scholars who believe that it is inadequate in accounting for the presence of a worldwide system of exploitation of cheap labor provided by poor people for the development of a capitalist system of economy. This perspective centering on internal-international colonialism claims that colonialistic and imperialistic forces unleashed by major Western powers, including the United States, generated both in sending and receiving countries socioeconomic conditions for mass emigration of Asian people, who sold their labor willingly or unwillingly.

This internal-international colonial model, loaded heavily with a Marxist method of class analysis, was applied to the study of the nineteenth-century Asian labor emigration to the United States by Lucie Cheng and Edna Bonacich in their edited work, *Labor Immigration under Capitalism.*[24] This model has provided research scholars with a new theoretical framework by which they can reinterpret the Asian American experience. In spite of the contributions the model has made, it also has left scholars of a different theoretical persuasion with a number of serious questions that are yet to be answered. For instance, how does one go about explaining the immigration of the Japanese to Hawaii in 1868? This first group of Japanese laborers who came to Hawaii to work on its sugar plantations was recruited by Eugene Van Reed. According to a study done on this particular group by Masaji Marumoto, this group, known as *Gan-nen-mono,*[25] was made of people with diverse socioeconomic backgrounds. Some of them were former samurais, while others were people with more education than normally found among the Japanese at that time. It would be difficult to state that they were victims of the Western capitalist exploitation, which motivated them to leave their country.

More important, there is the question of when Japan came under the influence of a capitalist system of exploitation. It was only in 1854, when Japan concluded a treaty with the United States to open the Port of Shimoda to American ships for securing wood, water, coal, and other provisions. It is highly questionable if a capitalist exploitation system had enough time to be deeply rooted in the Japanese economy and to uproot this particular group of people who decided to come to Hawaii. In a study of the emigration of Japanese workers between 1885 and 1894, when a total of 29,069 Japanese arrived in Hawaii, Alan Moriyama suggested that the recruiting practices used in Japan, by agents representing the labor interest of the Hawaiian Sugar Planters Association, had as much to do with Japanese workers' decision to emigrate as factors such as land tax and conscription laws.[26] Again, the capitalist exploitation model is unable to explain why a small group of Japanese political exiles came to Golden Hill, California, in 1869 and established the Wakamatsu Silk and Tea Colony.

The Korean immigration to Hawaii that lasted for a few years, between

1902 and 1905, brought approximately 8,000 laborers, who were from diverse socioeconomic backgrounds. Considering that the literacy rate among this group of people was higher than that of their countrymen in Korea, all of them were not poverty-stricken peasants. In fact, there were former soldiers, people of the literati class, and former government officials among these immigrants.[27] Korea was forced to establish diplomatic relations with Japan in 1876. In 1882 a treaty of commerce was concluded between the United States and Korea. However, it is highly questionable if a capitalism of Western or Japanese brand had enough time to be firmly established in the Korean economy to be used as a means of exploitation of poor Korean peasantry. To date, there is no clear evidence to suggest that Koreans who decided to immigrate to Hawaii did so only because they had become victims of capitalist exploitation. Even if an exploitative capitalism was established to force them out of their country, there is still the question of why they, and not others, decided to leave their country. These are empirical facts that do not neatly fall within the theoretical framework of the internal-international capitalist exploitation model.

It may be argued that the push-pull and the internal-international capitalist exploitation models are mutually complementary in that the latter attempts to account for global political and economic forces within the world capitalist system that exploited cheap labor for capitalist economic growth, whereas the former does explain local conditions under which particular groups of people decided to emigrate from Asia to North America. Some of these local conditions might have been created by a capitalist system of exploitation. It is assumed here that all conditions that contributed to the emigration of people from Asia to North America cannot be explained by a theory that focuses only on one single factor. To do so is to manipulate historical facts to fit them into a particular theory.

In the present volume, a legal history of Asian Americans is presented for the following purposes. It is intended, first, to examine both legislative and political goals of various immigration laws passed by Congress within the context of the evolutionary changes in American social and economic institutions. In view of the fact that the Supreme Court of the United States handed down some major decisions that had an impact on the administrative as well as legislative actions concerning Asian Americans' rights, the interplay and counterplay among the three branches of the U.S. government will also be examined. Furthermore, this legal history seeks to delve into the agonizing question of why Congress has been bent so long on passing legislation after legislation to discriminate against Asian immigration. For this inquiry, two major concepts that have served as principal rationale for congressional legislative actions will be carefully examined within the general theoretical perspective of the two-category system of superiority versus inferiority, inclusion versus exclusion, and people's domain versus plural domain. One is the concept of quality of people to be allowed to immigrate to America, and the other is that of quantity of people to be admitted into the country.[28] Subsumed under the first concept is a wide range of ideas concerning the character of people worthy of entry into America, although the desirable character of the immigrant shifted now and then to accommodate the political climate of the time. In view of the evolutionary development of ideas and attitudes in America, which were either against or for immigration, the present study will examine how they influenced debates on Asian immigration and how they might have been integrated into legislative actions taken by Congress.

Early debates on immigration during Colonial America centered around the concept of quality of the immigrant. Most colonies passed legislation to keep out the morally undesirable. These debates continued to persist into Revolutionary America and finally found their way into legislation; first, regulating naturalization, and later excluding undesirable aliens. When it was found that immigration to America could not be effectively regulated and controlled by laws addressing only the desirable character of the immigrant, Congress decided to control immigration through a quota system by which predetermined numbers were inequitably assigned to countries in favor of Western Europeans. Thus, Congress used a double-edged sword of quality and quantity to carve out American immigration policies that were, for all practical purposes and intent, against Asian immigration. This policy of discrimination continues today.

PERIODIZATION

In studying the history of immigration in general, and of immigration policies of Congress in particular, scholars seem to agree on five or six distinctive periods. But the present study divides the history of immigration in America into seven periods: (1) the colonial period (1609–1775), during which most immigrants in America came from the British Isles with little legal problem, as colonies did not have effective control over them, although there were some restrictive laws and heated debates on who should be admitted; (2) the American Revolutionary period (1776–1840), when European immigration was slowed due to war at home and in Europe, and when antiforeign feelings ran high even among the Founding Fathers; (3) the "old" immigration period (1841–1882), during which local governments exercised their autonomy in recruiting and bringing to their states large numbers of people from the British Isles, Germany, and Scandinavia. (However, there developed an increasing emphasis on the federal government's role in regulating and controlling immigration. In 1876, the

Supreme Court ruled that Congress had the sole power to regulate immigration. During this period the Chinese also immigrated to America without encountering many legal problems.); (4) the regulation period (1882–1920), when the Chinese were excluded from the class of people allowed to immigrate to America, and when large numbers of people from Central, Eastern, and Southern European countries were admitted; (5) the restriction and exclusion period (1921–1952), when a quota system was established to restrict the number of immigrants from Central, Eastern, and Southern European countries to America, and when all Asians were excluded from the class of people admissible to America due to their ineligibility for U.S. citizenship; (6) the partial liberalization period (1952–1965), when countries in Asia were given the same quota assignment as was given to nations in Central, Eastern, and Southern Europe, and when Asian immigrant residents were allowed to be naturalized; and (7) the liberalized policy period (1965–present), when the quota immigration policy was repealed to allow immigrants from the Third World countries, who now outnumber those from Europe.

SUMMARY

This book is written for a number of purposes. Chapter 1 focuses on earlier studies on American immigration in order to acquaint the reader with basic theoretical perspectives on immigration study. Furthermore, the reader is provided with a number of theoretical models to use in studying and analyzing the Asian American experience. Particularly, a number of two-category systems are explained in detail to help the reader see how the Asian American experience may be interpreted within the context of superiority versus inferiority, inclusion versus exclusion, and people's domain versus plural domain. It is claimed that Congress has attempted to bring immigration under its control by using two criteria. One is the quality of people, and the other is the quantity of people. These criteria have been used to keep out people who were considered undesirable.

Chapter 2 covers the period between 1609 and 1775. The reader is provided with a historical background of how immigration started from the English Isles to the North American colonies and of how different colonies were subsequently peopled by both English and non-English European immigrants. What is more important for the reader to understand is English colonists' perceptions and attitudes toward black slaves, American Indians, and non-English European immigrants, for out of these came both debates on the desirability of certain groups of immigrants and restrictive policies during Colonial America. What becomes clear through examination of the colonial immigration practice and policies is that there developed early in American history strong sentiments against people of color, of lower social class, of different religion, and of non-English origin.

In Chapter 3, which covers the period from 1776 to 1840, it is argued that the Founding Fathers harbored a strong resentment against foreigners, and their antiforeign attitudes became the foundation for the legislative action taken to confer U.S. citizenship. The Constitution, which specifies varying numbers of years of residence required of political candidates for public office, speaks partially for this antiforeign sentiment. A dual system that separates citizens from noncitizens was established by law during this period of American history. More important for the purpose of this book, it is claimed that the antiforeignism of Americans toward non-English Europeans was now directed against the Chinese, who were considered inferior to Americans in almost every aspect of their civilization. Given this ethnocentric attitude, the hostile federal legislations that followed were no big surprise. What is surprising is that they came as late as 1882. Had the Chinese immigrated to North America in large numbers, earlier and particularly to the eastern states in American history, Congress would have passed anti-Chinese immigration laws much sooner.

In Chapter 4, which deals with the period between 1841 and 1882, information is presented to show how the federal immigration policies have evolved through a number of judicial actions taken by the Supreme Court before the passage of the Immigration Act of August 3, 1882. Furthermore, the reader is provided with a historical background relating to political pressure that existed both inside and outside Congress, which passed the Chinese Exclusion Act of 1882. Included in this brief history are legislative measures taken against the Chinese by the California state legislature, in addition to local and municipal actions against Chinese residents and a number of judicial decisions by both federal and state courts.

Chapter 5 spans the period between 1882 and 1920, during which time major legislative and judicial events took place. It was during this period that Congress passed a number of laws to restrict and to stop the trans-Pacific immigration to America. Congress passed two major immigration laws either restricting or eliminating the trans-Pacific immigration before the passage of the Nationality Origins Act of 1924. It is important to analyze circumstances that existed both inside and outside Congress that led it to put a *coup de grace* to Asian immigration to America. Congress formulated its immigration legislation to restrict the number of people to be admitted for the first time in American history. It was also during this period that many Supreme Court decisions were made to rule on the constitutionality of immigration laws, including the Chinese Exclusion Act of 1882.

Chapter 6 examines legislative and judicial actions taken against Asian

Americans between 1921 and 1952. During this period a number of Supreme Court cases were decided against resident aliens of Asian ancestry, denying them the right to become naturalized citizens. It was also during this period that persons of Japanese ancestry, regardless of their citizenship status, were incarcerated due to the Pacific War. In 1952 Congress passed a law allowing a limited number of Asians to immigrate to America. It also gave resident aliens of Asian ancestry the right to be naturalized.

Chapter 7 deals with the period between 1952 and 1965, during which time major national and international changes occurred to compel America to overhaul its immigration policies. The two wars America fought against Asian Communist countries had a critical impact on the composition of people immigrating to America. The passage of the Immigration and Naturalization Act of 1965 finally put an end to the unrealistic dream of keeping America white.

Chapter 8 spans the period between 1965 and the present. Three major immigration laws were passed by Congress during this period. The Immigration Act of 1965 enabled large numbers of Asians to come to America as it did away with restrictions based on national origin. But it has also created some major problems among Asian Americans. A critical problem that needs to be addressed immediately is what to do with a large backlog of petitions that have not been approved. The other two immigration laws have begun to affect Asian immigration adversely. Although all the facts are not in yet, it is reasonable to conclude, with what evidence we have, that the Immigration Reform Law of 1986 has not been working effectively in curbing large numbers of undocumented Asians, particularly Chinese aliens, being smuggled into America. The Immigration Act of 1990 is discriminatory against Asian immigration. Since the Supreme Court handed down major decisions on Asian American rights with regard to their language, education, and employment, the reader is provided with analyses of these cases.

NOTES

1. John King Fairbank, "America and China: The Mid-Nineteenth Century," in *American-East Asian Relations: A Survey,* Ernest R. May and James C. Thomson, Jr. (eds.) (Cambridge, Mass.: Harvard University Press, 1972), pp. 19–23.

2. Hubert Howe Bancroft, *Retrospection, Political and Personal* (New York: The Bancroft Company, 1912), p. 357.

3. John Higham, *Strangers in the Land: Patterns of American Nativism* (New York: Atheneum Press, 1965), p. 22.

4. Arthur M. Schlesinger, "The Significance of Immigration in American History," *American Journal of Sociology,* 27 (July 1921), pp. 71–85.

5. Mary Roberts Coolidge, *Chinese Immigration* (New York: Henry Holt and Company, 1909).

6. Bruno Lasker, *Filipino Immigration to the Continental U.S. and Hawaii* (Chicago: University of Chicago Press, 1931).

7. Yamato Ichihashi, *Japanese in the United States* (Stanford, Calif.: Stanford University Press, 1932).

8. Elmer Clarence Sandmeyer, *The Anti-Chinese Movement in California* (Urbana: University of Illinois Press, 1939).

9. Stuart C. Miller, *The Unwelcome Immigrant: The American Image of the Chinese, 1785–1882* (Berkeley: University of California Press, 1969).

10. R. E. Park, "Our Racial Frontier on the Pacific," *Survey Graphic,* 9 (May 1926), p. 196.

11. Rose Hum Lee, *The Chinese in the United States of America* (Hong Kong: Hong Kong University Press, 1960).

12. Betty Lee Sung, *The Story of the Chinese in America* (New York: Collier Books, 1967).

13. Harry H. L. Kitano, *Japanese Americans: The Evolution of a Subculture* (Englewood Cliffs, N.J.: Prentice Hall, 1969).

14. R. E. Park, "Human Migration and the Marginal Man," *American Journal of Sociology,* 33 (May 1928), pp. 881–93.

15. Ibid.

16. Everett V. Stonequist, *The Marginal Man* (New York: Charles Scribner's Sons, 1937).

17. Stanley Sue and Derald W. Sue, "Chinese American Personality and Mental Health," *Amerasia Journal,* 1 (February 1972), pp. 60–65.

18. Lucie Cheng and Edna Bonacich, *Labor Immigration under Capitalism: Asian Workers in the United States before World War II* (Berkeley: University of California Press, 1984).

19. Edna Bonacich, "A Theory of Middleman Minorities," *American Sociological Review,* 38 (October 1973), pp. 583–94. Also see her 1972 article, "A Theory of Ethnic Antagonism," *American Sociological Review,* 37 (October 1972), pp. 547–59.

20. This term (two-category system) was used by Lloyd Warner in his 1953 work, *American Life: Dream and Reality* (Chicago: University of Chicago Press, 1953), p. 69.

21. Harry H. L. Kitano and Roger Daniels, *American Racism: Exploration of the Nature of Prejudice* (Englewood Cliffs, N.J.: Prentice Hall, 1970).

22. Donald G. Baker, "Identity, Power and Psychological Needs: White Responses to Non-Whites," *The Journal of Ethnic Studies,* 1 (Winter 1973), pp. 16–44.

23. Benjamin B. Ringer, *"We the People" and Others: Duality and America's Treatment of its Racial Minorities* (New York: Tavistock Publications, 1983).

24. Cheng and Bonacich, *Labor Immigration under Capitalism.*

25. Masaji Marumoto, "First Year Immigrants to Hawaii and Eugene Van Reed," in *East Across the Pacific,* Hilary Conroy and T. Scott Miyakawa (eds.) (Santa Barbara, Calif.: ABC Clio Press, 1972).

26. Alan Takeo Moriyama, *Imingaisha: Japanese Emigration Companies and Hawaii* (Honolulu: University of Hawaii Press, 1985), pp. 87–88.

27. For an excellent study on Korean immigration to Hawaii, see Wayne Patterson's work, *The Korean Frontier in America: Immigration to Hawaii, 1886–1910* (Honolulu: University of Hawaii Press, 1989).

28. For a more comprehensive treatment of this idea, see Saeed Ahmad Nizami's study, "The Law of Immigration in the United States," an unpublished Ph.D. dissertation, Southern Illinois University, 1968, 275 pp.

—2—

The Colonial Period
(1609–1775)

Myths die hard. In particular, the American myth of free immigration, open to all people, has been lingering in the deep psyche of the American public. This myth has a ring of truth when it is put within the context of the legal system that has allowed the trans-Atlantic immigration of Europeans to make America white and European. But it becomes a hollow litany of racial ideology when it is examined against the trans-Pacific immigration. From the beginning, this nation's social attitudes and institutions began to be firmly established in colonies where immigration of people of color was considered undesirable. Contributing to this development of negative attitudes was the British people's feeling of superiority toward themselves and their institutions.

A powerful myth centering on how the wealth of a nation is created drove many European nations to search for foreign colonies toward the end of the fifteenth century. Underlying the European desire for colonization abroad at this time was the mercantilist view of economy that was deeply embedded in the psyche of the ruling class in Europe. According to this view, the wealth of a society is based on the accumulation of precious metal (namely bullion), establishing colonies abroad, maintaining a merchant marine, and developing industry and mining in order to create a favorable trade balance.[1] It is no wonder then that many European nations attempted to develop commerce and industry. They also went into severe competition against each other to develop naval forces to be used in colonizing people and land abroad. During the sixteenth and seventeenth centuries Great Britain, Spain, Portugal, France, Germany, the Netherlands, and Sweden established colonies around the world, and many of these colonies were kept until after the end of World War II.[2]

Among European powers that vied for the colonization of North America at the beginning of the seventeenth century, Britain was proven most successful. After the initial attempts by Sir Humphrey Gilbert and Sir Walter Raleigh to found colonies failed, the Virginia Company, incorporated in London, sent a total of 120 colonists aboard three ships, *Susan Constant, Godspeed,* and *Discovery.* They sailed on December 20, 1606, and arrived in Virginia on April 26, 1607, under the leadership of Captain Christopher Newport. Newport led the colonists to establish a settlement on the James River that marked the beginning of a new nation, a nation that was definitely British in its foundation. Virginia, New England, Pennsylvania, New Jersey, Maryland, the Carolinas, and Georgia were first settled by the British, and Virginia, New England, and Maryland remained almost exclusively British throughout the seventeenth and eighteenth centuries. Other foreigners trickled into these colonies, but these non-English immigrants were actually from the British Isles. So much of the life in these colonies was similar to that of Britain that an observer remarked that "these colonies reproduced . . . the towns, the estates, the homes of Englishmen of that day. They were organized and governed by Englishmen under English customs and laws."[3]

Britain was going through profound social changes when these colonies began to take roots in the New Continent. Economically, agrarianism (deeply rooted in the traditional British social structure) was struggling against the newly developed capitalism for economic supremacy; religiously, churchmen were at war with dissenters for the control of celestial power; and politically, the traditional autocracy locked its horns with the representative system for the control of terrestrial power. The *ancien regime* was definitely changing, but only after attempts were made to revive itself by passing labor, poor, or corn laws, all of which made British social and economic problems worse. Towns and villages were abandoned and desperate people roamed through the streets. Under these conditions the British felt that their country was overpopulated, and they considered the New Continent as an outlet for surplus people.

Unlike Central and South America, where Spain and Portugal found rich minerals and raw material for exploitation and export to their home country, North America did not produce easy and quick riches for Britain. Instead, colonies in North America developed agriculture, which was often in competition against the economic interests of the mother nation.[4] As North American colonies further developed agriculture to raise cash crops for export, more people were needed as laborers. As the population in the colonies grew rapidly—it was 85,000 in 1670, but grew to become 1.5 million in 1754—more manufactured goods were shipped to the colonies for consumption.

COLONIAL PRACTICE

For reasons that were either natural, social, or both, the early practice of bringing immigrants from Europe to the New Continent followed the patterns already established by the natural endowments of the colonies and the folkways of the immigrant. Since all the colonies were engaged in agriculture (which developed in a reciprocal interplay of availability of vast lands and scarcity of labor), there quickly followed, in the early development of the colonies, an insatiable desire for labor. In fact, throughout American history the desire for cheap labor to turn a quick profit, both in agriculture and industry, has dominated American society. Englishmen willing to supply labor to colonists even resorted to kidnapping people and having them shipped to the New World, but this method could not be relied on as a permanent solution to the labor problem. Even convicts were sent to the New Continent, and colonists protested this.

As a more reliable method of recruiting laborers, colonists used three systems. First, there emerged in the colonies the system of free wage labor, by which an individual simply hired himself out for wage. This, of course, meant that he had to be brought to the New Continent. But this system of labor supply could not meet the increased demand, and therefore the Virginia Company (and later the British government) promised free land to colonists who would bring white settlers to the New Continent. Colonists devised a system of recruiting white laborers willing to cross the ocean but who could not afford to. This was the second system of indentured servitude, through which large numbers of lower-class British people came to the New Continent to work for a master under contractual obligation. Their contract normally specified that they would work for four to seven years as payment for their ocean passage. Such additional provisions as a house, tools, and a share of crops were provided. When they fulfilled their contract, they gained the rights of a free man and were able to hold title to their own land. The third system was chattel slavery. Virginia settlers resorted to this system in 1619, only twelve years after the first settlement, because their attempt to recruit Native Americans had failed.

Indentured servitude was mainly responsible for bringing to the New Continent large numbers of white settlers. It is estimated that the Virginia Company, which initiated the system, brought in as many as 1,500 bonded laborers per year throughout the seventeenth century. This system of labor recruitment proved beneficial both for the colonial economy, which needed to expand the market for farmers and businesspeople, and for the British government, which saw prosperous colonies as a sign of its national strength. For those who were destined to serve out their years of servitude, however, their life was no more than that of a slave. They were driven hard by masters who were bent on getting as much labor out of them as possible, and the overseers hired to supervise them were not known for their human kindness. They meted out punishment to a servant as if he were an animal, "hanging him by the heels as butchers do for the slaughter."[5] In spite of the inhuman treatment they were subjected to, many indentured servants came to the New Continent because it offered economic opportunities that were not readily available to lower-class English people in their country in those days. Although their life in indentured servitude was harsh, when their term ended they had a real chance of improving their lot. It is estimated that as many as two-thirds of all white laborers in the colonies before the American Revolution came as indentured servants.[6]

Enterprising businesspeople are usually preoccupied with money making in any society when they are left to pursue their own interests. Colonists in Virginia and other Southern colonies were no exception to this general rule. When it was found that tobacco turned a big margin of profit in the British market, colonists in Virginia went into a mad rush to raise tobacco as a cash crop for export. For some time in the Southern colonies, tobacco was the king before it was replaced by cotton. It enriched many colonists, who related their personal stories of going from rags to riches; one person said that by himself he was able to raise a crop that brought in £200, while another claimed that he was able to bring in £1,000 in one year, with six hired men working for him. Furthermore, there was the story of Samuel Argall, who had come to Virginia with nothing in his possession but took home £3,000.[7] These success stories whetted colonists' greedy appetites for more tobacco; Virginia sent to England 50,000 pounds of tobacco in 1618. This mad rush to raise more tobacco, however, resulted in an economic crash, as Britain took legal measures against the importation of tobacco. The British government passed the first of its Navigations Acts in 1650 and 1651 to regulate trade within the empire, and by 1665 the government required that tobacco be shipped in English ships only and be exported to nowhere but England. But colonists continued to raise tobacco as a cash crop, and the overproduction ultimately drove down the tobacco price in the English market; this proved financially disastrous to many colonists. Added to this plight was the British government's policy of discouraging its people from leaving England. These factors compelled colonists, particularly those with larger Southern plantations, to look elsewhere to recruit cheaper labor.

Blacks were brought into Virginia in 1619, but they were not treated as slaves. Although black slaves were treated somewhat like white indentured servants in the beginning, a conventional system of slavery began to emerge in Virginia by 1640, and by the 1660s the first slave codes were enacted in Virginia and Maryland.[8] These early slave codes dealt with economic and social aspects of slavery. Slaves were prohibited from possessing weapons or liquor, from buying and selling anything unless specially allowed, from learning how to read, from marrying or meeting a free black person, from leaving the plantation without a pass indicating their destination and time of return, from inheriting anything, from purchasing real property, from using abusive language against whites, from entering into contract for business,[9] from marrying a white person,[10] and from testifying in court, unless such testimony was against another slave. Some of these slave codes were later applied to persons of Asian ancestry in California and in other states. For instance, the Chinese could not testify against a white person or marry one. Persons of Japanese ancestry could not purchase land in California.[11]

Germans, Scotch-Irish, Dutch, French, and Jews, among others, immigrated to flee from religious persecution, poverty, and lack of opportunity for economic improvement in their home countries. These immigrants moved into the Middle Colonies, a stretch of land sandwiched between Maryland and New England. Dutch traders came as early as 1610, and after the Dutch West India Company was established in 1621, the Dutch began to come in droves to claim their rightful place in New Netherland, which in 1626 had three trading posts—Fort Orange (Albany), New Amsterdam (New York), and Fort Nassau (Gloucester, New Jersey). Four years later, New Amsterdam became a town of 300 residents.

Another Middle Colony, Pennsylvania, took in large numbers of Germans, who were promised religious tolerance and personal freedom by William Penn (who went to Europe to advertise for immigration to the colony). His active campaign to bring Germans to Pennsylvania was so successful that by the 1760s they constituted one-third of the colony's population. Large numbers of Scotch-Irish also moved to Pennsylvania. They were different from English people in their religious faith and practice, but they spoke English. Some of them moved to New York and New Jersey, while still others ventured into the Southern colonies such as Georgia and the Carolinas, where they encountered Anglican hostility. Scotch-Irish continued to land in the New Continent despite the ill treatment against them. They became the largest non-English immigrant group by 1776.

Blacks had made their way to New Amsterdam as early as 1628, adding more diversity to the already variegated population in the Middle Colonies. But black slaves were not brought into New York until the 1650s, when colonists in New Netherland expressed active interest in the African slave trade. By 1665, a year after the English took over the Dutch colony, New York recognized slavery as service for life.[12]

Unlike the colonists who peopled the Middle and Southern Colonies, English Puritans came to the New Continent with a new vision to build "a City upon a Hill,"[13] as John Winthrop declared. The Plymouth Colony was founded in 1620 on this vision of a purer form of Puritanism, which was destined to affect every aspect of American life. Because of their need to enforce homogeneity, the Puritans were highly selective in bringing people to their colony. There was little advertising for general immigration, and labor recruitment was, by and large, limited to people with the same faith who had useful skills as yeoman, tradesman, gentryman, and artisan. Since their purpose was to build a community of people with the same faith, they refused to accommodate people who deviated even slightly from their religious practice. There was no tolerance toward the Quakers, who were sometimes "flogged, jailed or even hanged."[14] The Bible State, as New England was called, even restricted qualifications to vote for the members of the General Court, the colony's assembly. A statute of 1631 declared, "No man shall be admitted to the freedom of this body politic, but such as are members of some of the churches."[15]

Such enforced homogeneity notwithstanding, a few minority groups were also found in the Bible State. Scotch-Irish immigrants were found among Puritans, and by 1657 Scots founded the Scots Charity Box in Boston to take care of the less fortunate among their ranks. In the first two decades of the eighteenth century, Puritanism relented a little. Fifty-four ships loaded with immigrants from Ireland who were led by their own clergymen arrived in Boston between 1714 and 1720. The presence of such large numbers of Scotch-Irish immigrants in the Bible State prompted John Winthrop to be concerned about the colony's safety; he said, "I wish their coming so over do not prove fatall in the End."[16]

The Bible State was not free of black slavery, but partly because of its religious faith (which required conformity to its established practices and uniformity of culture) and partly because of lack of economic conditions requiring large numbers of black slaves, New England had relatively few black slaves. Until 1680 there were only a few hundred black slaves, and throughout the seventeenth century the black slave population did not exceed more than 3 percent of the colony's population. Probably because of their small number, black slaves in New England received better treatment from their white masters than their counterparts in the Middle and Southern Colonies. In the Bible State, black slaves were recognized as property, and as such they were sold and bought. But, unlike their brethren in the Middle and Southern Colonies, they were allowed to testify against whites in some cases. They were given a jury trial, which was unheard of in the Southern Colonies.

Despite conflicts and problems associated with the immigration of Europeans who differed in their religion, culture, and temperament, the colonies continued to lure Europeans by promising them economic opportunity in the form of free land, religious freedom, and personal liberty. Throughout Colonial America, methods of attracting immigrants were left to local governments and enterprising businesspeople. Importation of black slaves from Africa increased as the demand for their labor ran high, particularly in Maryland, Virginia, and South Carolina, where black slaves constituted 40 percent of the total population in 1770. Virginia alone had almost half of the slave population in Colonial America.[17]

Constant demand for labor in the colonies, social unrest, and lack of economic opportunity abroad in Europe worked together to increase the population in the colonies rapidly. In 1640 there were 25,000 people, but that number increased to 80,000 twenty years later. In 1721 the population in the colonies passed the half-million mark. That figure was doubled in twenty years. The two-million mark was achieved by 1767. The 1790 census, first taken in America after the Revolution, enumerated 3,929,000 souls, exclusive of Vermont and the territory northwest of Ohio.[18]

COLONIAL DEBATE

Early debates on immigration centered around a narrowly drawn conceptual terrain on the quality of people considered worthy of entry into the English colonies. Even then, the debates focused almost exclusively on the quality of non-English European immigrants. This does not mean that the English colonists did not harbor prejudices toward people of color. But prejudice did not find its way into public debate for obvious reasons. Since the American Indians were natives of North America, English colonists had to deal with them, first for their survival and later to take land away from them. Black slaves were necessary for agriculture, particularly in the Southern colonies. It was not until the beginning of the nineteenth century that whites in North America resorted to policies of isolation and expulsion to get rid of the American Indians.

Immigration to the New Continent was open as far as Europeans were concerned. While some Europeans came as free individuals, many of them came as servants in bondage to their masters. However, these two separate classes of people had one thing in common: They came to the colonies on their own volition. This commonality alone, however, was not strong enough to cement European immigrants with different ethnic backgrounds into a harmonious community of people willing to coexist. Group conflicts were probably inherent in the ethnic composition of European immigrants. Adding more complexity to this group conflict were black slaves, who were brought to Colonial America against their will and who accounted for 22 percent of the total population on the eve of the American Revolution. Another culturally and racially distinctive group of people indigenous to North America were the American Indians (or Native Americans, as they are now called), who were gradually conquered by and subjugated to whites (who brutalized them for economic, social, and religious reasons).

Hostile perceptions that English colonists developed toward racially and ethnically different people grew gradually out of the cultural miasma of Colonial America. Non-English settlers were perceived as being different and foreign, while black slaves and Indians were seen as being strange and inferior. Such peculiar perceptions, when reinforced by social and economic forces that prevailed at the time, were gradually transformed into attitudes and institutions and became firmly lodged in the American psyche, not to be easily dislodged from the minds of whites in America, even today.

One of the earliest attitudes that English colonists developed toward black slaves was that of separateness or apartness. English colonists considered themselves apart or separate from other peoples, who were further distinguished from each other in terms of not being English. Like the Chinese, who considered themselves and their ethnic group as holding the hub of the universe, English people strongly felt that they were located at the center of a widening concentric circle of peoples who were more different and separate from English people as they were removed from the center of the concentric circle. Given this perception, it was natural for English colonists to think of black slaves as being more different from them than non-English Europeans and even Indians.

This English sense of separateness was observed in three aspects of daily life in Colonial America. First, interracial sexual union between blacks and whites was discouraged, since they were two separate peoples who could not be bonded in sexual union. There is evidence of punishments meted out against individuals who practiced sex between races, strongly indicating that such behavior was discouraged. For instance, in 1630 a Virginia court ordered that Hugh Davis be whipped "for abusing himself to the dishonor of God and shame of Christians, by defiling his body in lying with a negro."[19] In Maryland a man was sued in 1651 for having been responsible for the birth of a black bastard.[20] Physical punishment and a monetary fine did not stop people from practicing interracial sex, and finally Virginia passed legislation against miscegenation in 1691.[21] Another area of colonial life in which racial separateness was observed was the inability of black slaves to bear arms. The ban came as early as 1640 in Virginia, thus separating blacks from whites in a crucial area of civic obligation. Whether the ban had anything to do with whites' fear of black slaves is unknown, but it is probable that blacks were not considered as part of the white community to the extent that they would have the duty to defend it. Blacks were apart from whites in a third aspect of colonial life. Generally speaking, white women were not used for field work, but black women were, even if they were not slaves. Furthermore, free black women were required by the Virginia Assembly to pay taxes.[22]

This British sense of separateness seems to have been used extensively as a means of distinguishing the English from the non-English, and particularly from people of color. To use Ringer's model of People's Domain versus Plural Domain, as discussed briefly in Chapter 1, the English colonists thought of their community as the People's Domain, in that it consisted of people with common backgrounds in language, religion, and, above all, physical characteristics. Naturally, those who came from strange backgrounds, different from English, were considered alien, and they were placed in the Plural Domain. Thus, from the beginning of English colonization in North America, there rapidly developed a two-category system that established an unequal treatment of people on the basis of color and culture.

The air of superiority of the English colonists toward black slaves probably originated from their European cultural background. Even before Europe came into contact with Africa, there had been in the minds of Europeans a mental association of blackness with evil. In fact, the *Oxford English Dictionary,* published before the sixteenth century, stated that black meant "soil, dirty, foul . . . atrocious, horrible, wicked."[23] From this perception of blackness, it must have been rather easy for English colonists to infer that white meant good and pure. Therefore, white was superior, and black inferior. In the collective psyche of the English colonists, white meant not only good and pure, but also Christian. It is ironic that for some time during early Colonial America, colonists made unsuccessful efforts to Christianize Indians and blacks, although Indians and blacks were basically considered savages and heathens, respectively. A few blacks and Indians were converted, but their conversion made them neither free nor equal. English colonists believed in their cultural and racial superiority and later transformed it into natural superiority. Again, as Kitano and Daniels suggested in their work *American Racism,* a two-category system of discrimination was established in Colonial America that considered all whites superior to all nonwhites.

Black slaves were not the only people of color who were considered strange and inferior. Indians, who were indigenous to the Americas and who had established complex cultures before the Americas were "uncovered" by Europeans, were the first people who came into contact with the European conquerors. In the English colonies in North America, Indians had first suffered from European conquest before blacks were subjected to whites' brutalizing forces of racism. Which of the two groups had more intense bittersweet relations with whites is yet to be determined. What is definitely clear, however, is that after repeated contacts with European civilization, native Indian cultures were nearly destroyed and were never to be restored to their past glory.

The English colonists, unlike their Spanish and Portugese counterparts in Central and South America, adopted a rather aloof attitude toward the American Indians. Spanish and Portugese colonists intermingled with the natives and married them. One might speculate on reasons why there were happier relations between Spanish and Portugese colonists and their hosts in South America. It is likely that the colonists and the natives were both responsible for the less hostile relations they mutually enjoyed. Indians in South America were agricultural people who were settled in villages and who were less given to warfare. They did not resist Spanish and Portugese colonization as actively as their brethren did in North America, and therefore it was easier for the Spanish and Portugese to colonize them. In addition, the Catholic Spanish colonists were less stringent in their standards for converting Indians than Protestant English colonists. To support this claim, historians point out that the tradition of regarding a converted Indian as a Noble Savage was prevalent in Latin countries.

Another reason why English colonists adopted an aloof attitude toward their hosts was that they brought their families with them, which changed the complexity of their relations with the Indians. The Spanish and Portugese, however, came to South America as traders, leaving their families behind.

Both in New England and Virginia individual Indians extended their helping hands to white colonists, but as large numbers of white colonists became farmers, they needed more land quickly. In Virginia, tobacco cultivation required extensive land so rapidly that white settlers began to force Indians off their land. Many small and large battles were fought to decide land ownership. An attitude of mutual suspicion between white colonists and American Indians regarding land continued throughout Colonial America. In particular, after King Philip's War (which lasted from 1675 to 1676), white colonists were convinced that the Indians—including those who had been converted to Christianity—were treacherous savages who were always willing to kill white women and children. The Indians' perceptions of white colonists were no more amicable; they considered the colonists dangerous and greedy invaders whose desire for land could never be satisfied.

The English colonists in North America were not without prejudice against non-English European immigrants, and they frequently voiced their opinions of various white ethnic groups in their midst. The numerical strength of these ethnic groups seemed to have influenced the English colonists' attitudes toward them. Generally, the greater the number of a group, the stronger the negative attitude of the English colonists toward it. The German immigrants in Pennsylvania had their share of English prejudice against them. Although initially they were perceived as being quiet, industrious, and thrifty, Pennsylvania English colonists soon came to resent the large numbers of Germans who moved to Pennsylvania from New York because of the ill treatment they had received there.

Even Benjamin Franklin expressed his ethnic pride when he wrote, "The Germans who come hither are generally the most stupid of their own nation."[24] He believed that Germans were not able to exercise freedom because they had not been used to it, and he was convinced that if their immigration was left unchecked, "they will soon outnumber us, [so] that all the advantages we have will not be able to preserve our language and even our government will become precarious."[25] The notion that immigrants present a political and social danger to the stability and security of existing institutions has been a persistent theme in American history. Franklin was perhaps one of the first assimilationists, for he said, "All that seems to me necessary is, to distribute them more equally, mix them with the English, establish English schools where they are now too thick settled."[26] The negative attitude of the English in the New World toward German immigrants in Pennsylvania was not immediately translated into any legal measures to prevent them from coming to the colonies, since their labor was needed.

EARLY IMMIGRATION LAWS

English colonists seemed less tolerant of religious than ethnic differences, and their intolerance found its way into immigration legislation on religious grounds. Most colonies had laws against immigration of people who practiced religion that was different from that of the dominant group. For instance, the General Assembly of Massachusetts passed a law in 1637 requiring any town or person not to keep any newcomer for more than three weeks without permission of the authorities.[27] In 1656, the Assembly passed another law to keep out the Quakers, Protestants, and Catholics.[28] Catholics seemed to have been more subjected to restrictive laws in many colonies than any other religious group. The Quakers were prevented from entering Virginia and the New England colonies, with the exception of Rhode Island; and Maryland passed a law in 1699 entitled, "An Act for Raising a Supply towards Defraying of the Publick Charge of this Province and to Prevent too Great a Number of Irish Papists being Imported into this Province."[29]

Early colonial legislations against immigration seemed to have originated from English colonists' hostility toward people who were considered undesirable on moral grounds. As early as 1639, Massachusetts colonists ordered the removal of foreign beggars and later required indemnity from shipmasters who brought them. Feelings of resentment against the importation of the idle poor ran high, particularly after a law passed by the English Parliament in 1663 that allowed Justices of the Peace to send the idle poor to the colonies. Rogues, beggars, and vagrants were rounded up to be shipped to North America, and boys and girls of the poorer classes were kidnapped and were sent to the colonies. In 1717, the British government took another decisive step to rid the British Isles of criminal elements by shipping them to the colonies. It is estimated that as many as 50,000 criminals were sent to North America from 1717 until the beginning of the American Revolution, when such practices ended. Maryland had more than its share of these felons, and its General Assembly reacted quickly by enacting a law in 1676 requiring all shipmasters to report any criminal on board.[30] The law was intended to stop the entry of criminals into its territory. Judging from the stiff fine (which was set at 2,000 pounds of tobacco) to be imposed on anyone attempting to bring felons into Maryland, this practice must have been either very lucrative and/or widespread before the law was adopted. Not only were shipmasters to be fined if they brought criminals aboard their ship, but they were held responsible for the good conduct of their passengers, according to a proclamation issued on December 9, 1676.[31] In 1722, Pennsylvania followed suit by requiring every landed criminal to pay tax and the ship owner to be responsible for the good conduct of his passengers.[32]

The immigration of Germans into Pennsylvania stirred up ill feelings against them, as mentioned earlier. But as large numbers of them continued to move into the colony, arguments gradually developed that the security and peace of the colony was endangered by the presence of foreign people whose language and culture were different from those of the English. This concern with the immigration of people of a different culture found its way into legislation on September 21, 1727, when Pennsylvania passed a law requiring the immigrant to "take the oath of allegiance to the king, and of fidelity to the proprietary of the Province."[33] Two years later the colony passed another law requiring a tax of forty shillings—a form of head tax—on every immigrant in order "to discourage the great importation and coming in of foreigners and of lewd, idle and ill-affected persons."[34] This was probably one of the first head taxes imposed on the immigrant in American history.

SUMMARY

From the beginning, when the English began to develop colonies in North America, they adopted an attitude of aloofness and superiority over people of color and of different ethnic, religious, and social origins. This superior attitude toward other non-English Europeans found its way into legislation to restrict and curtail the immigration of people who were different from the English colonists. But these restrictive laws were passed on supposedly moral grounds. The colonial practice of not allowing people of color to testify against whites was carried over into the middle of the nineteenth century, when the Chinese were not permitted to do the same. Another colonial practice of imposing a head tax to discourage the immigration of certain groups of people was revived in California in the 1850s, when the Chinese were required to pay a head tax.

NOTES

1. Mercantilism is now defined by the *American Heritage Dictionary of the English Language* as "the theory and system of political economy prevailing in Europe after the decline of feudalism, based on national policies of accumulating bullion, establishing colonies and a merchant marine, and developing industry and mining to attain a favorable balance of trade" (Boston: Houghton Mifflin Co., 1973, p. 821). Robert Leckie, in a recent book, *George Washington's War: The Saga of the American Revolution* (New York: HarperCollins, 1992, pp. 22–25), states that mercantilism was partially responsible for the American Revolution.

2. It is interesting to note that powerful countries in Europe were able to maintain peace during the Concert Period, which spanned from 1815 to 1914. While peace was being maintained in Europe, these countries competed against each other to colonize Asia, Africa, and other parts of the world. For a more complete discussion of European colonialism and world order, see *The Quest for a Just World Order,* by Samuel S. Kim (Boulder, Colo.: Westview Press, 1984). For a more informative discourse on the Concert Period, see *The Great Transformation: The Political and Economic Origins of Our Time,* by Karl Polanyi (Boston: Beacon Press, 1944).

3. Roy L. Garis, *Immigration Restriction: A Study of the Opposition to and Regulation of Immigration into the United States* (New York: Macmillan, 1927), p. 3.

4. The underdevelopment of Latin American countries in comparison with the development of the United States and Canada is carefully analyzed in *Dependence and Underdevelopment,* by Andre Gunder Frank, James D. Cockcroft, and Dale L. Johnson (Garden City, N.Y.: Doubleday Anchor, 1972).

5. Leonard Dinnerstein, Roger L. Nichols, and David Reimers, *Natives and Strangers: Ethnic Groups and the Building of America* (New York: Oxford University Press, 1979), p. 13.

6. Ibid.

7. Samuel Eliot Morison, *The Oxford History of the American People,* Vol. 1 (New York: New American Library, 1965), p. 90.

8. Winthrop D. Jordan, *White over Black: American Attitudes towards the Negro, 1550–1812* (Baltimore, Md.: Penguin Books, Inc., 1968), p. 78.

9. Richard T. Schaefer, *Racial and Ethnic Groups* (New York: HarperCollins, 1993), p. 188.

10. Jordan, *White over Black,* p. 79.

11. J. B. Kessler, "The Political Factors in California's Anti-Alien Land Legislation, 1912–1913," an unpublished doctoral dissertation, Stanford University, 1958.

12. Ibid., p. 84.

13. Morison, *Oxford History,* p. 106.

14. Ibid., p. 180.

15. Adolphe E. Meyer, *An Educational History of the American People* (New York: McGraw-Hill, 1957), p. 24.

16. Garis, *Immigration Restriction,* p. 6.

17. Dinnerstein, Nichols, and Reimers, *Natives and Strangers,* p. 17.

18. Garis, *Immigration Restriction,* p. 1.

19. Jordan, *White over Black,* p. 78.

20. Ibid.

21. Ibid., p. 80.

22. Ibid., p. 77.

23. Dinnerstein, Nichols, and Reimers, *Natives and Strangers,* p. 17.

24. Madison Grant and Chas. Stewart Davison (eds.), *The Founders of the Republic on Immigration Naturalization and Aliens* (New York: Charles Scribner's Sons, 1923), p. 28.

25. Ibid., p. 29.

26. Ibid., p. 30.

27. Garis, *Immigration Restriction,* p. 16.

28. Ibid., p. 17.

29. Ibid.

30. Ibid., p. 15.

31. Ibid.

32. Ibid., p. 14.

33. Ibid.

34. Ibid., p. 15.

—3—

The Revolutionary Period
(1776–1840)

FOUNDING FATHERS

Eminent historians often praise the Declaration of Independence as one of the greatest political documents in human history. Samuel E. Morison declared that the words in the statement, "We hold these truths to be self-evident, that all men are created equal" are "more revolutionary than anything written by Robespierre, Marx, or Lenin, more explosive than the atom, a continual challenge to ourselves, as well as an inspiration to the oppressed of all the world."[1] This might have been true for white colonists who were considered members of the community called America, and this continues to be true for most white Americans today. But Morison either overlooked important implications of the document or was oblivious to them. This great document, declaring the birth of a new nation, defined the American peoplehood in its opening statement: "When in the Course of human events it becomes necessary for one People to dissolve. . . ."[2] When the Founding Fathers spoke of "one People," they did not have in mind a plurality of peoples from around the world who came to live on the new continent. Instead, they envisioned the emergence of a new peoplehood made up of northern and western European immigrants who had been assimilated enough to be accepted as members of the community. The expression "that all men are created equal" should be examined within this context. As Morison stated, Jefferson did not mean that blacks were created equal to whites;[3] he probably meant that people in a political community should be considered equal. Consequently, people who were considered outsiders of that political community were unequal and were accorded a different treatment.

This sentiment of separateness between members of the community and nonmembers was well articulated by John Jay, first Chief of the

Supreme Court, in the *Federalist Papers* "Providence has been pleased to give this one connected country, to one united people, a people descended from the same ancestors, speaking the same language, professing that same religion, attached to the same principles of government, very similar in their manners and customs."[4] John Jay, however, went beyond the boundaries of a political community. To him, a community was more than a body politic; it was also a cultural unity with its common language, religion, political ideology, manners, and customs. Above all, a people who made up a cultural community had to have the same ancestors, meaning that they had to be of the same racial stock.

John Jay was not the only one who expressed this new sense of peoplehood based on the common cultural bond. Jean de Crevecoeur, in his *Letters from an American Farmer* (first published in 1782 in London, but written probably a decade before the Revolution) asked, "What, then, is the American, this new man?" In answer to this self-imposed question, he pointed to the many biological and cultural ingredients that were European in origin and that could be amalgamated into a new national character that would transcend Europe.[5] Crevecoeur envisioned the character of a new American peoplehood distinctly different from that of Europe when he said, "Here, individuals of all nations are melted into a new race of men, whose labors and posterity will one day cause great changes in the world."[6] This assimilationist view was not too dissimilar from what Benjamin Franklin thought Pennsylvania had to do with the German immigrants in 1753, and it was popularized in the nineteenth century in the form of the melting-pot theory.

A new peoplehood on the new continent was more of a vision of the nation to be rather than of the nation that actually was at the time of the Revolution. Probably because of this quest to create a community built on a common culture, the founders of the nation voiced their fear of foreigners and their adverse influences. George Washington not only expressed his own antiforeign sentiment but perhaps set the tone for others to follow suit. He was suspicious of foreigners, particularly those who did not have family with them. He ordered his officers not to post any foreigner as sentry unless he had a wife or family in the country. This order, issued on July 7, 1775, was followed by another, three days later, in which Washington ordered his recruiting officers not to enlist any foreigner who did not have a wife or family in the country.[7] He was afraid that any person not born in the country would not have enough loyalty to keep secret any important document in his possession. Therefore, he wanted only native-born soldiers as his personal guards, as he confided in his letter of April 30, 1777, to Colonel Spotswood.[8] In another letter to Colonel Baylor he warned against the moral character of foreigners:

You should be extremely cautious in your enquiries into the character of those who are not natives who offer to enlist. Desertions among men of that class have been so frequent that unless you find 'em on examination to be of good and unsuspicious conduct, they should not be taken by any means. Otherwise, most probably, they will deceive you—the Public account and upon first opportunity will join the Enemy.[9]

John Adams was no less antiforeign than Washington. As early as 1780, when he proposed that a consul be stationed at Nantes, France, he strongly believed that the consul should be an American, although there were many French applicants.[10] He was convinced that French men could not serve very well because they lacked the knowledge of "our language, our laws, customs, and even the humors of our people, for even these must be considered, they never would be able to give satisfaction or to do justice."[11] Adams's fear of foreigners, particularly foreign agents in American politics, along with the antiforeign policies of the Federalists, was responsible for the passage of a number of laws against foreigners during the Fifth Congress.

Thomas Jefferson, the author of the Declaration of Independence, was not free from this antiforeign sentiment. He suggested that Virginia wait with patience for twenty-seven years rather than immediately bring in foreign immigrants whose governments were established on different principles from those of the English constitution.[12] In his "Notes on the State of Virginia," he concluded that the population of Virginia, which was 567,614 in 1781, would reach 1,135,228 in 1808 if Virginia was to rely on one stock of people for its natural increase. He believed that it would be better for Virginia to wait that long than to try to double its population immediately by bringing in people of different stock. His position against increasing the population of Virginia through immigration is evident in the following quote:

They [foreign immigrants of a different stock] will bring with them the principles of the governments they leave, imbibed in their early youth; or, if able to throw off, it will be in exchange for an unbounded licentiousness, passing, as is usual, from one extreme to another. It would be a miracle were they to stop precisely at the point of temperate liberty.[13]

AMERICAN NATIVISM AND THE CONSTITUTION

The Constitution, adopted on September 17, 1787, reflected this racist and nativistic sentiment in two ways. First, it established two separate categories or classes of people in the United States in its preamble, "We the

People of the United States." As already mentioned in relation to the Declaration of Independence, the People's Domain (which included the community made up of whites) was separated from the Plural Domain (which
consisted of black slaves and American Indians). Within the Plural
Domain human beings were deprived of their personhood. Thus, in Section Two, Article One, the Constitution hid the then prevailing racist ideology in a cryptic statement in reference to the apportionment formulas for
political representation and taxation, as "the whole Number of free Persons, including those bound to Service for a Term of years, and excluding
Indians not taxed, three fifths of all other Persons."[14] In other words, a
black slave was not a whole person deserving a full membership in the
American political community. Seventy years later, the Supreme Court of
the United States not only confirmed this racist political ideology, but also
transformed it into property rights in its decision on *Dred Scott v. Sanford*
in 1857.[15] Chief Justice Taney, who delivered the Court's opinion, declared
that "black persons had been regarded as beings of an inferior order,"
even before the Declaration of Independence and the U.S. Constitution
were framed, and that they were "altogether unfit to associate with the
white race, either in social or political relations." He asserted that blacks
"had no rights which the white man was bound to respect."[16] When the
Constitution was drafted, the Founding Fathers simply reconfirmed their
understanding of peoplehood in a political community, which they had
already stated in the Declaration of Independence. These people were to
be given certain rights to be framed in the Constitution.

Second, foreign-born citizens were required to have certain qualifications for holding public offices. For instance, Section Two of Article One
of the Constitution requires that a Representative be a citizen of the
United States for seven years before his election to Congress. Section
Three of the same article states, "No person shall be a Senator who shall
not have attained the Age of thirty Years, and been nine Years a Citizen
of the United States."[17] More important, the Constitution specifies citizenship and residence requirements for the President of the United States as
follows:

No Person except a natural born Citizen, or a Citizen of the United States, at the
time of the Adoption of this Constitution, shall be eligible to the Office of President; neither shall any person be eligible to that Office who shall not have attained
to the Age of thirty five years, and been fourteen Years a Resident within the
United States.[18]

Section Eight of Article One of the Constitution authorized Congress to
establish a uniform rule of naturalization. Congress went to work on a bill

with encouragement from President George Washington, who suggested that Congress form a committee to look into this matter. Evidently, there was a need for a uniform standard for naturalization throughout the nation, as different states adopted different rules for conferring U.S. citizenship. Unfortunately, Congress was embroiled in factional party politics between the Federalists and Republicans. The Federalists believed that aliens, when allowed to vote, would vote for the Republicans over the treatment of foreigners, and it passed no less than five separate laws between 1790 and 1798. During the second session of the First Congress, a three-man committee was appointed to consider a uniform standard for naturalization, and it presented to Congress its recommendations that "all free white persons" with one year of residence be given the right of citizenship. Congress did not debate the racial restriction, but it changed the one-year residence requirement into a two-year requirement. Congress passed the bill, and it became "An Act to establish an uniform Rule of Naturalization" on March 26, 1790.[19] This law recognized the principle of *jus sanguinis,* as it stated that "the children of citizens of the United States, that may be born beyond sea, or out of the limits of the United States, shall be considered as natural born citizens."[20]

The 1790 naturalization law established in America two separate classes of people. One group of people, who were free and white, were included in the political community called America as citizens who were entitled to the rights and privileges of citizenship. The other group of people, who were nonwhite, were ruled ineligible for membership in the community. The "free white persons" clause continued to be an inseparable part of American government policy against the naturalization of persons of Asian ancestry until 1952. This law had a lasting impact on the experience of Asian Americans, who were deprived of their right to become members of the community due to their race. The Supreme Court did not rule on the constitutionality of the "free white persons" clause until 1922, when the case of *Ozawa v. U.S.* was decided by the Court against Ozawa, who was denied his right for naturalization.

The 1790 naturalization law was repealed on January 29, 1795 when Congress passed "An Act to establish an uniform rule of Naturalization; and to repeal the act heretofore on that subject."[21] This law declared that "any alien, being a free white person, may be admitted to become a citizen of the United States."[22] However, it required such an alien to declare his intention to become a citizen three years prior to admission. He was also required to be a resident in a state or territory for one year, which could be counted toward a five-year residence requirement before he could be admitted. Such an alien was required to be sworn in to support the Constitution of the United States and to renounce his former allegiance, title, or nobility. Children of American citizens were to be considered citizens of the United States, regardless of their place of birth, as long as their parents had been residents of the country, thus maintaining the *jus sanguinis* principle adopted in the 1790 law. Congress had not yet finished its work on naturalization laws, and the factional struggle between the Republicans and Federalists during the Fifth Congress had an adverse impact on foreigners who wished to become U.S. citizens.

A number of factors generated a stronger sentiment against foreigners, particularly against the French, during the 1790s. The Jay's treaty, signed in London on November 19, 1794, prevented war with England and opened the door to the West. But it also brought the country to the brink of war with the aggressive French Directory, which considered America as a British satellite. It suspended diplomatic relations with America and refused to accept Monroe's successor, and it used threatening language toward the United States. The Jeffersonian Republicans refused to go along with the Federalist policy of strengthening national defense by building more frigates in preparation for war with France. While these events were taking place internationally, large numbers of radical emigrés came to America, establishing themselves politically. Albert Gallatin, a European emigré, became the Republican minority leader, and a French botanist, Michaux, spied for his government. It was estimated that there were as many as 25,000 French refugees in the United States in 1798. There were also refugees from the Irish rebellion of 1798. All of these gave the Federalists enough reason to feel that the nation would not be secure unless radical foreigners were brought under strict control. In addition, John Adams's sentiments toward foreigners might have had some influence on the Fifth Congress (1797–1799). As President of the United States, he strongly voiced his opposition to foreign interference and foreigners' influence because, according to him, they tend to "excite and ferment the natives into parties and factions."[23] His definition of the American character, articulated on June 25, 1798, may have been related to the passage of "An Act concerning Aliens" on the same day and the passage of the Alien Enemy Act on July 6, 1798. According to Adams, a true American was a person who had no attachments or exclusive friendship for any foreign nation.[24] It is also possible that Federalists wanted to require a longer period of residency before foreigners could be naturalized because they believed that once foreigners were given their franchise, they would vote for the Republicans.

Given this environment of suspicion of foreigners, it would have been politically unwise for the Federalists not to pass a number of laws designed to exclude or expel foreign immigrants considered dangerous for national security. The Fifth Congress, during its second session, saw a flurry of activities that resulted in passage of three pieces of antiforeign legislation. The first of these, passed on June 18, 1798, had seven sections.[25] Section One required foreigners to be in the United States for a period of fourteen years before admission to U.S. citizenship. It stipulated that a foreigner had to file her intention to become a U.S. citizen five years before her admission. It excluded any foreigner from becoming a U.S. citizen if her nation was at war with the United States at the time of her application. Section Four required registration of all alien white persons who resided in the territory of the United States, and a fee of 50¢ was charged to the alien. A $2 fine was to be imposed on any alien for failing to register.

A week later, on June 25, 1798, Congress passed another antiforeign legislation entitled, "An Act concerning Aliens."[26] This law was, however, much different from the three previous laws, as it authorized the president to take drastic measures against "undesirable foreigners." Although the bill at the time of its introduction in the Senate had many sections, the law included only six sections in its final form. Section One empowered the president to expel from the United States any alien who was considered "dangerous to the peace and safety of the United States." When an alien was found residing in the United States without permission, after she was ordered deported she was to be imprisoned for no more than three years. Section Three required every master or commander of any ship carrying aliens to report them in writing to the collector (a government official), specifying their name, age, place of nativity, occupation, and physical description. Section Six set the term of the law at two years.

The Federalists, who controlled Congress, were not satisfied with the Aliens Act. They pressed for more drastic measures to be used against dangerous aliens in the event of war, presumably with France. Congress passed another law entitled, "An Act respecting Alien Enemies," on July 6, 1798.[27] The law had three sections in its final form. It included some draconian methods of dealing with citizens of nations hostile against the United States. Section One of the law authorized the president to make public proclamation in the event of war or actual invasion of the country by a foreign nation. Following such proclamation, the president was empowered to take the following steps, if necessary, by the law: "All natives, citizens, denizens, or subjects of the hostile nation or government, being males of the age of fourteen years and upwards, who shall be within the United States, and not actually naturalized, shall be liable to be apprehended, restrained, secured and removed, as alien enemies."[28] The law passed with such expediency (to stifle criticism against the Adams administration by French and Irish newspaper editors) was used to arrest twenty-five men, but only ten were found guilty. Included among them were a member of Congress and several Republican editors. David Brown was sentenced to a four-year prison term for his agitation, and that was the severest penalty meted out to a journalist in accordance with this law. The law, however, did not succeed in silencing journalists, as they continued to criticize the Federalists for their infringement on personal liberty and for heavy taxes. The Federalists paid a heavy political price in the 1800 presidential election, when they were defeated by the Jeffersonian Republicans.

The Alien Enemies Act was a forerunner of various pieces of legislation passed by Congress to control and regulate alien enemies, particularly persons of Japanese ancestry during the Pacific War. It serves notice to all aliens in America that they could be targeted and rounded up for deportation or incarceration, depending on America's political relations with their nations of origin.

SENTIMENT AGAINST IMMIGRATION

In the Declaration of Independence there is a grave charge against the king of England. He was accused of attempting to prevent the population of the colonies from increasing through immigration. To accomplish this purpose, according to the claim, he obstructed the Laws for Naturalization of Foreigners, refused to encourage people to immigrate to the United States, and raised the conditions for acquiring land in the United States. These charges were probably made for political gains, but those who were involved in drafting the Declaration of Independence were not active supporters of immigration. As early as 1787, Benjamin Franklin claimed that America had a right to restrict immigration whenever it was proven harmful. Thomas Jefferson was no friend of immigration, as he expressed his anti-immigration opinion in his "Notes on the State of Virginia." George Washington was no friend of immigration either. In his letter to John Adams on November 17, 1794, he stated, "My opinion, with respect to emigration, is that except of useful mechanics and some particular descriptions of men or professions, there is no need of encouragement."[29]

Today there are a number of studies on early immigration that leave the reader with the impression that immigration was encouraged from the beginning of the nation. This might have been true with regard to those who were actually involved in the business of recruiting immigrants, financing their transportation from Europe to America, and finding employment for them. These people had a vested interest at stake. It is one thing to say that these businesspeople were supporters of immigration. But it is quite another to claim that the federal government established policies to encourage immigration. Between 1800 and 1840

Congress did not pass any immigration laws, although it passed three pieces of legislation that had some bearing on immigration.

On April 14, 1802, Congress passed the Naturalization Act,[30] which shortened the residence requirement from fourteen years to five. In 1819 Congress passed a law, "An Act Regulating Passenger Ships and Vessels,"[31] requiring them to carry the required amount of provisions, such as water, vinegar, and bread. Congress enacted this law after a report of a high mortality rate among European immigrants who came to America aboard ships that were ill prepared to carry passengers. In 1848 Congress upgraded provisions written into the 1819 law by passing another law that required ventilation standards and improved conditions for sanitation, cooking facilities, and food and water supplies.[32] In 1834 Congress passed a law granting thirty-six sections of land in Illinois and Michigan to exiles from Poland.[33]

Despite the concerns expressed with regard to the health and safety of passengers brought into the United States aboard ships whose proprietors' pecuniary interests were better served when more passengers were crammed into each square feet, Congress was deliberate with its legislative responsibility to bring the states' various practices under some uniformity and control. In the absence of a national policy for immigration, individual states regulated immigrants by setting up standards for screening immigrants. For instance, on February 11, 1824, the Legislature of New York passed a law, "An Act concerning passengers in vessels arriving in the port of New York,"[34] requiring shipmasters to pay $1.50 for cabin passengers and $1.00 for those in steerage. The fees paid were spent to maintain a marine hospital. Shipmasters were also required to report the name, age, birthplace, occupation, and physical conditions of each passenger. This attempt by New York State to screen passengers was challenged by Miln, master of a ship transporting immigrants, who believed that the New York regulations were in violation of Section Eight of the Constitution (which gives Congress alone the power to regulate commerce with foreign nations).

The case of *The Mayor, Alderman, and Commonality of the City of New York v. George Miln,*[35] decided by the Supreme Court on February 16, 1837, by a vote of six to one, was the first major Commerce Clause case. (The Commerce Clause, Section Eight, Article One of the Constitution, regulates commerce with foreign nations.) The Court's decision gave individual states certain powers to regulate immigrants entering their state boundaries in the absence of a federal policy for controlling immigration. Justice Barbour, representing the Court's majority opinion, stated that "the end and the means here used are within the competency of the States, since a portion of their powers were surrendered to the federal government." Defending further the rights of states to screen passengers, he stated, "We think it as competent and as necessary for a State to provide precautionary measures against the moral pestilence, vagabonds, and possibly convicts, as it is to guard against the physical pestilence that may arise from unsound and infectious articles imported."[36] Justice Thompson, who filed a separate opinion in defense of New York, warned against any attempt to declare the New York law unconstitutional, or any law similar to it, because it would be "productive of the most serious and alarming consequences, and ought not to be done unless demanded by the most clear and unquestioned construction of the Constitution."[37] He believed that the states should retain the exercise of powers to regulate immigration until Congress asserted its power to regulate commerce.

In general, federal policies for encouraging European immigration actively were not established until Congress passed the Homestead Act of 1862[38] and "An Act to Encourage Immigration" in 1864.[39] These policy measures were necessitated by changed political, economic, and industrial conditions that began to alter both America's landscape and mindscape in the 1840s. The number of European immigrants entering the United States from 1790 to 1840 partially supports the claim that the social climate in America did not encourage a massive immigration of people from Europe. Between 1790 and 1820, European immigrants trickled into the United States at a rate of less than 10,000 annually.[40] Throughout the 1820s, less than 100,000 came to the United States, and more than half of them were from Ireland. From 1831 to 1840, it is estimated that 470,000 Europeans entered America, and most of them were either from Ireland or Germany. But between 1841 and 1850 the number of European immigrants, most of whom were Irish and German, tripled the number of immigrants of the previous decade.[41]

SUMMARY

The racial separation practiced in Colonial America continued into Revolutionary America. From the beginning of the nation, the two important documents, the Declaration of Independence and the Constitution, created a discriminatory legal system of separating the People's Domain from the Plural Domain by conferring U.S. citizenship only to "free white persons." All nonwhite people were excluded from membership in the community, thus establishing a two-category system of inclusion and exclusion. This exclusion was legally constituted by the Congress of the United States when it passed a number of laws relating to naturalization between 1790 and 1798. These laws were highly antiforeign.

Contemporary studies on early immigration suggest that even non-

English Europeans were actively encouraged to come to America. But even a cursory examination of speeches and letters written by founders of the nation suggest that they did not encourage immigration. In fact, they were against immigration. Included among this group of people who were antiforeign and nativistic were George Washington, John Adams, Benjamin Franklin, and Thomas Jefferson. This does not mean that there were no people actively engaged in the immigration business. These people were, however, outside any formal government structure established to encourage immigration. They were engaged in the business of importing people largely for a profit.

NOTES

1. Samuel E. Morison, *The Oxford History of the American People,* Vol. 1 (New York: New American Library, 1965), p. 296.

2. Carl Becker, *The Declaration of Independence: A Study in the History of Political Ideas* (New York: Vintage Books, 1922), p. 5.

3. Morison, *Oxford History,* p. 295.

4. Edward Mead Earle, *The Federalist: A Commentary on the Constitution of the United States* (New York: Modern Library, 1941), p. 9.

5. Richard J. Meister (ed.), *Race and Ethnicity in Modern America* (Lexington, Mass.: D. C. Heath, 1974), p. 6.

6. Ibid.

7. Madison Grant and Chas. Stewart Davison (eds.), *The Founders of the Republic on Immigration Naturalization and Aliens* (New York: Charles Scribner's Sons, 1928), pp. 82–83.

8. Ibid., p. 84.

9. Ibid., p. 86.

10. Ibid., p. 1.

11. Ibid.

12. Ibid., pp. 58–59.

13. Ibid., p. 60. In his "Notes on the State of Virginia," Jefferson expressed his racial prejudice against blacks: "A black after hard labor through the day, will be induced by the slightest amusements to sit up till midnight, or later, though knowing he must be out with the first dawn of the morning. . . . They are more ardent after their female; but love seems with them to be more an eager desire, than a tender delicate mixture of sentiment and sensation. . . . In general, their existence appears to participate more of sensation than reflection. To this must be ascribed their disposition to sleep when abstracted from their diversions, and unemployed in labor. An animal whose body is at rest, and who does not reflect, must be disposed to sleep of course. Comparing them by their faculties of memory, reason, and imagination, it appears to me that in memory they are equal to the whites; in reason, much inferior, as I think one could scarcely be found capable of tracing and comprehending the investigations of Euclid; and that in imagination they are

dull, tasteless, and anomalous." See Jefferson's "Notes on the State of Virginia," in *The Writings of Thomas Jefferson,* H. A. Washington (ed.), Vol. VIII (New York: Riker, Thorneanc Co., 1854).

14. Donald E. Lively, *The Constitution and Race* (New York: Praeger, 1992), p. 1.

15. *Scott v. Sanford,* 60 U.S. 393, 407 (1857).

16. Ibid., p. 407.

17. Constitution of the United States, Article One, Sections Two and Three.

18. Constitution of the United States, Article Two, Section One.

19. 1 Stat. 103.

20. 1 Stat. 104.

21. 1 Stat. 414.

22. Ibid.

23. Grant and Davison, *The Founders,* p. 5.

24. Ibid., p. 6.

25. 1 Stat. 566.

26. 1 Stat. 507.

27. 1 Stat. 577.

28. Ibid.

29. Grant and Davison, *The Founders,* p. 60.

30. 2 Stat. 153.

31. 3 Stat. 488.

32. 9 Stat. 220.

33. E. P. Hutchinson, *Legislative History of American Immigration Policy, 1798–1965* (Philadelphia: University of Pennsylvania Press, 1981), p. 25.

34. 36 U.S. 101.

35. Ibid.

36. Ibid.

37. Ibid.

38. 12 Stat. 392.

39. 13 Stat. 385.

40. Luciano Mangiafico, *Contemporary American Immigrants* (New York: Praeger, 1988), pp. 6–7.

41. Ibid.

—4—

The Beginning of Federal Control
(1841–1882)

The cultural character of a people is difficult to judge, because people and their character (as well as their culture) change constantly. When a people is evaluated and judged, what is usually created is the passing impression the people have left on the mind of the observer, whose encounter with them might have been casual, temporary, and short lived. Certainly, character judgments may become more reliable if the encounter is more frequent and enduring. But such a lasting encounter is rare when two peoples of different cultural backgrounds develop only casual relations, be they in business, religion, diplomacy, or government.

The American public's encounter with China and its people began in the 1780s, when American traders, diplomats, and Christian missionaries went to China to carry on their business. While in China, or upon their return, they reported on their observation of Chinese culture and society for a variety of reasons. Some wrote to gain support from their sponsors, while others did so to "enlighten" the American public. Their impressions of China left in the American mind such negative stereotypes of the Chinese that they ultimately led to congressional legislative action against the Chinese in 1882, according to Stuart Miller, author of *The Unwelcome Immigrant*. Miller's discourse in the first chapter of that book was developed in response to the California thesis presented by Mary Coolidge in her book, *Chinese Immigration*. Coolidge argued for the idea that a number of political, economic, and social conditions prevailing in California created political pressure on Congress, which finally passed the Chinese Exclusion Act of 1882. In arguing against the California thesis, Miller pointed out that the California phenomena were part of the nationwide anti-Chinese sentiments, and the public opposition to Chinese immigration was so widespread that Congress could no longer resist the popular demand for Chinese exclusion.

CHINESE IMAGES IN AMERICA

Even before Chinese immigrants began to arrive in California and elsewhere in the United States, Americans had been exposed to reports prejudiced against the Chinese and their civilization through printed media such as newspapers, magazines, and books. Prejudiced opinions were also expressed in private letters and diaries. The earliest reports on China came from American traders, many of whom harbored racial and cultural prejudices against Chinese merchants and government officials. Some of the comments they made about the Chinese may have been justifiable, as they inevitably must have dealt with corrupt government officials and unscrupulous merchants. Thus, in a letter written by Thomas Randall to Alexander Hamilton in 1791, Randall criticizes Chinese merchants for their fraudulence and Chinese government officials for their harassment and false promises. But traders such as Randall were not too shy to make a generalized charge against the whole nation of China. Randall complained that "the Chinese are considered by most persons who have seen them, as very contemptible, however importantly they think of themselves."[1] Stuart Miller examined the writings of fifty American traders who were involved in the China trade between 1785 and 1840 and summarized his findings. According to Miller, American traders reported consistently on "Chinese peculiarities, dishonesty, xenophobia, vices, cowardice, technological and military backwardness, and the static condition of Chinese society."[2]

China, its people, and their institutions did not fare any better in the hands of American missionaries. They should have known better not to express disdain toward Chinese culture if they were to be effective with their soul-saving mission. But they were not free from the weakness of human hubris. Missionaries had no respect for Confucius and his philosophy. Thus, the Reverend David Abeel condemned anything Confucian because he considered it "a function of ignorance."[3] Others who were more vociferous against what Confucius had to offer used stronger words in condemning him, saying that all the flaws of Chinese society were attributable to Confucian influence. Included among these flaws were "pride, self-righteousness, blind inconsistency, shameful dissoluteness, lurking atheism, and a hungering and thirsting after unrighteous gain."[4]

American missionaries also criticized other aspects of Chinese culture. They were critical of Chinese men's treatment of their women and of the practice of infanticide. Concerning infanticide, Abeel claimed that "before the carts go around in the mornings to pick up the bodies of infants thrown in the streets, . . . dogs and swine are let loose upon them."[5] He estimated that 70 percent of all female infants were murdered by their parents, while Samuel Wells Williams, an American missionary who published *The Chinese Repository* in China, gave a more conservative estimate at 40 percent. Missionaries on home leave back in the United States gave speeches at local church and civic organizations and were also critical of the character of the Chinese, who were found deficient because of "their lechery, dishonesty, xenophobia, cruelty, despotism, filth and intellectual inferiority." Even an official pamphlet published by the American Board of Commissioners for Foreign Mission asserted that foreigners found Chinese "cunning and corrupt, treacherous and vindictive."[6]

The negative image of China and its civilization was popularized in America by means of the penny press, which came into being in the 1830s to compete against the more well-established Wall Street press. Even before the Opium War, which was forced on China as a result of the Chinese refusal to accept the British opium trade, the penny press ran numerous articles describing China as a nation populated by less than human beings (by American standards). The *Port Folio* magazine, edited by Charles Caldwell, Professor of Natural History at the University of Pennsylvania and an important figure in the early development of racist theory, claimed that "the Chinese never can become a great and independent people because they do not possess that energy of soul and physical conformation, which are necessary to produce such a result."[7] A number of magazines ran damaging articles suggesting that the Chinese used cats, dogs, and rats in their cuisine. Some even claimed, in 1830, that young girls were killed so that the Chinese could drink certain fluids from their bodies (Miller, p. 87).

The competition between the penny press and its counterpart reached a climax in 1840, when China was fighting against the British Empire for its survival. The Opium War of 1839–1842 was brought to the American public through the penny press, as the Vietnam War was brought to the American conscience through television more than a century later. Most of the editorials and articles published in the penny press were unfavorable toward China. For instance, a Boston penny press ran an article on the Opium War on its front page depicting China as "the land of many letters, many lanterns, and few ideas. Peopled by the long eared, elliptic-eyed, flat-nosed, olive colored, Mongolian race, it offers a population singularly deficient in intellectual physiognomy; though to its absurd ugliness."[8]

Even prominent political leaders got into the limelight by expressing their opinions on the Opium War in public. John Quincy Adams defended the British right to force the opium trade on China in a public lecture. He opened the lecture by claiming that cultivation of commerce was part of the "natural rights and duties of men." He asserted that while China was a nation of selfish morals, Christian nations had altruistic moral principles. Adams supported the then prevailing ideology of Western colonialism of plundering Africa, Asia, and other parts of the world, and he claimed that England did China a favor by extending "her liberating arm to the farthest bound of Asia."[9] Adams concluded his lecture by claiming that England had the righteous cause in the war, thus grounding the British aggression on the principle of "Just War," which the Catholic Church had advocated for centuries.

CAUSES FOR CHINESE IMMIGRATION

Chinese immigration to the Americas began at a time when China and the Western powers were going through major social, economic, and political changes. The rapid expansion of industrial and commercial capitalism in Europe and the United States created great demands for cheap labor and a world market where Western-manufactured goods could be sold. Ironically, the slavery system that had supplied the Western capitalist system of production with cheap labor came to an end in 1833 under the British Empire, when there was a greater demand for labor. Therefore, Western powers were compelled to look for other means of finding cheap labor.

China fell victim to this Western imperialistic search for labor and market. England defeated China in the Opium Wars of 1839–1842 and 1856–1860, forcing China to open treaty ports for British-manufactured goods in accordance with treaties concluded in 1842 and 1843. Following the English example, other Western powers rushed into China, demanding unequal treaties. Thus, the United States concluded with China the Treaty of Peace, Amity and Commerce, signed in Wanghia in 1844. In the same year, France and China concluded an unequal treaty. Through these treaties Western nations received privileges of anchoring their warships at treaty ports, of sending their missionaries to proselytize the Chinese, of buying land and selling their manufactured goods, of stationing their military and civilian government officials in Peking, and of protecting themselves against prosecution in China by extraterritoriality.

Although the Ch'ing ruling class in Peking was forced to make concessions to Western powers for trade and diplomacy, it refused to collaborate with them for developing active trade and emigration of the Chinese from their country. The government was, however, powerless to prevent private Chinese from conducting business with Westerners. These private Chinese were located in treaty ports, particularly those in the Guandong Province in China, where a number of conditions were favorable for them. This region had a long-established tradition of overseas trade and emigration;

it also was the most commercially developed, due to transportation facilities made available by inland and coastal navigation; its market economy was the most advanced due to many manufacturing centers; it was the most socially and politically active region; and, finally, it had the greatest population concentration in China.

The Guandong Province was under a great population pressure. In 1787 the province's population was estimated at 16,014,000, but it made a net gain of 75.6 percent in less than eighty years. The province had 28,181,000 residents in 1850. The Pearl River Delta, and particularly its Hsin-ning district, from which most early Chinese came to California, was more densely populated than the rest of the province.[10]

Given the Ch'ing government's resistance to trade with foreigners and its official policy of forbidding Chinese emigration until 1860, Western powers had to find other ways of trading and acquiring the much needed labor. Sometimes they relied on local Chinese merchants for trade, and they frequently resorted to extralegal methods of recruiting Chinese peasants to go abroad. The Western powers gradually devised two ways of recruiting and sending Chinese laborers abroad. The first was the legalized contract labor system. This system was used in 1845 when Chinese laborers were sent to the island of Burbon on a French vessel from Amoy.[11] Although the system is labeled as contract labor, it was, for all practical purposes, a slavery system because each laborer was bound by strict terms of contract that required him to work under a system of bondage for a specific number of years (usually for a seven-year period). In return, he was provided transportation, room and board, and a minimum wage. Between the mid-1840s and 1874, approximately 542,000 Chinese were sent to the Americas by this method: 152,000 to Cuba from 1847 to 1875, 120,000 to Peru from 1847 to 1875, 65,000 to the British West Indies from 1852 to 1874, 30,000 to Hawaii from 1852 to 1895, and 10,000 to Australia between 1848 and 1878.[12]

The second system was the credit-ticket labor system for indenture, which was never legalized, at least in the United States. However, this method of recruiting and sending Chinese laborers to foreign plantations was widely used by many Western powers; Chinese laborers were sent to the plantations of Dutch Sumatra in the 1870s, the 1880s, and the 1890s; British North Borneo plantations acquired Chinese laborers in the 1880s. Singapore and Penang plantations imported Chinese in the 1890s.[13] Chinese immigrants to California used this method as early as the 1850s, and they continued through 1882 to obtain their passage through this method. The credit-ticket system was tacitly recognized by the United States in the 1868 Burlingame Treaty with China. Under this system, the recipient of a credit ticket that allowed him a passage to California was liable for the terms he accepted. He was not only liable for the principal and interest, but also any commission charged against him. But the eager emigrant promised to pay as much as $100 for a ticket that originally cost him $40. Upon arrival in California, he was subjected to more restrictions, including his mobility, until he was able to clear the debt.

STATE VERSUS FEDERAL CONTROL

The Chinese immigration to Hawaii and California was an integral part of international trade in labor service that Western powers exploited in colonialist economic development during the nineteenth century. From this perspective, the method of integrating Chinese merchants into the trade of manufactured goods and labor service, of recruiting Chinese laborers from within China by means of contract labor or the credit-ticket system, and of shipping laborers to their destinations in America was part of the general practice used in China, and it did not have any peculiar characteristics. If there were any unique features in the experience of the nineteenth-century Chinese immigration to America, they occurred after the Chinese arrived in California, where they encountered the naked prejudice and legal discrimination of their white hosts.

As already mentioned, individual states were given a great deal of latitude in regulating and controlling immigration into their territories by the decision of the Supreme Court on the case of *City of New York v. Miln.* Congress moved deliberately into passing laws pertaining to immigration, because it did not want to interfere with rights of state. However, Congress did pass legislation when the health and safety of passengers on all ships carrying immigrants were in question: In 1819, Congress passed a law, "An Act Regulating Passenger Ships and Vessels,"[14] requiring ships and vessels to carry the required amount of provisions, such as water, vinegar, and bread. This law was upgraded in 1848 by another piece of legislation that required certain standards for ventilation, sanitation, cooking facilities, food, and water supplies ("An Act to Provide for the Ventilation of Passenger Vessels, and for other Purposes," May 17, 1848).

For the first time in American history, Congress enacted a law with ten sections, some of which specified the number of passengers to be carried by certain types of ships and the number of pounds of bread, rice, oatmeal, wheat flour, and potatoes, among others. The captain of any vessel carrying immigrants was authorized by the law to maintain discipline and keep "such habits of cleanliness among such passengers, as will tend to the preservation and promotion of health."[15] The following year, on March 3, 1849, Congress extended the 1848 legal provisions to the Pacific immigration in anticipation of Chinese immigration to America.[16]

Chinese immigrants began to trickle into California in the 1820s, although their number remained small until 1850. Between 1820, when the U.S. government began to keep immigration records, and 1848, when the *Bald Eagle* brought two Chinese men and one Chinese woman to San Francisco, only forty-three Chinese were recorded to have come to America. After the news of gold discovery at Sutter Creek on January 28, 1848, reached Hong Kong, the Chinese began to come to California in large numbers. The first group of Chinese immigrants in California were merchants, who came to establish the mechanism for continued emigration of laborers from China and to handle their employment and livelihood. In 1849, Chinese merchants established import houses to bring food and other provisions from China. They also started restaurants and laundries for a society dominated by single males. In 1850, an important business organization, the Chew Yick Kung Saw, was created in San Francisco to promote Chinese merchants' business interests.[17]

In 1849, when the forty-niners began to stake claims in California gold mines, 715 Chinese entered the United States; some of them worked in California gold mines, where they met with white miners' hostility. The following year saw a quantum jump in the number of Chinese entering the United States; California alone received 4,000 Chinese immigrants. In 1851 the Chinese population in California rose to 25,000, and another 20,000 were added to this in 1852. By the end of the decade there were 34,933 Chinese in California. In some counties of California the Chinese population was almost half that of the white residents. Eldorado County had the most number of Chinese (4,762), while San Francisco County had only 2,719 Chinese; these figures probably reflected the number of Chinese engaged in gold mining.[18]

White responses to the presence of the large number of Chinese, particularly Chinese miners (who were perceived as unfair competitors), were swift and ugly. Contrary to some reports that the Chinese were "welcomed, praised and considered almost indispensable"[19] during the first few years of their immigration, the Chinese became immediate targets of both legal and extralegal actions taken by white miners against them to discourage their presence in California. First, a mob action occurred in Tuolumne County at a British company that employed a group of sixty Chinese workers, who were forced out of their work camps by rioting white miners.[20] This was the first anti-Chinese riot in California and was followed by many more in subsequent years.[21] Second, the California state legislature reacted strongly against Chinese miners by passing a Foreign Miners' Tax in 1850, requiring all foreign miners ineligible for U.S. citizenship to pay a monthly tax of $20. This drastic measure brought about a number of undesirable consequences. Sometimes miners put up a stiff resistance and expelled tax collectors from their camps. But many of them left the mines, which resulted in a depopulation of mining camps. Because of such adverse results, the 1850 law was repealed in 1851. In the following year, however, the legislature passed a Foreign Miners' License Tax, this time requiring foreigners who were not citizens of the United States to take out a license for $3 a month. Collectors received 10 percent of the revenues collected, while the state and county shared the rest equally.[22]

Some Chinese merchants had a vital interest in maintaining this system of taxing their compatriots engaged in mining. Since Chinese miners were in debt to them for their passage from China, they had to work to clear their debt, and they usually found work in the mines. These Chinese merchants were willing to assist in tax collection by providing interpreters, and they even requested that the tax be raised from $3 to $4. This was granted by the California legislature, which passed another Foreign Miners' License Tax in 1853. The Foreign Miners' License Tax of 1853 not only raised the tax to $4, but also added $2 per month each succeeding year after October 1855. This law was ruled unconstitutional in 1870, but during the two decades that the law was enforced, Chinese miners carried the burden, as 98 percent of $4,919,536.40 was collected from them.[23] The revenues from the Foreign Miners' License Tax proved to be a great source of the state's income, constituting one-half of the total income from all sources between 1850 and 1870.

In addition, California's judicial system worked against the Chinese. In 1854, the California Supreme Court handed down a decision on *The People v. George Hall*[24] that was not only discriminatory but also irrational. The defendant, George Hall, was convicted of murder on the basis of testimony given by Chinese witnesses. The defendant appealed, claiming that evidence against him was inadmissible because it was given by Chinese. This claim was based on Section 304 of the Civil Practice Act, which stated, "No Indian or Negro shall be allowed to testify as a witness in any action in which a white person is a party."[25] In applying this law to his decision, Chief Justice Hugh C. Murray argued that such terms as *Indian* and *Negro* are generic in nature, and therefore, when they are broadly interpreted, should include the Chinese. For justification of his line of reasoning, he invoked the name of Columbus:

We have adverted to these speculations for the purpose of showing that the name of Indian, from the time of Columbus to the present day, has been used to designate, not alone the North American, but the whole of the Mongolian race, and that the name, though first applied probably through mistake, was afterwards continued as appropriate on account of the supposed common origin.[26]

The same court handed down another decision similar to *People v. George Hall* in the same year. In *The People v. Brady,*[27] the California Supreme Court ruled that forbidding a Chinese person to testify for or against a white person is not in violation of the Fourteenth Amendment of the Constitution. These ludicrous decisions apparently embarrassed the California state legislature, which decided in 1873 to repeal all laws forbidding the Chinese from testifying against whites.

The Foreign Miners' License Tax alone did not satisfy the California state legislature, although the tax became a major source of its revenues. It took further steps to prevent Chinese immigration into its territory. On April 28, 1855, "An Act to Discourage the Immigration to This State of Persons Who Cannot Become Citizens" was passed, but it was ruled unconstitutional in 1857. In the following year, the California legislature enacted yet another law, "An Act to Prevent the Further Immigration of Chinese or Mongolian to This State," and in 1862 the same legislature passed "An Act to Protect Free White Labor Against Competition with Chinese Coolie Labor." Also in 1862, the California legislature closed up any potential loopholes in the California Foreign Miners' License Tax by passing another law. This law, commonly known as the California Police Tax, was a head tax imposed on every Chinese who was eighteen years of age or older; it required such individuals to pay $2.50 monthly if they were not engaged in the production of rice, sugar, tea, or coffee or if they had not paid the California Foreign Miners' License Tax. The law was challenged in 1863 in the case of *Lin Sing v. Washburn*[28] on the grounds that such a law was in violation of the state's constitution. The state's highest court ruled in favor of Lin Sing.

In 1862, Congress took positive steps to encourage European immigration while it passed legislation to ban the Chinese coolie trade. First, Congress passed "An Act to prohibit the 'Coolie Trade' by American Citizens in American Vessels,"[29] which President Lincoln signed on February 19, 1862. Presidents Pierce, Buchanan, and Lincoln had informed Congress of atrocities committed by coolie traders or "pig traders" against Chinese coolies transported in American vessels, which carried them to Latin American countries. Between 1847 and 1859, 116 American ships were involved in the coolie traffic between Macao and Havana, with a total 90,081 tonnage. During this period 50,122 coolies, with an 18 percent rate of casualty, were transported aboard these ships.[30]

One of the main reasons for concerns with the American and European coolie trade involved the safety of the lives and property of white people in China. Lord John Russell related his concerns to Lord Lyons in a letter that was included in President Lincoln's message to the Thirty-Seventh

Congress. In this letter Russell observed that European contractors hired agents to kidnap the Chinese, who were collected and put into barracoons before they were shipped to overseas destinations. He remarked that the circumstances under which the Chinese coolies were assembled and shipped abroad had "borne only too close a resemblance to the corresponding circumstances connected with the African slave trade."[31] He warned European coolie traffickers against their trade: "If such abuses were suffered to continue unchecked, the exasperation created thereby amongst the Chinese population would seriously endanger the safety of the lives and property of the whole European community in China."[32]

The coolie trade bill was introduced by Congressman Eliot of Massachusetts during the second session of the Thirty-Seventh Congress, and it was passed by the House on January 15, 1862. The Senate took action on the bill with an amendment to prohibit the coolie trade entirely. The bill was cleared through Congress and was signed into law on February 19, 1862. The bill had seven sections. Section One prohibited any American citizen or foreign resident in the United States from transporting Chinese coolies aboard a ship registered and licensed in the United States from China to any foreign port. Section Two set the terms of punishment to be meted out to violators at $2,000 and an imprisonment not exceeding one year. Section Four included an important provision for future Chinese emigration to the United States, as it declared that the law should not be "construed to apply to or affect any free and voluntary emigration of any Chinese subject, or to any vessel carrying such person as passenger on board the same."[33] Thus, a free emigration was open to the Chinese as long as they received a permit signed by an American consular agent residing at the port of departure.

Congress passed "An Act to secure Homesteads to actual Settlers on the Public Domain."[34] The bill, signed on May 20, 1862, made unappropriated public land available to immigrants who were eligible for U.S. citizenship. Section One of the law stipulated the qualifications of people eligible for application for homesteading. According to the law, "any person who is the head of a family, or who has arrived at the age of twenty-one years, and is a citizen of the United States, or who shall have filed his declaration of intention to become such . . . and who has never borne arms against the United States" was qualified to "enter one quarter section or a less quantity of unappropriated public lands."[35] He was to pay $1.25 or less per acre, and he was to pay $2.50 per acre if he was to homestead eighty acres or less. Section Two required a homesteader to settle on the land and cultivate it for five years before he received a title to the land. Section Five declared that such public land reverted to the government if the homesteader abandoned the land for six months.

The Homestead Act attracted land-hungry European farmers, who came to America in increasing numbers. Throughout the 1860s, more than 2 million Europeans came to the United States. Most of them were Germans, English, and Irish. The total number of immigrants from these three ethnic groups was 1,445,923. But this ethnic pattern of European immigration changed modestly during the next decade as more than 200,000 Scandinavians, many of whom were Swedes, immigrated to America.[36] Since the Chinese were not eligible for U.S. citizenship, they could not benefit from the Homestead Act of 1862.

At the opening of the Thirty-Eighth Congress on December 8, 1863, President Lincoln urged Congress to establish a system whereby immigration of farmers and laborers to America could be encouraged. He pointed out the need for labor in many fields of industry that could be met by cheap labor available abroad. In accordance with this presidential message, a select committee was established in the House that included Congressmen Washburne of Illinois, Grinnell of Iowa, Law of Indiana, Baldwin of Massachusetts, and Rollins of Missouri. The committee reported out its own bill, which the House passed promptly. The Senate worked on its own bill independently of the House, and it too passed the bill. The two bills then went to conference, and a compromise was reached for a bill that was signed on July 4, 1864, by the president to become "An Act to encourage Immigration."[37]

The law had eight sections. Section One authorized the president to appoint a commissioner of immigration to be placed under the direction of the Department of State. The term of his office was to be four years, with a salary of $2,000 per annum. The commissioner was allowed to have no more than three clerks. Section Two approved a system of contract labor immigration whereby emigrants, before departure for America, could pledge their wages to pay for their transportation from their homeland to the port of entry in the United States. But the term of their wage contract was limited to no more than one year. The wage contract was ruled legally valid; therefore, it was enforceable in the courts of the United States. But the wage contract approved by the law did nothing to create a condition of slavery or involuntary servitude. Section Seven required the commissioner of immigration to submit a detailed annual report to Congress on foreign immigration, and the final section authorized an appropriation of $25,000 to carry out the provisions of the law.[38]

The Act of July 4, 1864, was important for Chinese immigration in at least two ways. First, the credit-ticket system used by Chinese immigrating to America was considered legitimate, although it was not legalized. As already mentioned, the credit-ticket system was a form of contract labor, as Chinese pledged their wages for transportation and other incidental expenses. There were, of course, many abuses by those who sponsored the Chinese immigrants. Nevertheless, the credit-ticket system was an effective method that large numbers of Chinese immigrants used to come to America. Second, the law paved the way for a new treaty, the Burlingame Treaty of 1868, between the United States and China. The Treaty of Tientsin had been concluded between America and China on June 18, 1858. But this 1858 treaty did not have any provisions for Chinese emigration or trade with America. Therefore, it was revised as the Burlingame Treaty and included eight additional articles. Articles Five and Six included the most important provisions, as they pertained to Chinese rights for emigration to America and naturalization. Article Five guaranteed free emigration of the Chinese as follows:

The United States of America and the Emperor of China cordially recognize the inherent and inalienable right of man to change his home and allegiance, and also the mutual advantage of the free migration and emigration of their citizens and subjects, respectively, from the one country to the other, for purposes of curiosity, of trade, or as permanent residents.[39]

Article Six, however, denied the Chinese their right to become naturalized citizens of the United States, stating that "nothing herein contained shall be held to confer naturalization upon citizens of the United States in China, nor upon the subjects of China in the United States."[40] This treaty also retained the foundation of the 1858 treaty, which was unequal in that it recognized the extraterritorial rights of the United States in China.

On February 9, 1869, Congress amended the Act of 1862 that prohibited American citizens from transporting coolies in American vessels. The amendment was extended to include "the inhabitants or subjects of Japan, or of any other oriental country, known as coolies."[41] In view of the fact that the first group of Japanese laborers, recruited by Eugene Van Reed to work on sugar plantations in Hawaii, arrived in Honolulu on June 19, 1868, Congress acted to head off the business of transporting any coolies from countries other than China.

Stuart Miller characterized the year 1870 as "a crucial one in crystallizing anti-Chinese sentiment on the East Coast" (p. 194). His reasoning for this claim is based on the examination of many newspapers published on the East Coast during this period. Most editors of these newspapers were apprehensive about Chinese immigration and wanted to have Chinese immigrants restricted to the West Coast, to deny them citizenship, and to send them home when they fulfilled their economic function. When they heard that Chinese workers were in Massachusetts, they immediately called for Chinese exclusion.

This anti-Chinese sentiment was reflected in a congressional debate between the proponents of citizenship for Chinese immigrants and its opponents. Leading the battle for the debate on behalf of the Chinese was Senator Charles Sumner of Massachusetts. He seized an opportunity to introduce an amendment to delete the word *white* from "all acts of Congress relating to naturalization" when the Senate considered a bill designed to eliminate and punish fraudulent practice in naturalization proceedings. Sumner's bill proposed to strike out the word *white* so that no distinction of color or race could be made in naturalization law, particularly the word *white* in the Act of April 14, 1802, which had repealed all previous naturalization laws.[42] In support of his amendment, Sumner presented a powerful argument based on a new interpretation of the meaning of the Declaration of Independence. He insisted that the opening statement of the Declaration of Independence, which proclaims the equality of all men, means actually, "all men" with no respect to color or race. Sumner stated,

It is "all men," and not a race or color that are placed under protection of the Declaration; and such was the voice of our fathers on the 4th day of July, 1776. Sir, such was the baptism vow of this nation. According to this vow all men are created equal and endowed with inalienable rights. But the statutes of the land assert the contrary; they declaring that only all white men are created equal.[43]

Sumner's passionate plea for the Chinese right to naturalization not only fell on deaf ears but met with the stiff resistance of Sumner's senatorial colleagues, who voted against the Sumner bill. However, the Senate voted to give the right to naturalization to aliens of African nativity and to persons of African descent. This provision was included in Section Seven of the law, passed on July 14, 1870, known as "An Act to amend the Naturalization Laws and to punish Crimes against the same, and for other Purposes."[44]

On December 7, 1872, President Grant sent a message to Congress emphasizing the need to legislate against the evils associated with the coolie trade and the importation of women for prostitution. In response to the presidential call for legislation, Congress worked on a bill introduced by Representative Myers of Pennsylvania, and both chambers cleared the bill for the president to sign into law on March 3, 1875. The law, known as the Immigration Act of 1875,[45] was the first federal legislation aimed at regulating and controlling the immigration of aliens. Section Two of the law prohibited importation of aliens without their free and voluntary consent, while Section Three made it unlawful to bring in women for the purpose of prostitution. Section Four outlawed any contract made with intent to supply coolie labor to another person. Section Five enumerated two classes of people who were prohibited from coming to America as immigrants: persons convicted of felonious crimes, and women "imported for the purposes of prostitution."[46]

During the 1870s, California outdid the federal government in its effort to pass anti-Chinese legislation and to enforce it. Even after California's highest court handed down a number of decisions that ruled California's anti-Chinese laws unconstitutional, the California legislature passed yet another law in 1870 authorizing the Commissioner of Immigration to remove from the state those who were considered lewd, idiotic, dumb, blind, crippled, infirm, or unable to support themselves. The law also authorized the commissioner to remove "debauched women" from California. This particular law was challenged by twenty-one Chinese women, who were refused permission to land because the commissioner considered them as belonging to this class of people. The Pacific Mail Company, the owner of the ship that had brought these women from China, filed a petition for a writ of habeas corpus to free them, but the state's lower court supported California's statute in question. The petitioner then filed another petition, this time with the Supreme Court of the State of California, which ruled that the statute in question was neither in violation of the Burlingame Treaty of 1868 nor in violation of the Fourteenth Amendment of the U.S. Constitution.

The petitioner then asked for a third habeas corpus, this time with the U.S. Circuit Court, which ruled in favor of the petitioner. Justice Stephen Field recognized the state's traditional police power of excluding paupers and convicts but claimed that such power is limited. He ruled that the California statute in question was not only in violation of the Burlingame Treaty, but also in violation of the Fourteenth Amendment and the Civil Rights Act of 1870.[47] The case of *Chy Lung v. Freeman*[48] developed from this and tested a major constitutional question on whether the power to regulate and conduct commerce and trade with foreign nations belonged solely to the Congress of the United States.

The case of *Chy Lung v. Freeman* went to the Supreme Court of the United States on a writ of error to the Supreme Court of California. It was argued before the Court on January 14, 1876, and was decided on March 20, 1876, the same day that the Court handed down its decision on *Henderson v. Wickham, Mayor of the City of New York*.[49] The Court recognized a major difference between the two cases that stemmed from a difference in laws passed by California and New York. Whereas New York's law required a bond for every passenger landing in New York, California's law required a bond for certain classes of people who were considered "debauched women" and others. In its ruling on *Henderson v. Wickham*

(92 U.S. 259 [1875]), the Court recognized the need to develop a "uniform rule applicable to all the seaports of the United States," but it found New York's law unconstitutional because it came into conflict with the Commerce Clause specified in Section Eight, Article One, of the U.S. Constitution. Thus, the Court reversed its decision on the case of *City of New York v. George Miln* and placed immigration under congressional control.

Justice Miller, in delivering the opinion of the Court on the case of *Chy Lung v. Freeman,* characterized the California statute in question as being extraordinary and suggested that it placed in the hands of one man the power to prevent vessels from "carrying passengers, or to compel them to submit to systematic extortion of the grossest kind."[50] He then described a hypothetical situation wherein the commissioner, authorized to enforce the statute, could extort money from Chinese ignorant of "our language and our laws." Justice Miller clarified the constitutional question pertaining to this case when he stated,

We are not called upon by this statute to decide for or against the right of a State, in the absence of legislation by Congress to protect herself by necessary and proper laws against paupers and convicted criminals from abroad; nor to lay down the definite limit of such right, if it exist. Such a right can only arise from a vital necessity for its exercise, and cannot be carried beyond the scope of that necessity. When a State statute, limited to provisions necessary and appropriate to that object alone, shall, in a proper controversy, come before us, it will be time enough to decide that question. The statute of California goes so far beyond what is necessary, or even appropriate, for this purpose, as to be wholly without any sound definition of the right under which it is supposed to be justified. Its manifest purpose, as we have already said, is not to obtain indemnity but money.[51]

CALIFORNIA AGAINST CHINESE IMMIGRATION

The highest court's decision did not set right with anti-Chinese agitators in California, who felt that they were betrayed and that they had to put pressure on Congress and the state legislature to do something about their Chinese problem. A number of factors contributed to the escalation of anti-Chinese feelings among white laborers in California. First, in 1873, more Chinese came to California than any single year since 1852; this aroused ill feelings among white laborers, who felt that the Chinese were pitted against them. Second, the general depression that had plagued the East for several years finally reached California, which in 1873 was suffering from one of the severest droughts in history. Hundreds of thousands of people who had come to California in search of gold were disappointed, as mining could no longer support them. The decline in mining was followed by a ruinous crash in stocks that wrecked careers and lives. Unemployment soared subsequently, and white labor reacted to economic downturns with mob actions. These factors contributed to the birth in California of the Workingmen's Party, led by Denis Kearney, who cried out, "Chinese Must Go!"

Against these social and economic backgrounds, the Second Constitutional Convention, called almost exclusively to deal with the Chinese problem, was held on September 28, 1878, and lasted until March 3, 1879. From the beginning, the Convention was dominated by anti-Chinese feelings, as more than one-third of the 152 Convention delegates were members of the Workingmen's Party of California. They took the lead in writing a number of racist anti-Chinese clauses into the California Constitution that were adopted on March 3, 1879, by the Convention and ratified by the Californian people the following May. In addition, the delegates sent a memorandum to Congress to stop Chinese immigration. This newly adopted California Constitution was discriminatory against the Chinese. First, Section Two of Article XIX on the Chinese prohibited corporations then existing or companies to be formed under the laws of California from hiring any Chinese or Mongolians. Section Three forbade the Chinese from being employed by any state, county, municipal, or other public work, except in punishment for crime. The Constitution also forbade the Chinese from purchasing land or inheriting it, as they were aliens ineligible for U.S. citizenship. Section One authorized the state legislature to "prescribe all necessary regulations for the protection of the State, and the counties, cities and towns thereof, from the burdens and evils arising from the presence of aliens."[52] In accordance with this authority, on April 23, 1880, the California legislature passed an act entitled, "An Act Relating to Fishing in the Waters of This State," "prohibiting all aliens incapable of becoming electors of this state . . . from fishing, or taking any fish, lobsters, shrimp, or shellfish of any kind for the purpose of selling or giving to another person to sell."[53]

The constitutionality of Article XIX was tested on two separate cases. The first was the case of *In Re Tiburcio Parrott*,[54] which was decided in the United States Circuit Court, District of California, on March 22, 1880. Parrott, president and director of the Sulpher Bank Quicksilver Mining Company, was arrested on charges of having violated Section Two of Article XIX of the California Constitution. He petitioned for a habeas corpus, challenging the constitutionality of the law in question. The Court ruled that Article XIX of the California Constitution was in violation of the Burlingame Treaty of 1868 and of the due process clause of the Fourteenth Amendment of the U.S. Constitution. The second case was *In Re Ah Chong*,[55] which was decided on June 9, 1880, at the U.S. Circuit Court, District of California. Ah Chong was arrested for taking fish in San Pablo

Bay and selling them in violation of the law passed on April 23, 1880. He was tried, convicted, and sentenced to spend thirty days in jail. Ah Chong petitioned for a habeas corpus, claiming that his imprisonment was in violation of the Burlingame Treaty of 1868 and of the Fourteenth Amendment of the U.S. Constitution. The Court ruled in favor of Ah Chong.

CONGRESS AND THE CHINESE EXCLUSION LAW OF 1882

While courts handed down decisions in support of the constitutional protection of Chinese residents in America, a great deal of political pressure was exerted on Congress to pass legislation against Chinese immigration. As early as 1870, when Congress considered naturalization laws, a resolution was introduced in the Senate that included emotional statements regarding the undesirable qualities of the Chinese and the danger of Chinese immigration. In the same year, Representative Mungen of Ohio introduced a resolution calling for an appointment of a committee of two senators and five representatives to look into the danger of Chinese immigration. The following year, the same legislator gave a long anti-Chinese address in the House. The Senate received a bill in February 1871 redesigned to regulate Chinese immigration, but Congress did not act on it.

Between the passage of the 1875 Immigration Act and the 1882 Chinese Exclusion Law, a number of attempts were made in both chambers of Congress, mainly by lawmakers from the Western states, to legislate against Chinese immigration on several grounds: They were being cruel and indifferent to their sick, they were unwilling to conform to American institutions, and they refused to become citizens by accepting the rights and assuming the responsibilities of citizenship. In 1876 there was a swelling tide of presidential and congressional politics against Chinese immigration. Several factors contributed to this turn of events. First, there was a nationwide economic depression, which generated anti-Chinese feelings among white workers. Second, both the Republican and Democratic parties adopted an anti-Chinese immigration policy as they were preparing to face each other in the presidential election that year. Third, congressmen from California resumed in Congress their attack against Chinese immigration. Fourth, the report submitted by the Special Committee on Chinese Immigration of the State of California to Congress, "Chinese Immigration; Its Social, Moral and Political Effect," was widely circulated among politicians and labor leaders to create negative opinions toward Chinese immigration.[56]

In 1876 there were a number of attempts in Congress to modify existing treaties in favor of Chinese exclusion. For instance, Representative Piper of California introduced a joint resolution in January calling for modification of existing treaties. In February, the Senate received a resolution of the California legislature asking for revision of treaties with China. In April, Senator Sargent of California introduced a resolution asking the president to enter into negotiations with Great Britain and China to control the influx of Chinese coolies and criminals. Sargent depicted the Chinese immigrants as a social, economic, and political threat to American civilization. He charged that they did not share republican ideals or practice them. Furthermore, he insisted that Chinese women were prostitutes who corrupted American youth.

However, Sargent was challenged in the Senate by Senators Merrimon and Hamilton, both of whom felt that America should remain as an asylum for the oppressed of the world. After considerable debate on the merit of Sargent's resolution, the Senate decided on July 6, 1876, to accept a substitute resolution presented by Senator Morton, who called for a Senate committee to investigate the character, extent, and effect of Chinese immigration to this country. This committee, as originally organized, was comprised of three senators: Morton of Indiana, Sargent of California, and Cooper of Tennessee. But it was made into the Joint Special Committee to Investigate Chinese Immigration when the House decided to join the Senate in the investigation. The committee's membership was enlarged to include three representatives: Piper of California, Meade of New York, and Wilson of Massachusetts. The committee was headed by Senator Oliver P. Morton of Indiana, but he was too ill to be active with the committee's work. Consequently, the two members of the committee from California, Senator Sargent and Representative Piper, took on the responsibility of carrying out the committee's investigation. These two men had served on the Anti-Coolie Union of San Francisco as vice-presidents and were staunch opponents of Chinese immigration.[57]

The committee spent eighteen days in San Francisco, between October 18, 1876, and November 18, 1876, for its investigative effort. Throughout the entire hearings, Sargent and Piper did their utmost to create an environment of hostility against Chinese immigrants. The committee heard 130 witnesses who presented personal testimonies both for and against Chinese immigration. Although the Chinese community was asked to send its representatives, they did not appear; rather, the Chinese community sent Colonel Frederick Bee, one of its lawyers, to read a letter from the Chinese Six Companies (an organization that represented Chinese interests).

The committee searched for a great deal of information and collected more than 1,000 pages of testimony, with over 100 pages of supporting documents. These became the basis for a six-page committee report written by Senator Sargent. The report, submitted to Congress in late February 1877 as *Senate Report 689,* recommended that the president enter into negotiation with China to modify existing treaties and that Congress pass laws to restrict the great influx of Asians into America. In its general tenor, the report was highly anti-Chinese. In particular, it characterized the Chinese as an undesirable people who cannot assimilate in America:

The testimony seemed to be concurrent that the Chinese are non-assimilative with the whites; that they have made no progress, during the quarter of a century in which they have been resident on the Pacific coast, in assimilation with our people; that they still retain their peculiar costume and follow their original habits in food and mode of life; that they have no social intercourse with the white population; that they work for wages which will not support white men and especially white families; that they have no families of their own in this country.[58]

In response to the recommendations of the Joint Special Committee, the Chinese Six Companies sent a memorial to Congress on December 8, 1877. In this 53-page appeal the Chinese community leaders pointed out that they had been deprived of the opportunity to present their viewpoints on the question of Chinese immigration during the hearings held by the Legislative Committee of the Senate of the State of California. They claimed that the investigation by the California Senate was, therefore, one wholly and entirely ex parte. Suggesting that the report, including "An Address to the People of the United States upon the Evils of Chinese Immigration," was misleading at best and false at worst, the memorial argued against some of the statements made during the hearings by various witnesses. The memorial concluded by asking Congress to have "a careful consideration of all its bearings" and to take whatever action is deemed necessary in "justice and fairness."

In 1879, Congress passed a bill[59] forbidding ships from bringing more than fifteen Chinese at a time, but the bill was vetoed by President Hayes, who believed that such a measure was in violation of the Burlingame Treaty. However, Hayes was faced with the upcoming Presidential election in 1880, and he had to make an important political decision. He decided to modify the treaty, which had hitherto allowed free immigration of the Chinese to the United States. He dispatched a team of commissioners headed by James B. Angell, who was reluctant to accept the appointment because he did not believe that absolute prohibition was the solution to the problem of Chinese immigration. But Agnell was assured that his government was seeking only limited restrictions, and not total exclusion. The Angell Commission went to China in June 1880 and successfully renegotiated to revise the Burlingame Treaty. The Chinese government was afraid that the American government would move toward absolute prohibition, so it concluded a treaty on November 17, 1880, that recognized the right of the American government to regulate, limit, and suspend Chinese immigration. The Chinese government received a concession from the U.S. government that assured protection of Chinese residents who were already within its territory.

This modified treaty failed to ease political pressure on Congress for legislation against Chinese immigration. Immediately following the treaty, Congress received twenty-five petitions from across the country. In addition, many civic organizations, such as the Methodist Church and the New York Board of Trade, sent petitions to Congress asking for legislation to restrict Chinese immigration. In December 1881, Senator Miller of California introduced a bill during an emotional speech that urged his colleagues to pass the bill immediately. Miller was convinced that Chinese immigrants, if they were allowed to come to America in large numbers, would create havoc in American society because their civilization would inevitably be in direct conflict with American society. Conflict in human history, according to Miller, was not one of classes, as Karl Marx postulated, but one of races. This racial conflict theory was clearly reflected in Miller's statement, "In truth, the history of mankind is for the most part descriptive of racial conflicts and the struggles between nations for existence." [60] Miller warned his colleagues against a potential collapse of American civilization:

History teaches no lesson with greater clearness or persistence than this: that nations once powerful have degenerated and gone into decay, generally, in consequence of, and in proportion to, the admission and incorporation into their bodies-politic of inferior or heterogeneous races; and this we may apply with peculiar fitness to a nation like ours, whose government is a government of the people.[61]

The Miller bill was sent through the usual legislative process before it was reported by the responsible committee. The bill, suspending immigration of both skilled and unskilled Chinese laborers for twenty years, was passed by Congress, but President Arthur vetoed it on April 4, 1882, on the grounds that it was not in conformity with treaty obligations. In his veto message, however, the president urged Congress to pass a bill that he could sign, because he strongly felt that there was a need for some legislation on the subject. Accordingly, Congress began to work on a number of bills that included shorter periods of suspension, and finally a bill, "An act to execute certain treaty stipulations relating to Chinese," [62] which provided a ten-year suspension, was passed by Congress and was signed into law on May 6, 1882. The law in its final form, which had fifteen sections, suspended immigration of Chinese laborers for ten years and prohibited naturalization of the Chinese for American citizenship. It also denied entry to wives of Chinese laborers already in the United States.

In its preamble, the law (22 Stat. 58) stated that the immigration of Chinese laborers "endangers the good order of certain localities within the territory," probably referring to the West Coast. Section Four of the law required Chinese laborers to carry a certificate of identity, which listed the name, age, occupation, and last place of residence of the carrier. This biographical description was to conform to the information entered into the registry book, which the collector of customs was required to keep in the custom house in the district where Chinese laborers landed or departed. Section Five allowed every Chinese laborer to acquire a certificate of identity, free of cost, which he could carry in his possession before departure from the United States. Section Six was written into the law in an attempt to differentiate Chinese laborers from those Chinese who were not laborers. The latter group was also required to carry a certificate of identity, and it was to be used as prima facie evidence of information listed on the required certificate. Section Fourteen denied the Chinese the right to naturalization, stating "that hereafter no State court or court of the United States shall admit Chinese to citizenship; and all laws in conflict with this act are hereby repealed" (22 Stat. 61). The last section defined the word *laborer* to mean "both skilled and unskilled laborers and Chinese employed in mining."[63]

Chinese laborers were not the only class of people who were excluded from immigrating to America in 1882. Congress passed another immigration law on August 3, 1882, known as "An act to regulate Immigration,"[64] that excluded certain classes of people from entering America as immigrants. This law expanded the number of excluded classes of people listed in the Immigration Act of 1875. Whereas women, brought into America for prostitution, and convicts were excluded in the 1875 law, Section Two of the 1882 immigration law enumerated any convict, lunatic, idiot, or any person unable to take care of himself or herself without becoming a public charge as people who could not enter America as immigrants. One may wonder if there was a mental or psychological association in the minds of lawmakers between the undesirable characteristics of the Chinese laborers and those of the people listed in Section Two of the bill passed on August 3, 1882.

The original Chinese exclusion law, passed on May 6, 1882, was revised on July 5, 1884, when Congress passed "An Act to amend 'An Act to execute certain treaty stipulations relating to Chinese,' "[65] requiring the Chinese to produce a certificate of identity as "the only evidence permissible to establish [the] right of re-entry" into the United States. This was specified in Section Four of the Chinese Exclusion Law, because Congress was concerned with the "notorious capabilities of the lower classes of Chinese for perjury." Section Six of the revised law allowed "every Chinese person other than laborer" to enter America, provided that he had received a certificate of identity from the Chinese government or any foreign government of which he was a subject. In the same section, a class of Chinese known as "merchants" was defined not to include "hucksters, peddlers, or those engaged in taking, drying, or otherwise preserving shell or other fish for home consumption or exportation." Section Fifteen was revised to state that the Chinese Exclusion Law was not only applicable to all subjects of China, but to all Chinese, regardless of their nationality.[66]

As evident in the Act of July 5, 1884, Congress made continuous efforts to close any loopholes in the original Chinese Exclusion Act, which left certain words or concepts ill defined. Government officials, even those with good intentions, were confused by this wording regarding the classes of Chinese excluded by the law. Furthermore, immigration and customs officials, due to their personal prejudices against the Chinese, were often bent on preventing them from entering America, even if they possessed the proper papers. In addition, the Chinese devised rather clever extralegal methods to enter America. In this process of resorting to illegal means of entry or reentry into America, many of them ran afoul of immigration law. Those Chinese who felt that they had been unjustly denied entry or reentry into the United States appealed to the American judicial system, as evidenced in the following chapters.

SUMMARY

The Chinese immigrants who came to America were part of the general immigration of Chinese laborers to many areas of the world. They provided much needed labor for the Western powers in their colonialistic and imperialistic expansion. Although the Chinese were allowed to enter America when their labor was needed, America refused to accept them into its community membership. From the beginning of their immigration, the Chinese were considered undesirable and therefore unassimilable in America. Even before Congress acted to exclude Chinese laborers legally, many Americans had excluded them psychologically. Laws were just a convenient social means by which the psychological fear of the unknown and unfamiliar was concretized and legitimated in the form of exclusion.

It is evident that between 1840 and 1882, Congress strove to establish a national policy of immigration based on the idea that people worthy of entry into America had to have a certain personal and/or collective quality. Those who were considered fit for immigration because of their quality were, of course, Europeans. Once Congress established the quality of people on the basis of their race as the singularly most important criterion for immigration, it continued to apply this criterion to other Asian groups (Japanese, Koreans, Filipinos, Asian Indians), regardless of their nationality. Thus, Congress passed legislation in 1917 and 1924 excluding all Asians from entry into America as immigrants.

NOTES

1. Stuart C. Miller, *The Unwelcome Immigrant: The American Image of the Chinese, 1785–1882* (Berkeley: University of California Press, 1969), p. 20.
2. Ibid., p. 26.
3. Ibid., p. 63.
4. Ibid., p. 66.
5. Ibid., p. 67.
6. Ibid., p. 76.
7. Ibid., p. 87.
8. Ibid., p. 84.
9. Ibid., p. 95.
10. Ping-ti Ho, *Studies on the Population of China, 1368–1953* (Cambridge, Mass.: Harvard University Press, 1959), pp. 278–83.
11. Persia C. Campbell, *Chinese Coolie Emigration to Countries within the British Empire* (London: Oxford University Press, 1923), p. 113.
12. Leigh Bristol-Kagan, "Chinese Migration to California, 1851–1882: Selected Industries of Work, the Chinese Institutions and the Legislative Exclusion of a Temporary Labor Force," an unpublished Ph.D. Dissertation, Harvard University, 1982, pp. 11–12.
13. Ibid., pp. 13–15.
14. E. P. Hutchinson, *Legislative History of American Immigration Policy, 1798–1965* (Philadelphia: University of Pennsylvania Press, 1981), pp. 21–22.
15. 9 Stat. 221–22.
16. 9 Stat. 399.
17. Bristol-Kagan, "Chinese Migration to California," p. 35.
18. Elmer Clarence Sandmeyer, *The Anti-Chinese Movement in California* (Urbana: University of Illinois Press, 1973), p. 19.
19. Mary Roberts Coolidge, *Chinese Immigration* (New York: Henry Holt and Company, 1909), p. 21.
20. Kil Young Zo, *Chinese Emigration into the United States, 1850–1880* (New York: Arno Press, 1978) p. 86.
21. For a thorough study on American labor and its reaction to Chinese residents in California, see *The Indispensable Enemy: Labor and the Anti-Chinese Movement in California,* by Alexander Saxton (Berkeley: University of California Press, 1971).
22. Bristol-Kagan, "Chinese Migration to California," p. 11.
23. Ibid., pp. 5–16.

24. 4 Cal. 399, October 1854.

25. This law was based on the colonial tradition that forbade Negroes and Indians from testifying in court.

26. 4 Cal. 402.

27. 4 Cal. 198.

28. 20 Cal. 535, July 1862.

29. 12 Stat. 340.

30. Other studies reported higher mortality rates. For instance, the four-year period from 1860 to 1863 saw the mortality rate running as high as 29.59 percent, 22.58 percent, 41.55 percent, and 29.13 percent, respectively. See *Ch'ing Policy Toward the Coolie Trade, 1847–1878,* by Robert L. Irick (San Francisco: Chinese Materials Center, 1982), p. 210.

31. Executive Document No. 16, House of Representatives, Second Session, Thirty-Seventh Congress, p. 17.

32. Ibid.

33. 12 Stat. 340–41.

34. 12 Stat. 392–93.

35. Ibid.

36. Leonard Dinnerstein, Roger L. Nichols, and David Reimers, *Natives and Strangers: Ethnic Groups and the Building of America* (New York: Oxford University Press, 1979), p. 101.

37. 13 Stat. 385.

38. 13 Stat. 387.

39. William L. Tung, *The Chinese in America, 1820–1973* (Dobbs Ferry, N.Y.: Oceana Publications, 1974), p. 88.

40. Ibid.

41. 15 Stat. 269.

42. Benjamin B. Ringer, *"We the People" and Others: Duality and America's Treatment of its Racial Minorities* (New York: Tavistock Publications, 1983), p. 625.

43. Ibid., pp. 627–28.

44. 16 Stat. 256.

45. 18 Stat. 477.

46. Ibid.

47. 16 Stat. 140. Section Sixteen of the Civil Rights Act of 1870 stated, "And be it further enacted, That all persons within the jurisdiction of the United States shall have the same right in every State and Territory in the United States to make and enforce contracts, to sue, be parties, give evidence, and to the full and equal benefit of all laws and proceedings for the security of person and property as is enjoyed by white citizens, and exactions of every kind, and none other, any law, statute, ordinance, regulation, or custom to the contrary not withstanding. No tax or charge shall be imposed or enforced by any State upon any person immigrating thereto from a foreign country which is not equally imposed and enforced upon every person immigrating to such State from any other foreign country; and any law of any State in conflict with this provision is hereby declared null and void."

48. 92 U.S. 275 (1876).

49. 92 U.S. 259 (1876).

50. Ibid.
51. 92 U.S. 278 (1876).
52. Tung, *Chinese in America,* p. 57.
53. L. S. B. Sawyer, *Reports of Cases Decided in the Circuit and District Courts of the United States for the Ninth Circuit,* Vol. III (San Francisco: A. L. Bancroft and Company, 1877), pp. 451–58.
54. Ibid., pp. 349–89.
55. Ibid., pp. 451–58.
56. Shirley Hune, "The Issue of Chinese Immigration in the Federal Government, 1875–1882," an unpublished Ph.D. Dissertation, George Washington University, 1979, pp. 50–59.
57. Coolidge, *Chinese Immigration,* p. 97.
58. Ringer, *"We the People,"* p. 633.
59. Coolidge, *Chinese Immigration,* pp. 135–40.
60. Ringer, *"We the People,"* p. 646.
61. Ibid., p. 647.
62. 22 Stat. 58.
63. 22 Stat. 61.
64. 22 Stat. 214.
65. 23 Stat. 115.
66. 23 Stat. 118.

—5—

The Regulation Period
(1882–1920)

Congress may have been so institutionalized that it was more susceptible and vulnerable to the electoral politics and lobbying of interest groups than any other branch of the federal government. Because of the way it was organized and the people who had been elected to serve, Congress has probably curried favor with a certain class interest and class ideology over others. From its inception, Congress, as a political institution of advice and consent, was organized for a more adversary than unitary democracy.[1] It has been a political arena in which agents have participated in the bargaining process to represent their district, as well as special group interests. Seldom has it functioned to bring about a common or national interest that would serve the good of all Americans.

A number of factors have contributed to the weakening of the potential power of Congress to serve for the common good. First, its internal organization, particularly its committee and seniority structure, has been partially responsible for the unequal distribution of legislative power. At times, Congress has given the American public the impression that it is in the hands of a few people who misuse or abuse power to advance their own interests or the interests of the group they represent. Second, interest groups represented by lobbyists tend to push their own legislative agenda at the expense of the common good. Third, the biographical backgrounds of people elected to Congress seem to have been responsible for legislation that is often biased against certain social classes and ethnic and racial groups.

In a study of the social backgrounds and personalities of 180 members of Congress between 1947 and 1957, it was found that they did not represent "a good cross section of United States citizens."[2] The person chosen to serve in Congress for the common good of all Americans usually came from different social and economic backgrounds than the average American voter. He came from a family that was richer, more educated, and less urban. He was native born, white, and usually Protestant. Of the 9,618 people who served in Congress until 1949, only 4 percent, or 374, were foreign born; and of those, four out of five came either from Canada or Western Europe. It was only after the end of World War II that any Asian American was elected to serve in Congress. Due to a lack of information on the social backgrounds and personalities of those people who served in Congress during the 1870s and 1880s, it would be difficult to state unequivocally that they had very similar social backgrounds, as their colleagues had during the decade between 1947 and 1957. But it would be safe to assume that the lawmakers who served in Congress during the last three decades of the nineteenth century were not radically different from those who served before or after the ten-year period. If the assumption is valid, then it could be further assumed that there was not much sympathy in Congress toward Asian immigration in general, and Chinese immigration in particular.

The entire federal judiciary system, and the Supreme Court in particular, has not been immune to political, cultural, and institutional forces that favored a certain class interest and class ideology. Due to the pressure of the legal professional on judicial decision making, federal judges were constantly reminded of the presence of certain normative standards, criticism by their colleagues, and the public's scrutiny. These forces tended to put pressure on federal judges to be conservative in their decision making. Another source of judicial conservatism stems from the system and method of appointment. Since all federal judges are appointed by the president with the consent of the Senate, they tend to come from a certain class or group of people with prescribed qualifications in terms of their training, legal experience, and political orientation. Few of them are nominated by the president, are approved by the Senate, and finally are appointed to the federal courts by advocating a too radical or reactionary judicial or political philosophy.[3]

Judges go through common socialization experiences, through which they learn certain political cognitive maps, values, and expectations. At the end of the socialization they are inducted into the political system, where they are to assume certain specialized roles. Grossman describes role alternatives available to judges as follows:

The socialization of judges necessarily involves a variety of factors. After the obvious ones such as adequate legal training and experience, basic honesty, and judicial temperament, we can identify such basic role expectation alternatives as devotion to the procedure versus concern for substantive issues, judicial self-restraint versus judicial activism, concern for "the law" as an abstract doctrine versus concern for arriving at "just" settlements of individual cases, and a view of the courts as instruments for social change versus a view of the courts as conservators of the status quo.[4]

Judges appointed to serve in the Supreme Court have not come from the average American family. Throughout the history of the Supreme Court, over 90 percent of the justices came from economically well-to-do families, and they represented the "socially prestigious and politically influential gentry class in the late eighteenth and early nineteenth century." One author describes a typical Supreme Court justice as being "white, generally Protestant, with a penchant for a high social status domination, usually of ethnic stock origin from the British Isles, and born into comfortable circumstances."[5] The same author claims that approximately two-thirds of the justices of the court, in American history, were children of "American political families":

It would be a serious mistake, however, to conclude that the background factors have had no influence upon judicial behavior whatsoever. The social attitudes of families in the gentry class or professionalized upper-middle class, and particularly the traditions of the families with judicial associations, may be accounted subtle factors influencing the tone and temper of judicial decision making. While such influence cannot ordinarily be traced in cause-and-effect formulas in specific decisions, it frequently emerges in the careers of individual justices as setting implicit limits on the scope of theoretical decision-making possibilities.[6]

Given their family background, education, legal experience, and socialization, a great majority of the Supreme Court justices were far removed from the daily experiences of struggling immigrants, and they were not able to develop any strong sense of empathy with them. Furthermore, since they saw themselves as protectors of a white America, they had little sympathy for the Asian immigrant. Indeed, Asian immigrants have had very little advocacy in the Supreme Court for their legal rights to come to America and enjoy "liberty and the pursuit of happiness."

Since the passage of the first Chinese exclusion law in 1882, many Chinese immigrants challenged various aspects of exclusion laws under the auspices of the Chinese community, mainly the Chinese district association known as the Chinese Six Companies. The exclusion laws were written in such vague terms, and Congress disposed of them so expeditiously without careful scrutiny, that Congress had to enact a number of Chinese exclusion laws. As a result, officers responsible for enforcing these laws were confused about the various meanings of terms, which they had to interpret and apply to the administration of justice. Some officers were blatantly prejudiced against the Chinese seeking entry into America. The leaders of the Chinese community were frequently appealed to by their compatriots, who were either denied entry or were ordered deported. They skillfully used, with the help of their American lawyers, the American judicial system to rectify the injustices their compatriots had suffered at the hands of local, state, or federal officers.

EXCLUSION, EXPULSION, AND DEPORTATION

Between 1882, when the first Chinese exclusion act was passed, and 1921, when Congress passed the first quota immigration law in the history of America, more than fifty major cases were brought to the Supreme Court by Chinese litigants for a variety of reasons. Most of these cases dealt with legal issues of exclusion, expulsion, and deportation, although there were a few cases dealing with other legal matters. The Supreme Court has differentiated these three terms from each other in handing down the decisions concerning immigration laws. The Supreme Court has used the term *exclusion* to mean "preventing someone from entering the United States who is actually outside of the country or is treated as being so." Expulsion has been used to mean "forcing someone out of the United States who is actually within the country or is treated as being so." Deportation has meant "the moving of someone away from the United States, after his or her exclusion or expulsion." Frequently, however, deportation has been used to mean "the forced expulsion from the nation of aliens already in the United States."[7] Since the passage of the first Chinese exclusion law in 1882, there was, until 1965, a continuous legal and litigious interplay and counterplay among three interest groups. Congress enacted increasingly restrictive legislation to exclude and expel the Asian immigrant. In response to congressional legislative actions, the leaders of the Asian American communities turned to the federal courts to seek justice, and the Supreme Court was compelled to interpret the laws and adjudicate litigations.

The first exclusion case, *Chew Heong v. U.S.,*[8] which involved the Chinese Exclusion Law of 1882 as revised on July 5, 1884, came to the Supreme Court, which was petitioned by Chew Heong to determine the following: (1) whether Section Four of the said law was applicable to Chew Heong, who had resided in the United States from November 1880 to May 6, 1882, and who stayed out of the country until after July 5, 1884; (2) whether the petitioner had the right to reenter the country under the provision of the restrictions; and (3) whether the petitioner had the right to reenter the country without producing the certificate prescribed in the said law.

The case was argued on October 30, 1884, and was decided on December 8 of the same year. Arguing on behalf of the petitioner, attorneys H. S. Brown and Thomas D. Riordan stated that the treaty between the United States and China gave the petitioner, at the time of his departure to Hawaii on June 18, 1881, the right to go from and come back to the United States. The government, however, argued that if the petitioner was to be admitted into the country without the required certificate, as prescribed in the said law, then it would be against the intention of Congress. Justice Harlan, delivering the majority opinion of the Court, reasoned that "the courts uniformly refuse to give statutes a retrospective operation, whereby rights previously vested are injuriously affected."[9] Justice Harlan continued, "It would be a perversion of the language used to hold that such regulations apply to Chinese laborers who had left the country with the privilege, secured by treaty, or returning, but who, by reason of their absence when those legislative enactments took effect, could not obtain the required certificate."[10]

Justices Field and Bradley filed separate dissenting opinions. When he presided as circuit justice over a judicial panel including Justices Sawyer, Hoffman, and Sabine,[11] Justice Field had ruled that Chew Heong had no right to reenter the United States without the certificate of identity required by law. As Justice of the Supreme Court, Stephen J. Field defended the power of Congress to exclude the Chinese even if it came in conflict with treaty provisions:

If, however, the act of Congress be in conflict with the treaty upon the immigration of Chinese laborers, it must control as being the last expression of the sovereign will of the country . . . if the legislative department sees fit for any reason to refuse, upon a subject within its control, compliance with the stipulations of a treaty, or abrogate them entirely, it is not for this court or any other court to call in question the validity or wisdom of its action, and impute unworthy motives to it.[12]

Justice Field's judicial interpretation of the power of Congress to exclude Chinese was probably tainted by his personal prejudice against the Chinese, whom he characterized as people who "cannot assimilate with our people, but continue a distinct race amongst us, with institutions, customs and laws entirely variant from ours."[13] He was of the opinion that a restriction on Chinese immigration was necessary to "prevent the degradation of white labor, and to preserve to ourselves the inestimable benefits of our Christian civilization."[14] In fact, Justice Field, a Californian, continued to express strong anti-Chinese sentiments in his subsequent judicial opinions in relation to Chinese immigration cases.

Justice Bradley, however, dissented from the majority opinion on much narrower grounds. From his point of view, every Chinese laborer wishing to enter the United States was required by the 1882 Chinese Exclusion Law to present a certificate of identity as evidence for his former residence in the United States. He further reasoned that because "Chinese of lower class have little regard for the solemnity of an oath," Congress passed another law amending the first act to make "the said certificate the only evidence permissible to establish his right of re-entry."[15] According to his construction of the original legislative intent of the law, everyone coming into the country was required to have a certificate of identity, and there was no exception to this requirement. Chew Heong did not have such a certificate and therefore could be excluded. But there was in the law an exempt clause that stated that the act should not apply to those who were already in the United States on November 17, 1880. Since Chew Heong was in the country before the date specified, he belonged to the exempt class. Perhaps Justice Bradley accurately interpreted the purpose of Congress when it decided to amend the original Chinese exclusion law; he said that Congress had a basic distrust of the Chinese of low class for their willingness to comply with an oath they had taken. It is also possible that he was prejudiced against Chinese of low class. Either way, there seemed to have been a certain element of class or racial prejudice against a certain class of Chinese people in Congress as well as in the Supreme Court.

U.S. v. Jung Ah Lung[16] was another exclusion case similar to the first one. This case involved a Chinese laborer who was initially denied reentry to the United States because he did not carry a certificate of identity. Jung Ah Lung, a lawful resident in San Francisco between November 17, 1880, and October 23, 1883, left for China on the latter date for a visit. Before he left he obtained a certificate of identity in conformity with Section Four of the Chinese Exclusion Act of 1882. He was absent from the United States between October 23, 1883, and August 25, 1885, when he attempted to reenter the country. He was detained by the local customs authority because he was unable to produce the certificate of identity he was required to present. He claimed that his certificate was stolen from him by pirates who attacked the ship he was aboard. While he was absent from the United States, Congress revised the Chinese Exclusion Act of May 6, 1882, to make Section Four of the original law more restrictive as it specified the certificate "the only evidence permissible to establish his [Chinese laborer] right of re-entry" (23 Stat. 116).

The case was decided on February 13, 1888. Justice Blatchford delivered the opinion of the Court, and three of his colleagues filed a dissenting opinion. The majority opinion in favor of the petitioner was decided on the following facts: (1) The petitioner obtained a certificate of identity as prescribed by law before his departure, having given his physical description; (2) his certificate was stolen from him by pirates; (3) the certificate remained outstanding and was not canceled as a result of someone reentering the United States with the certificate; and (4) the petitioner corresponded, in all aspects, to the description made in the registration books kept by the customs authority. In his opinion, as Justice Blatchford pointed out, "the certificate was not the only evidence permissible to establish the right of re-entry"; it was issued merely "for the purpose of properly identifying the laborer"; it was proper evidence of his [the Chinese laborer's] right to go from and come to the United States; and it entitled him to "return to and re-enter the United States." [17]

Justice Harlan dissented, filing a separate opinion with which Justices Field and Lamar concurred. In their opinion, Congress intended to "exclude from the country all Chinese laborers of the class to which the appellee belongs, unless they produced to the collector the certificate issued as evidence of their right to re-enter the United States." As Jung Ah Lung claimed, if his certificate was taken away by force from him, that was his misfortune, according to the three justices. That fact should not defeat "the intention of the legislative branch of the government" (124 U.S. 638–39).

The following year the Supreme Court ruled on what is known as "the Chinese Exclusion Case," [18] which involved a Chinese laborer, Chae Chan Ping. He lived in San Francisco from 1875 until June 2, 1887, when he left for China. Before he left, he obtained a certificate of identity that gave him, at the time when it was issued, the right to reenter the United States. The appellant returned to San Francisco aboard the steamship *Belgic* on October 8, 1888, and he presented his certificate, asking permission to land. Captain Walker, master of the ship that brought him, refused permission on the ground that his certificate had been made null and void by the law passed by Congress on October 1, 1888.[19]

During the appellant's absence, Congress had considered two separate bills on Chinese immigration and passed them with deliberate speed. The Senate Committee on Foreign Relations introduced a bill on July 11, 1888, and it was passed by the Senate without debate. The House had an identical bill but chose to send the Senate bill to its Foreign Affairs Committee, and the House passed the bill on August 20, 1888. Congress spent forty days passing another Chinese exclusion bill, which was signed into law on September 13, 1888. The law repealed both the 1882 and 1884 exclusion acts, provided that the pending treaty with China was executed. The law suspended Chinese immigration for twenty years, but suspension was to be made void if the Chinese government refused to ratify the treaty, thus making the exclusion of the Chinese immigration permanent.

Congress acted swiftly to pass another bill, this time spending only four days to legislate a law that would have a major impact on the lives of tens of thousands of Chinese immigrants. On September 3, 1888, Representative William Scott of Pennsylvania, reacting quickly to a London dispatch of the preceding day (which reported that the Chinese government rejected the treaty negotiated between China and the United States), introduced a bill that would make the certificate of identity issued to Chinese alien residents, in conformity of the Chinese Exclusion Act of 1882 and as amended by the 1884 Chinese Exclusion Act, null and void. It was reported that there were as many as 20,000 Chinese who were in transit at the time of the passage of the bill.[20]

Attorneys representing the appellant presented an oral argument, and two separate briefs were filed to present main propositions, which were grouped into three divisions. First, it was stated that if the appellant who was imprisoned had the right to land on American soil, then the judgment of the lower court was erroneous and should be reversed. Having argued that the appellant was held without any judicial review of any court, his attorneys claimed that their client was deprived of due process of law. The appellant's attorneys conceded that a sovereign government had the right to prohibit foreign aliens from immigration, but Congress did not have power to prohibit the "return to this country of the appellant. He had a vested right to return, which could not be taken from him by any exercise of mere legislative power" (130 U.S. 585).

Justice Field brushed aside the argument that denial to Chae Chan Ping of his right to land in the United States would be in violation of existing treaties between the United States and China. With regard to the rights conferred to Chae Chan Ping by treaties between the United States and China, the Court relied on a doctrine articulated in the Head Money Cases[21] decided in 1884. The Court had ruled that "so far as any treaty made between the United States and any foreign power can become the subject of judicial cognizance in the courts of this country,"[22] the treaty was subject to the Congressional mandate. This meant that a treaty was no higher than a statute passed by Congress. In view of the fact that the U.S. Constitution places treaties and Congressional legislation on equal footing, this ruling was rather controversial. But since the Constitution failed to provide a clear resolution of the conflict between prior treaties and subsequent Congressional acts, the Court argued that laws made by Congress after the treaty had been concluded and ratified should control. This doctrine was further buttressed by the Chinese Exclusion Case, when the Court ruled against Chae Chan Ping on May 13, 1889.

Justice Field, in delivering the Court's unanimous opinion, supported the position that Chinese laborers were a threat to the interest of the country and its good order. He was sure, as he had been convinced on previous occasions, that the Chinese could not either assimilate with American people or change their habits or modes of living. He gave his own idea of who should become members of the community called America when he quoted from a statement made by Marcy, Secretary of State under President Pierce, who said that "every society possesses the undoubted right to determine who shall compose its members."[23] Undoubtedly, Justice Field believed that the Chinese should not become members of American society. His prejudicial feelings might have been infused into his judicial opinion, which asserted the power of sovereign nations:

The power of exclusion of foreigners being an incident of sovereignty belonging to the government of the United States, as a part of those sovereign powers delegated by the Constitution, the right to exercise at any time, when, in the judgment of the government, the interests of the country require it, cannot be granted away or restrained on behalf of any one. . . . Whatever license, therefore, Chinese laborers may have obtained, previous to the act of October 1, 1888, to return to the United States after their departure, is held at the will of the government, revocable at any time, at its pleasure.[24]

According to Justice Field, the power to exclude aliens was incident of the sovereignty that was delegated to the national government. But the question of whether all incidents of sovereignty were delegated by the Constitution to the federal government was not answered until the Court ruled on the case of *United States v. Curtiss-Wright Corporation*[25] in 1936. The Court declared that the powers of external sovereignty vested in the federal government did not depend on the Constitution, and the president of the United States had plenary powers in international relations independent from congressional delegation. What the Court had done between 1889 and 1936 was to expand progressively the powers of the national government in its role in international affairs, thus weakening the doctrine of enumerated powers—the notion that the federal government enjoys only enumerated powers. In 1893, Justice Gray asserted in his majority opinion on the *Fong Yue Ting v. U.S.* case that the federal government was vested with all the powers of government in international relations. Justice Gray's ruling was part of this gradual process of expanding the role of the federal government in international affairs.

The following year *Wan Shing v. U.S.*[26] and *Quock Ting v. U.S.*[27] reached the Court. The former involved a Chinese who, upon arrival in San Francisco on August 7, 1889, was refused the right to land in the United States because he was considered a laborer. He was detained by the captain of the ship that brought him to San Francisco, and he applied for a habeas corpus in order to obtain his release from detention. Wan Shing claimed that he was a merchant, having done business on Dupont Street in San Francisco while he lived in America between November 17, 1880, and sometime before June 6, 1882. He left for a visit to China on April 19, 1882. The petitioner maintained that he had the right to land in the United States because he was a former resident and was engaged in business. Justice Field, in delivering the opinion of the Court on May 11, 1891, ruled that the evidence the petitioner presented before the Court was insufficient and that the only evidence permissible was the certificate of identity issued by the Chinese government indicating that he was not a laborer. Since Wan Shing could not produce such a certificate, he had no right to land in the United States.

On the same day, Justice Field handed down the Court's opinion on *Quock Ting v. U.S.* Quock Ting, the petitioner, came back to San Francisco after a visit to China in February 1888 but was denied his right to reenter the United States because he was deemed a Chinese subject. He claimed, however, that he was born on Dupont Street in San Francisco and that the Chinese Exclusion Act of 1882 was not applicable to him because he was a citizen of the United States. In his defense, his attorneys presented evidence that included the testimony of the petitioner's father that he had bought tickets for his son and his wife to go to China. Justice Field, in delivering the majority opinion, ruled that the evidence presented before the Court was not conclusive. Furthermore, the testimony given by the petitioner's father was not believable because of doubts of his sincerity, according to Justice Field, who was probably inclined to discredit any testimony given by a Chinese person. Justice Brewer, dissenting from the majority opinion, criticized the government because it "rested on the assumption that, because the witnesses were Chinese persons, they were not to be believed."[28]

One of the first Supreme Court cases involving persons of Japanese ancestry was *Nishimura Ekiu v. U.S.*,[29] which was decided on January 18, 1892. Nishimura Ekiu, a Japanese subject, came from Yokohama, Japan, to San Francisco aboard the steamship *Belgic* on May 7, 1891, and she requested permission to land in the United States. She was refused permission to land by William H. Thornley, Commissioner of Immigration of the State of California, who believed that permitting her to land would be in violation of the provisions of the act approved by Congress on August 3, 1882.[30]

This was the first general federal immigration law that departed from encouraging people from Europe to come to America. Although Congress had passed the Homestead Law in 1862 to encourage Europeans to immigrate, the same branch of government gravitated toward developing federal immigration policies beginning in 1864, when the Office of the Commissioner of Immigration was established by the Act of July 1864. As stated earlier, the Immigration Act of March 3, 1875 followed, establishing minor federal regulations on immigration for the first time in American history. Numerous states, which felt that they were deprived of head tax revenues but were held responsible for caring for unwanted immigrants, believed that the provisions of this law were not sufficient. Members of Congress from New York took the initiative in introducing bills at both legislative chambers. The House approved its bill and forwarded it to the Senate, which passed it without debate. President Arthur signed it into law on August 3, 1882. The main provisions of the law included, among others, a head tax of 50¢ imposed on every immigrant arriving by vessel; the money was to be used for regulating immigration and caring for immigrants. Section Four of the law stated that all foreign convicts, unless they were convicted of political offenses, "shall be sent back to the nation to which they belong, and from which they came" (22 Stat. 214). Section Two specified classes of people excluded from coming to the United States: "And if on such examination there shall be found among such passengers any convict, lunatic, idiot, any person unable to take care of himself or herself without becoming a public charge, they shall report the same in writing to the collector of such port, and such persons shall not be permitted to land."[31]

The inspecting officer, William H. Thornley, believed that the petitioner, Nishimura Ekiu, would be a public charge and therefore not permissible to land in the United States, although she had $22 in her possession. Her story that she was accompanied by her husband turned out to be untrue, and her claim that her husband was in the United States was discredited because she did not know his address. She was detained in the Methodist Episcopal Japanese and Chinese Mission, because the ship that brought her was considered an improper place for detention. When she filed for a habeas corpus to obtain her release, John L. Hatch, now appointed as Inspector of Immigration at the Port of San Francisco on May 14, 1891, inspected the detainee, as required by the Act of March 3, 1891,[32] and refused to give her permission to land. Furthermore, he made a report to the collector that was identical with that of Thornley, except that he cited the Act of March 3, 1891, rather than the Act of August 3, 1882, as having been violated.

Congress passed the Immigration Act of March 3, 1891, to supplement and strengthen provisions made in the Immigration Act of August 3, 1882, and the Contract Labor Act of 1885.[33] Section One of the act specified classes of people who were excluded from immigration. Those included in these classes were "idiots, insane persons, paupers likely to become a public charge, persons suffering from a loathsome or a dangerous contagious disease, persons who have been convicted of a felony or other infamous crimes or misdemeanor involving moral turpitude."[34] This provision, in essence, did not depart radically from the Immigration Act of August 3, 1882. What the former did was to add to the latter more classes of people declared excluded from immigration. Section Seven of the act established the Office of Superintendent of Immigration. The president was to appoint this officer, who, in turn, was to appoint a commissioner of immigration. This became the major point of attack in defense of Nishimura Ekiu.

Attorney Lyman I. Mowry argued on behalf of the petitioner that the appointment of John L. Hatch was illegal because the Secretary of the Treasury had appointed him, rather than the superintendent of immigration, as required by the Act of March 3, 1891. Mowry also claimed that the inspecting officers did not follow the instructions of the Act of March 3, 1891, as they had neither administered any oaths nor taken any testimony. Finally, Mowry argued that the decisions made by Thornley, Hatch, and the collector were arbitrary, irregular, and without testimony.

These three technical points were not to become obstacles to the government, which was bent on administering "justice" in ways to restrict Asian immigration. Justice Gray, in delivering the opinion of the Court, reiterated the power of a sovereign nation to exclude aliens, as Justice Field had insisted in the case of *Chae Chan Ping v. U.S.* Justice Gray upheld the constitutionality of the Act of March 3, 1891:

The result is, that the Act of 1891 is constitutional and valid; the inspector of immigration was duly appointed; his decision against the petitioner's right to land in the United States was within the authority conferred upon him by that Act; no appeal having been taken to the superintendent of immigration, that decision was final and conclusive; the petitioner is not unlawfully restrained in her liberty.[35]

The U.S. government's decision to exclude Nishimura Ekiu and deport her back to her country prompted Japan to negotiate for a treaty with Washington. In 1894, the United States and Japan concluded one of the most comprehensive treaties ever made between them. The treaty, known as the Treaty of Commerce and Navigation of 1894, included twenty-nine articles covering such subjects as mutual freedom of trade and travel, import and export duties, and port regulations. But the most important provision for Japanese alien residents in America was written into Article I of the Treaty, which stated that "the citizens of subjects of each of the two High Contracting Parties shall have full liberty to enter, travel, or reside in any part of the territories of the other Contracting Parties, and shall enjoy full and perfect protection for their persons and property."[36] In

1903 this treaty came under review by the Supreme Court of the United States in the case of *Yamataya Kaoru v. Thomas M. Fisher.*[37]

Ever since the Court handed down its decision on the Chinese Exclusion Case (i.e., *Chae Chan Ping v. U.S.*) in 1889, its interpretations of the rights of the Chinese to land in the United States became increasingly constrictive, allowing little latitude for immigration officials stationed at the port of entry. This is because some overzealous officials refused permission for the Chinese to land, even if they had the necessary documents giving them the right to reenter the United States. This was particularly true in the case of *Lau Ow Bew v. U.S.,*[38] which the Court reviewed.

Lao Ow Bew was a Chinese merchant who had been engaged in the wholesale and import business in Portland, Oregon, seventeen years before his departure, on September 3, 1890, for a short visit with relatives in China. Before he departed from the United States, Bew had obtained evidence of his status as a merchant in America. He came back to San Francisco aboard the *S.S. Oceanic* on August 11, 1891, and after presenting evidence of his former status, he asked for permission to land. The collector received the evidence and acknowledged that Lau Ow Bew was a merchant domiciled in America, but he refused to give him permission to land on the grounds that he did not have a certificate that the Chinese government was supposed to have issued in accordance with the requirements of Section Six of the Chinese Exclusion Act of May 6, 1882, as revised on July 5, 1884.

Because Lau Ow Bew was detained against his will, he sued for a habeas corpus to obtain his release, and the Circuit Court of Appeals for the Ninth Circuit reviewed the case and upheld the collector's decision on October 7, 1891. Lau Ow Bew then appealed to the Supreme Court, which issued a writ of certiorari to the Circuit Court, requiring it to send the case up for review and decision. Attorneys for the appellant argued that the Treasury Department issued instructions with regard to the reentry of the Chinese as follows:

Chinamen who are not laborers, and who have heretofore resided in the United States, are not prevented by existing law or treaty from returning to the United States after visiting China or elsewhere. No certificates or other papers, however, are issued by the department, or by any of its subordinate officers, to show that they are entitled to land in the United States, but it is suggested that such persons should, before leaving the United States, provide themselves with such proofs of identity as may be deemed proper, showing that they have been residents of the United States, and that they are not laborers, so that they can present the same to and be identified by, the collector of customs at the port where they may return.[39]

Assistant Attorney General Parker, in defense of the government's action, claimed that the appellant was about to come to the United States from China, and therefore he was subject to American laws governing Chinese immigration. Citing the case of *Wan Shing v. U.S.,* Parker considered it not unnatural for Congress to "require of a person in China who claims to be engaged in trade in the United States, that he shall be identified and show to be such by the Chinese government."[40] He reasoned that the purpose of Section Six of the Chinese Exclusion Law of 1882 was "one to stop and turn back the multitude of Chinese laborers who pay no respect to our wishes or our laws, and who are prompt to employ fraud and perjury in order to place themselves in the ranks of competition in our labor markets."[41]

Chief Justice Fuller delivered the opinion of the unanimous Court on March 14, 1892. He argued against the government's position, stating that all laws were to be construed as to avoid an unjust or an absurd conclusion. Evidently, supporting the government's claim that the appellant was required to have in his possession a certificate issued by the Chinese government appeared unjust and absurd to the justices. Although every Chinese person other than laborer who was already within the United States, or who was about to come to the United States, was required to obtain a certificate issued by the Chinese government, the appellant did not belong to that class of people who were about to come to the United States. Since the appellant was formerly a resident of the United States and wanted to return to the country of his residence and business, he should be allowed to land in the United States. The Court reversed the decision of the Circuit Court and instructed it to discharge the appellant.

The original Chinese Exclusion Act of May 6, 1882, was to expire at the end of the ten-year period of suspension, and Congress felt compelled to make a decision on Chinese immigration. The Chinese Exclusion Act was good for ten years, and it was up to Congress to renew or revise it. As the expiration date approached, there was a flurry of bills introduced in Congress to deal with the Chinese question. At least eight different bills were designed to prohibit Chinese immigration. Most of these bills were sponsored by congressmen from the Pacific Coast states, including Geary of California, Mitchell of Oregon, Cutting of California, Loud of California, Dolph of Oregon, and Wilson of Washington. Most of these bills proposed to prohibit Chinese immigration. One of the bills was finally reported out of the Committee on Foreign Affairs of the House, which passed the bill. The bill was then sent to the Senate Committee on Foreign Relations. The committee worked on the bill, which was reported back to the Senate with favorable recommendation. The bill was finally passed, and the president signed it into law, making it the Chinese Exclusion Act of May 5, 1892.[42]

The law included many provisions grouped into eight sections. Section

One stated that all laws now in force, prohibiting or regulating Chinese immigration into the United States, were to continue in force for ten years from the passage of the law. Sections Two, Three, Four, and Five specified procedures of appeal, deportation, and penalty for violation of the law. Section Six included the most critical legal requirement. It required all Chinese laborers residing in the United States, and who had the right to remain therein at the time of passage of the act, to apply for a certificate of residence to their district's collector of internal revenue within one year after passage of the law. Those who failed to obtain a certificate of identity within the prescribed period were subject to arrest and deportation unless they could establish to the satisfaction of the judge that they were unable to obtain the certificate by reason of accident, sickness, or other unavoidable cause and that they were proven residents of the United States at the time of passage of the act by at least one credible white witness and to the satisfaction of the Court.

The constitutionality of the Chinese Exclusion Act of May 5, 1892, also known as the Geary Act of 1892, was tested in the cases of *Fong Yue Ting v. U.S., Wong Quan v. U.S.,* and *Lee Joe v. U.S.*[43] Fong Yue Ting had been a lawful resident of the United States since 1879, and he had no intention of returning to China. He had, for more than a year, resided in the city, county, and state of New York after passage of the Chinese Exclusion Act of May 5, 1892. He had not, since passage of said act, applied for a certificate of residence, and he was arrested by the marshal who had authority to do so. In the case of *Wong Quan v. U.S.,* the petitioner failed to obtain a certificate of residence and was, therefore, arrested by the marshal who had authority. The petitioner also claimed that he was ordered deported without any hearing. The third petitioner applied for a certificate of residence but was refused by the collector because the witness he produced was Chinese, not a credible white witness. All petitioners claimed that they were deprived of due process of law and that Section Six of the Chinese Exclusion Act of May 5, 1892, was unconstitutional and void.

Justice Gray delivered the majority opinion of the Court on May 15, 1893, and Justices Brewer, Field, and Fuller filed their separate dissenting opinions. Justice Gray declared that "the right of a nation to expel or deport foreigners, who have not been naturalized or taken any step towards becoming citizens of the country, rests upon the same grounds, and is as absolute and unqualified as the rights to prohibit and prevent their entrance into the country."[44] This was a reiteration of the doctrine established in the Chinese Exclusion Case. Gray insisted that deportation was neither a punishment for crime nor a banishment. He characterized deportation as "a method of enforcing the return to his own country of an alien who has not complied with the conditions upon the performance of which the government of the nation, acting within its constitutional authority and through the proper departments, has determined that his continuing to reside here shall depend."[45] He also made a reference to the Chinese as being unwilling to assimilate and therefore dangerous to the country's peace and security. Justice Gray rested his opinion on the theory that the power to exclude or expel aliens is "an inherent and inalienable right of every sovereign and independent nation" (149 U.S. 698).

This power to expel aliens is the same as the power to exclude aliens, according to Justice Gray, which was already adjudicated in the Chinese Exclusion Case in 1889. According to Justice Gray, the power to expel aliens is an inherent power of the government, and such power was not derived from the Constitution. All sovereign governments have an inherent power to exclude or expel aliens. By implication, if a government did not have such a power, then it would be less than sovereign. In relation to this notion of sovereignty one is compelled to pose at least three questions. First, did the fact that the United States expelled powerless Chinese laborers prove that it was a sovereign nation? Sovereignty of a nation may have no compelling correlation with its power to expel aliens. Second, was it possible to establish the sovereignty of a nation by means other than expelling defenseless aliens? Third, was the power to expel aliens the only incident of sovereignty delegated by the Constitution, or did the Constitution delegate all incidents of sovereignty to the federal government? With regard to the first two questions, reasonable people would assert that there were alternative methods available to the government to assert its sovereignty. Regarding the last question, in Justice Gray's opinion such power was just another step toward expanding the role of the federal government in international affairs.

Justice Brewer based his dissenting opinion on three grounds: First, three petitioners who were placed under arrest were lawful residents of the United States; second, they were within the protection of the U.S. Constitution; and third, Section Six of the Chinese Exclusion Act of May 5, 1892, deprived them of liberty and imposed punishment without due process of law in disregard of the Fourth, Fifth, Sixth, and Eighth Amendments of the Constitution. He questioned the theory of the power of a sovereign nation, characterizing it as indefinite and dangerous. Again he questioned his colleagues' judgment:

Where are the limits of such power to be found, and by whom are they to be pronounced? Is it within legislation capacity to declare the limits? If so, then the mere assertion of an inherent power creates it, and despotism exists. May the courts establish the boundaries? When do they obtain the authority for this? Shall they look to the practices of other nations to ascertain the limits? . . . The expulsion of a race may be within the inherent power of a despotism.[46]

Justice Brewer characterized deportation of the three Chinese laborers as punishment, which, from his point of view, deprived them of life, liberty, or property without due process of law. This was certainly in violation of the Constitution, since the laborers had not been given due process, which requires that "a man be heard before he is condemned" (149 U.S. 741) (to use Justice Brewer's own words). Brewer emphatically pointed out that no person, including a Chinese person, who had once come within the protection of the Constitution could be punished without a judicial trial.

The majority opinion on this case did not agree with Justice Field, who had been known for his anti-Chinese feelings. Field filed a dissenting opinion that refuted the legal grounds covered by the majority. He briefly went over the decision on the *Chae Chan Ping v. U.S.* case (for which he had delivered the majority opinion four years earlier), and he pointed out the difference between the two. From his point of view, the government's power to exclude aliens from the country should not be denied whenever the public interest demanded it, but the government's power to deport from the country aliens who were admitted legally could not be defended unless it was punishment for crime. He challenged the theory of sovereignty expounded in the majority opinion and characterized it as an admission that "the government is one of unlimited and despotic power so far as aliens domiciled in the country are concerned."[47]

Justice Field may have been contradicting himself when he refuted the *Fong Yue Ting* majority opinion, which cited the ruling on the Chinese Exclusion Case as its supportive evidence. Justice Field, who had delivered the Court's unanimous decision, had grounded his reason on the theory of sovereignty of nation, which was now applied to the case of *Fong Yue Ting v. U.S.* Justice Field argued that there was a difference between the power of Congress to exclude aliens and to expel or deport them. According to Field, Congress did not have the power to deport aliens without regard to the guarantees of the Constitution. But was not Chae Chan Ping, who was ordered excluded by the Court, already in the United States when he was detained aboard an American ship docked in San Francisco? Perhaps Justice Field made an error in judgment when he authored the Court's opinion on the Chinese Exclusion Case.

Justice Field defined what sovereignty in America meant to him. Sovereignty was vested in the American people, and only in them. They have delegated certain sovereign powers to the government of the United States. There should be no argument on this point, as it was clearly stated in the Tenth Amendment of the Constitution, according to Field. Congress, therefore, should not exercise power when it is not found in express terms in the Constitution. Thus, Justice Field sided with the doctrine of constitutional limitations.

Another interesting point of refutation raised by Justice Field was his objection to the deportation of friendly aliens. He agreed with the majority opinion that enemy aliens were under the law of nations, while friendly aliens were under the municipal law. By implication, then, enemy aliens may be expelled without due process of law by a national government, while friendly aliens may be protected by due process. If this was Field's reasoning, then there remained an important question at the time of the decision: Who is an enemy alien and how do we determine this? The Court should have dealt with this question in 1893, because it reemerged in a different form to haunt the Court when it had to decide on Japanese internment cases during World War II.

Justice Field was so outraged by the outcome of the Fong Yue Ting case that he worked behind the scenes to have the decision reversed. He even suggested that the number of justices be increased because he felt he could get a justice appointed to vote with the dissenters. But his efforts failed, and finally he concluded his dissent as follows:

I will not pursue the subject further. The decision of the Court and the sanction it would give to legislation depriving resident aliens of the guaranties of the Constitution fills me with apprehensions. Those guarantees are of priceless value to every one resident in the country, whether citizen or alien. I cannot but regard the decision as a blow against constitutional liberty, when it declares that Congress has the right to disregard the guaranties of the Constitution intended for the protection of all men, domiciled in the country with the consent of the government, in their rights of person and property.[48]

Chief Justice Fuller, in his dissenting opinion, stated that the provisions of the Fifth and Fourteenth Amendments were meant to be universal in their application to any person in U.S. jurisdiction, regardless of race, color, or nationality. Furthermore, he pointed out that the legal principle established in the case of *Yick Wo v. Hopkins* applied to Congress under the Fifth Amendment and to the states under the Fourteenth Amendment. Justice Fuller reasoned that registration could be required through legislation by Congress for the purpose of identification of aliens, but to deport them for failing to coerce compliance with it was a legislative sentence of banishment that, in his opinion, was absolutely void.

On May 27, 1895, a decision was handed down by the Supreme Court of the United States that strengthened the authority of the executive branch of government in handling aliens seeking to enter the United States. The case[49] involved a Chinese merchant, Lem Moon Sing, a member of Kee Sang Tong and Company in San Francisco and a lawful alien resident of the United States, who had left for a visit to China on January 30, 1894. During his absence Congress passed (on August 18, 1894) a law that read in part as follows: "In every case where an alien is excluded from admission into the United States under any law or treaty now existing or hereafter made, the decision of the appropriate immigration or customs officers, if adverse to the admission of such alien, shall be final, unless reversed on appeal to the Secretary of Treasury."[50]

Lem Moon Sing returned to the United States, arriving in San Francisco by the steamer *Belgic,* and requested permission to land. However, his request was denied and he was detained against his will by John H. Wise, collector of the port. He filed for a habeas corpus to obtain release from detention. But the writ of habeas corpus was denied by the district court, and he appealed to the Supreme Court. The opinion of the Court (delivered by Justice Harlan, with Justice Brewer dissenting) reaffirmed the principle established in the case of *Nishimura Ekiu v. U.S.,* on which the Court ruled to the effect that an alien who left the country on his or her own will, upon returning to the country should be treated as any other alien seeking to enter the country. The Court also took sides with the executive branch of government, which had sought to increase immigrant or custom officers' latitude for making decisions on aliens arriving in the United States.

Three major factors contributed to the enactment of yet another Chinese exclusion law in 1902. First, Theodore Roosevelt was sworn in as the twenty-sixth president following the assassination of President McKinley in 1901. Upon assuming the office, he sent to Congress a strong message for changing immigration laws in order to keep out of the country anarchists or persons professing principles hostile to all government and to deport them back to the country from which they came. Second, Congress received Volume XV of the Industrial Commission report on December 5, 1901, submitted by the Commission chairperson, Albert Clarke. The report included recommendations on a wide range of legislative actions to be taken, including revision of immigration laws. Third, the Geary Act of 1892, which had extended the original Chinese exclusion for ten years, was to expire in May 1902, and therefore Congress was urged to extend Chinese exclusion for another ten or twenty years. Congress saw a flurry of bills, one of which called for prohibition and exclusion of persons of Chinese descent into the United States and its territories, including the Philippine Islands and Puerto Rico.

The final bill, passed on April 29, 1902,[51] had four sections. Section One stated that all laws in force that excluded the coming of the Chinese were reenacted, extended and continued until a treaty could be concluded between the two nations. It also stipulated that all exclusion laws would be applied to the island territory under the jurisdiction of the United States. It also prohibited the coming of the Chinese from such an island territory to the United States. Section Four required every Chinese laborer residing in any of the insular territories of the United States to obtain within one year a certificate of residence in the insular territory. This section was particularly aimed at Chinese residents in the Philippines, and the Philippine Commission was authorized to enforce the requirements.

The Fifty-Eighth Congress made Chinese exclusion laws as laws enacted without limitation when it approved a deficiency appropriation bill on April 27, 1904. Section Five of the law declared that "all laws in force . . . regulating, suspending, or prohibiting the coming of Chinese persons or persons of Chinese descent into the United States . . . are hereby reenacted, extended and continued, without modification, limitation, or conditions."[52] The language inserted into the 1902 law anticipated a treaty between the United States and China, but Congress decided to enact the 1904 Immigration Act, making the Chinese exclusion "a closed issue" as characterized by Samuel Gompers, the leader of the American Federation of Labor, which had been seeking a total and permanent exclusion of the Chinese laborers.

Between 1902 and 1922, the Supreme Court dealt with over twenty exclusion, expulsion, or deportation cases, most of which concerned the rights of aliens of Asian ancestry to enter the United States. With a few exceptions, most decisions went against them for a variety of reasons. First, the Supreme Court had already established some major ground rules through its decisions on *Chae Chan Ping v. United States, Nishimura Ekiu v. United States, Fong Yue Ting v. United States,* and *Lem Moon Sing v. United States.* The Court had consistently ruled to strengthen the discretionary power of the immigration officers representing the executive branch of the government. Second, even in the case of aliens claiming to be citizens of the United States, the Court ruled that the burden of proof is not on the government, but on petitioners. Third, the Court made it increasingly difficult for Asian aliens to have judicial hearings.

In the case of *United States v. Lee Yen Tai,*[53] the Court handed down a decision on April 21, 1902, against Lee Yen Tai, one of the three appellees in the case, who claimed that because the 1894 treaty between China and the United States abrogated the twelfth section of the Act of 1882, the Commissioner was without jurisdiction to order the appellees deported. The Court, however, ruled that if statutes are in conflict with each other, both must be in effect. On May 5, 1902, the Court handed down another ruling on the case of *Fok Yung Yo v. United States,*[54] declaring that transit passage of a Chinese person across the territory of the United States was subject to regulations of the U.S. government, and that the courts could not interfere with the action taken by the customs official against the appellee.

In the case of *Chin Bak Kan v. United States,*[55] two questions were raised before the Court. The first was whether a commissioner had authority to order deportation of a Chinese person who was found to be in the United States illegally. The second was whether a Chinese person who claimed to be a citizen of the United States had the burden of proving her citizenship. On June 2, 1902, the Court ruled that a commissioner was duly authorized to conduct deportation proceedings, thus strengthening the power of the executive branch of government in dealing with aliens. It also ruled that a Chinese person had to prove that she was a citizen of the United States. In the words of Chief Justice Fuller, who delivered the opinion of the unanimous Court, "by the law the Chinese person must be adjudged unlawfully within the United States unless he 'shall establish by affirmative proof, to the satisfaction of such justice, judge, or commissioner, his lawful right to remain in the United States.' "[56] In other words, all Chinese who were already in the United States were to be considered illegal residents, unless they could prove themselves to be otherwise. The Chinese were not accorded the privilege of common law that a person is innocent until proven guilty.

The Court softened the power of customs officers in dealing with the fundamental principles of due process of law guaranteed in the Constitution by declaring that aliens who were already in the United States, even though they entered illegally, should be given an opportunity for a hearing. This ruling was handed down by the Court in the case of *Yamataya Kaoru v. Fisher,*[57] also known as the Japanese Immigrant Case, on April 6, 1903. The case went to the Court as a result of a lower court's ruling that Yamataya must be deported to Japan because she was considered a pauper who would likely become a public charge. This deportation order was in conformity with the Act of March 3, 1891, which Congress passed to protect the general public against contact with dangerous or improper persons.

The attorneys for the appellant presented their brief on the following grounds: First, the Act of March 3, 1891, which gave immigration officers power over aliens, should be construed to have effect on those who were not already in the United States; second, the Act of March 3, 1891, was unconstitutional; third, the appellant was being deprived of her liberty without due process of law. The attorneys also claimed that a Japanese person who landed in the United States had all the rights that were accorded American citizens according to the treaty signed on November 22, 1894, between Japan and the United States. As mentioned earlier in relation to the case of *Nishimura Ekiu v. U.S.,* this treaty was negotiated and concluded between the two nations after the Supreme Court ruled against Nishimura. On the other hand, Assistant Attorney General Hoyt, arguing for the government, brushed aside the claim made by the appellant's attorneys and defended the government's position that the 1894 treaty did not necessarily exempt the Japanese from the excluded classes of aliens wanting to enter the United States.

Justice Harlan, in delivering the opinion of the majority, declared that "no person shall be deprived of his liberty without opportunity, at some time, to be heard" (189 U.S. 101), although such a hearing may not be either a regular or in the forms of a judicial procedure. But the appellant Yamataya had notice of the investigation to be undertaken to establish if she was in the country legally or illegally. Justice Harlan conceded that she "did not understand the nature and meaning of the questions propounded to her" (189 U.S. 102) because of her lack of English, but this fact alone could not justify the Court's intervention. If she did not understand English, "that was her misfortune,"[58] to borrow from Justice Harlan's words, and, of course, her want of English "constitutes no reason, under the acts of Congress, or under any rule of law, for the intervention of the court by habeas corpus."[59]

The Supreme Court took a dim view of the claim made by those Chinese who said that they were born in America, but because they were minors when Chinese laborers were required to register in accordance with the Chinese Exclusion Act of 1892 as amended in 1893, they did not have certificates to show that they had a right to stay in America. The Court ruled on *Ah How v. United States*[60] on February 23, 1904. Justice Holmes delivered the opinion of the majority, declaring that the claims of U.S. citizenship supported by the parole evidence of one appellant and by a certificate issued by a U.S. commissioner for another appellant were not acceptable evidence for judgment.

On March 21, 1904, however, the Supreme Court handed down its decision on the case of *Tom Hong v. United States*[61] on the basis of testimony presented on behalf of the appellants. This case involved three appellants, including Tom Hong, who were engaged in business in New York. They ran a company called the Kwon Yen Ti Company from 1891 to 1895, when the company ceased its operation. As you may recall, all Chinese laborers were required to register in accordance with the Chinese Exclusion Act of 1892 as amended in 1893, but Tom Hong did not register because he was a merchant, and no merchant was required to register by the said law. The appellants also failed to put their names on the list of the company.

After their company went out of business, they were found without a certificate and were brought before the commissioner, who ordered them deported because they were considered laborers in light of the absence of their names from the company's list. Justice William Rufus Day ruled that the appellants did not have to list their names as long as they could establish the fact that they were merchants.

A narrow interpretation of the rights of entry into the United States by Chinese claiming to be U.S. citizens was handed down by the Supreme Court when it ruled on the case of *U.S. v. Sing Tuck*[62] on April 25, 1904. In delivering the Court's majority opinion (with which Justices Brewer and Peckham dissented), Justice Holmes declared that a Chinese person claiming to be a U.S. citizen must establish his or her citizenship in a reasonable manner and that such a person should exhaust administrative remedies before resorting to judicial relief. As discussed earlier in relation to *Lem Moon Sing v. U.S.,* the decision of the appropriate immigration officers was to be final in every case where an alien was excluded from admission into the United States, and the Act of August 18, 1894, applicable only to aliens was now applied to a Chinese person claiming to be a U.S. citizen (28 Stat. 390).

Justice Brewer, in his dissenting opinion, chastised the majority for its discriminatory attitude:

Must an American citizen, seeking to return to [this] his native land, be compelled to bring with him two witnesses to prove the place of his birth or else be denied his right to return, and all opportunity of establishing his citizenship in the courts of his country? No such rule is enforced against an American citizen of Anglo-Saxon descent, and if this be, as claimed, a government of laws and not of men, I do not think it should be enforced against American citizens of Chinese descent.[63]

A still narrower interpretation of the rights of entry into America by Chinese claiming to be American citizens was made by the Supreme Court when it decided against Ju Toy[64] on May 8, 1905. Ju Toy was refused entry to the United States when he returned to the United States from a trip to China. He claimed that he was a native-born U.S. citizen, and he filed an appeal as he was required. The decision to deny him entry was affirmed by the Secretary of Commerce, and Ju Toy petitioned for a habeas corpus. The Federal District Court decided in his favor, but the government appealed. The Circuit Court of Appeals certified certain questions to be dealt with by the Supreme Court. The first question before the Court was whether a habeas corpus should be granted to a Chinese person claiming to be a U.S. citizen whose right to enter the United States had been denied by immigrant officers. The second question was whether such a person should be given a further hearing or whether the writ should be dismissed. The third question was whether the decision of the Secretary of Commerce was final.

Justice Holmes delivered the majority opinion, which stated that the answer to the first question was no, whereas the third question should be answered affirmatively. Of course, it followed that the writ was to be dismissed, given the answers to the first and third questions. The Court supported the government's decision to deport Ju Toy, even though he followed the procedures spelled out by the Court in its decision on *Sing Tuck v. United States.* Justices Brewer, Peckham, and Day dissented, and Justice Brewer filed a separate opinion, with which Justice Peckham concurred. Justice Brewer conceded the power of the executive officials to deny entry to Chinese aliens, but he argued that a Chinese person claiming to be a citizen of the United States had the constitutional right to receive judicial review. If an American citizen, albeit a person of Chinese ancestry, was to be deported then she was entitled to her Fifth Amendment rights because deportation is punishment, and "no person shall be held in answer for a capital or otherwise infamous crime, unless on a presentment or indictment of a grand jury."[65]

The Court's decision on *Ju Toy v. United States* became rather unpopular and was subject to severe criticism, both in America and China. It helped to fan a fiery rage among the Chinese, who felt that their country and their people had been unjustly treated by Congress, which made Chinese exclusions laws permanent in 1904. Chinese merchants in Shanghai and Canton, with the support of students, planned to stage a nationwide boycott of American-made goods. But Edwin H. Conger, American Minister in Beijing, was reported to have scoffed at such a plan, because he believed that the Chinese could not agree on anything and that Chinese merchants would not allow their emotions to interfere with their businesses. Tseng Shao-ch'ing, the leader of the boycott movement, proved him wrong, and the boycott started in Shanghai on July 20, 1905, as Tseng planned. The boycott was financed primarily by the Chinese in the United States, who sent approximately $90,000 to China in hopes of forcing America to change its exclusion policies against the Chinese.[66]

Perhaps because of the boycott and the unreasonable nature of the decision on the case of *Ju Toy v. U.S.,* subsequent decisions by the Court on cases involving Chinese claiming to be U.S. citizens who were denied entry into the United States required that the executive hearing on the question of their citizenship must be a fair hearing, but that the administrative decision should be final unless the Chinese were denied an opportunity to establish their citizenship at a fair hearing or the officers abused their authority. The first of these cases decided by the Supreme Court was *Chin Yow v. United States*[67] on January 6, 1908. Justice Holmes ruled that Chin Yow should have been given an opportunity to prove his citizenship at a hearing. Another case involving a Chinese person claiming to be a U.S. citizen was *Tang Tun v. Edsell, Chinese Inspector,*[68] which was decided on March 11, 1912. Justice Hughes delivered the opinion of the Court and ruled that Tang Tun had received an opportunity to prove his citizenship, but his proof was insufficient to establish his citizenship. Since he was given an administrative hearing to prove his citizenship, the Court was unable to intervene. A third case, *Kwock Jan Fat v. White,*[69] came to the Court on June 7, 1920. Justice Clarke handed down the Court's ruling to the effect that "a report which suppressed or omitted it [testimony by witnesses] was not a fair report and a hearing based upon it was not a fair hearing within the definition of the cases cited" (253 U.S. 464). Clarke declared, "It is better that many Chinese immigrants should be improperly admitted than that one natural born citizen of the United States should be permanently excluded from his country."[70]

PROTECTION OF THE FIFTH AND SIXTH AMENDMENTS

An important judicial principle was established on May 18, 1896, when the Supreme Court handed down its decision on the case of *Wong Wing v. United States.* The case involved four Chinese persons: Wong Wing, Lee Poy, Lee Yon Tong, and Chan Wah Dong, all of whom were found illegally in the country. They were taken to John Graves, a commissioner of the Circuit Court of the United States for the Eastern District of Michigan, who had ruled that they were unlawfully in the country. The commissioner then sentenced them to sixty days of hard labor in the Detroit house of correction, and the prisoners were to be deported to China after completion of their sentence.

The prisoners then sued for a habeas corpus, alleging that they were illegally detained by Joseph Nicholson, superintendent of the correction house. But the Circuit Court denied the writ, and the prisoners were remanded to the said superintendent. The prisoners then appealed to the Supreme Court. Attorney Frank H. Canfield, representing the appellants, argued that the fourth section of the 1892 Act, known also as the Geary Act, inflicts an infamous punishment and, therefore, it conflicted with the Fifth and Sixth Amendments of the Constitution. The fourth section of the Geary Act stated, in part, that "any such Chinese person, or person of Chinese descent, convicted and adjudged to be not lawfully entitled to be or remain in the United States, shall be imprisoned at hard labor for a period not exceeding one year, and thereafter removed from the United States."[71] The appellants had never been indicted by a grand jury, as required by the Fifth Amendment, nor had they been given a speedy and public trial, by an impartial jury, as required by the Sixth Amendment of the U.S. Constitution.

Justice Shiras delivered the opinion of the Court, with Justice Field concurring in part and dissenting in part. The Court upheld the government's action in detaining the appellants as it was part of the means necessary to give effect to the exclusion or expulsion of Chinese aliens. However, the Court ruled that even aliens were protected by the Fifth and Sixth Amendments of the U.S. Constitution, and therefore they should not have been subjected to a capital or other infamous punishment without an indictment of a grand jury, and they should not have been deprived of life, liberty, or property without due process of law. The Court concluded that the commissioner acted without jurisdiction and the Circuit Court made an error in not discharging the appellants from imprisonment.

FOURTEENTH AMENDMENT PROTECTION: *WONG KIM ARK V. U.S.*

Another major judicial principle was established by the Supreme Court of the United States on March 28, 1898, when the Court handed down its decision on the case of *Wong Kim Ark v. United States.*[72] Wong Kim Ark was born in 1873 at 751 Sacramento Street, San Francisco, California, to Chinese parents who were, at the time of their son's birth, Chinese subjects and were lawful residents of the United States. They were not employed in any diplomatic or official capacity representing the government of China. Wong Kim Ark lived at the same address until 1890, when he left for China for a visit. He returned to San Francisco on July 26, 1890, and was given permission to reenter the country without any difficulty. In 1894 he departed again for a visit to China and returned to San Francisco in August 1895, when he requested permission for landing. He was, however, denied permission on the grounds that he was not a citizen of the United States. Wong Kim Ark had never renounced his citizenship, and he had never committed any act that would have deprived him of his citizenship. A lower court had ordered him discharged after it had been ruled that he was a citizen of the country, and the government appealed to the Supreme Court.

Until 1898, there had never been in the history of the United States a case that tested the constitutionality of the Fourteenth Amendment as it applied to a person born in the United States of Chinese parents who were not citizens of the United States. The constitutional question before the Court then was whether a person born of Chinese parents was a citizen of the United States. In delivering the opinion of the Court, Justice Gray resorted to the common law as a means of understanding the language of the Constitution. He made a reference to the case of *Smith v. Alabama,* in which Justice Matthews had stated that "there is no common law of the United States, in the sense of a national customary law, distinct from the common law of England" (124 U.S. 478). He shared with Justice Matthews the idea that the interpretation of the Constitution can best be made when it is done within the context of English common law, and the Constitution should be read within the context of its history.

According to the practice of English common law, a person was considered a subject of the king if born within the king's domain. In other words, a person became a natural citizen by virtue of his place of birth, also known as *jus soli.* As pointed out earlier, the First Congress established an uniform standard for naturalization on March 26, 1790, giving all free white persons the right to become U.S. citizens, provided that they met certain requirements. It was not until Congress passed the Civil Rights Act of 1866 that a specific statute was enacted to clarify the acquisition of American citizenship by birth within the United States. The Act read as follows:

All persons born in the United States, and not subject to any foreign power, excluding Indians not taxed, are hereby declared to be citizens of the United States; and such citizens, of every race, color, without regard to any previous condition of slavery or involuntary servitude, except as punishment for crime whereof the party shall have been duly convicted, shall have the same right, in every State and Territory in the United States.[73]

This law clearly defined the conditions under which a person could be declared an American citizen; she was born in the United States, was not subject to any foreign power, and was an Indian who was taxed. There was no ambiguity of meaning in the statute insofar as Justice Gray was concerned. But if there was room for misinterpretation, then the Fourteenth Amendment of the Constitution was clear enough in its meaning to dispel any doubt or misinterpretation (so reasoned Justice Gray), for it stated that "all persons born or naturalized in the United States and subject to the jurisdiction thereof, are citizens of the United States and of the State wherein they reside." Justice Gray interpreted the opening words "all persons born" to be general, restricted only by place and jurisdiction, but not by race or color, as he wrote in his opinion for the majority in favor of Wong Kim Ark.

Justices Fuller and Harlan dissented, however, and filed a separate opinion. Their dissenting argument was constructed around three major points. First, the majority's construction of U.S. citizenship on the basis of

English common law was found misrepresented since, according to the two justices, the question of nationality or citizenship was essentially political in nature, and as such it belonged to the public law rather than the common law. If the question belonged to the sphere of public law, then it should be dealt with within the context of international relations. Second, the two justices were convinced that the Civil Rights Act of 1866, which used the words "all persons born in the United States and not subject to any foreign power," was misconstrued by the majority. The key words in the 1866 law, according to the dissenting justices, were "not subject to any foreign power, because they did not necessarily refer to territorial jurisdiction only." They insisted that these words should be construed to mean that all persons born in the United States and not owing allegiance to any foreign power are citizens. Since Wong Kim Ark and his parents were subjects of the Emperor of China, owing allegiance to him, Wong Kim Ark could not become a U.S. citizen. Third, the Fourteenth Amendment of the Constitution, which uses the words "all persons born, or naturalized in the United States, and subject to the jurisdiction thereof," was misinterpreted by the majority, according to Justices Fuller and Harlan. The words "subject to the jurisdiction thereof" meant to be "completely subject to their political jurisdiction" and owing "direct and immediate allegiance." The two justices were of the opinion that persons who were not subject to the jurisdiction of the United States at the time of birth could not become its citizens, unless they went through naturalization. Since the Chinese were not eligible for naturalization, they could not become U.S. citizens.

Another constitutional question that Justices Fuller and Harlan raised in their dissenting opinion was whether the Fourteenth Amendment had abridged the treaty-making power of the president. If it did not, then the president, with the consent of the Senate, could make a treaty prohibiting a person of Chinese ancestry born in the United States from becoming a U.S. citizen. By the same token, Congress, through its legislative power, could prohibit a person of Chinese descent born in the United States from becoming a U.S. citizen. The two justices were in unison in claiming that the treaty-making power of the president or the legislative power of Congress had not been abridged by the Fourteenth Amendment.

The *jus soli* principle, upheld by the Supreme Court of the United States in the case of *Wong Kim Ark v. U.S.,* opened the closed door for the Chinese born in the United States to make entry into the community called the United States, or the People's Domain, as it was called by Benjamin Ringer. It was an important victory for the Chinese, as it touched on their constitutional rights, but it did not have a major impact on the Chinese community in America, as there were not many second-generation Chinese. The majority of Chinese in America were still kept outside the People's Domain and were considered fit only to be permanent sojourners who had no vested rights of domicile, always subject to deportation (as evidenced in the Supreme Court's decision on *Fong Yue Ting v. U.S.*). But the Supreme Court wavered once in a great while between excluding the Chinese from the community of America absolutely and including them for particular reasons. The Supreme Court decision in 1886 on *Yick Wo v. Hopkins*[74] marked one of these rare occasions when the Court wavered.

FOURTEENTH AMENDMENT PROTECTION: *YICK WO V. HOPKINS*

The case of *Yick Wo v. Hopkins* reached the Supreme Court as a result of violation of Order No. 1569 by Yick Wo, who was subsequently found guilty and was fined $10. He was imprisoned until the fine was paid at the rate of $1 per day. Yick Wo petitioned the Supreme Court of the State of California for a writ of habeas corpus, but the Court upheld the constitutionality of the said ordinance. In its decision, the Court ruled as follows:

The board of supervisors, under the several statutes conferring authority upon them, has the power to prohibit or regulate all occupations which are against good morals, contrary to public order and decency, or dangerous to the public safety. Cloth washing is certainly not opposed to good morals or subversive of public order or decency, but when conducted in given localities it may be highly dangerous to the public safety. . . . The order No. 1569 and section 68 of order No. 1587 are not in contravention of common right or unjust, unequal, partial, or oppressive, in such sense as authorizes us in this proceeding to pronounce them invalid.[75]

Order No. 1569, passed on March 26, 1880, by the California state legislature, prohibited any person from conducting a laundry business within the corporate limit of the city and county of San Francisco, unless such business was housed in a building constructed either of brick or stone. Any person violating any part of this order and found guilty was to be fined $1,000 or less or to be imprisoned for six months or less. Section 68 of Order No. 1587, which was passed by the same legislature on July 28, 1880, included the same provision as found in Order No. 1549.

Attorneys Hall McAllister, L. H. Van Schaick, and L. Smoot presented their argument. They indicated that there were about 320 laundries in the city and county of San Francisco, of which 240 were owned and operated by Chinese. Furthermore, they pointed out that 310 of them were constructed of wood, as nine-tenths of all houses in the city of San Francisco were made of the same material. They mentioned that while the Chinese were denied permission to continue their laundry businesses, all other nonwhites, with one exception, were allowed to conduct their businesses. Then the attorneys charged that the purpose of the ordinance, and of its exclusion, "is to drive out of business all the numerous small laundries, especially those owned by Chinese, and give a monopoly of the business to the large institutions established and carried on by means of large associated Caucasian capital."[76] They asked the following question:

If the facts appearing on the face of the ordinance, on the petition and return, and admitted in the case, and shown by the notorious public and municipal history of the times, indicate a purpose to drive out the Chinese laundrymen, and not merely to regulate the business for the public safety, does it not disclose a case of violation of the provisions of the Fourteenth Amendment to the national Constitution, in more than one particular?[77]

Justice Matthews, who delivered the opinion of the Court on the case, agreed with Yick Wo's attorneys and ruled that the municipal ordinances under question were in violation of the Fourteenth Amendment of the Constitution. Brushing aside the argument that the police power of the State is indestructible and inalienable and that the State may construe her own laws, Justice Matthews stated that the power conferred on the supervisors of the city and county of San Francisco was a naked and arbitrary power that they could use without reason and without responsibility. In concluding his opinion, Justice Matthews stated as follows:

For the cases present the ordinances in actual operation, and the facts shown establish an administration directed so exclusively against a particular class of persons as to warrant and require the conclusion, that, whatever may have been the intent of the ordinances as adopted, they are applied by the public authorities charged with their administration, and thus representing the State itself, with a mind so unequal and oppressive as to amount to a practical denial by the State of that equal protection of the laws which is secured to the petitioners, as to all other persons, by the broad and benign provisions of the Fourteenth Amendment to the Constitution of the United States. Though the law itself be fair on its face and impartial in appearances, yet it is applied and administered by public authority with an evil eye and an unequal hand, so as practically to make unjust and illegal discrimination between persons in similar circumstances, material to their rights, the denial of equal justice is still within the prohibition of the Constitution.[78]

By the decision on the case of *Yick Wo v. Hopkins,* the Supreme Court restricted the state's sovereign power to construe its own laws so as to deprive any person of her Fourteenth Amendment rights. But the majority of the Court did not adhere to this same principle, in 1893, when it handed down its decision on *Fong Yue Ting v. U.S.* The majority of justices claimed that the sovereign power of the nation is absolute, suggesting that if it could not expel aliens, then the country would be considered as not having sovereign power. The minority insisted that the principle established by the decision on *Yick Wo v. Hopkins* should be applied to the case of *Fong Yue Ting v. United States.*

THE STRANGE CASE OF *BALDWIN V. FRANKS*

The unusual case of *Baldwin v. Franks*[79] came to the Supreme Court for a review of a judgment of the Circuit Court of the United States for the District of California, on a writ of habeas corpus. The criminal proceedings against Baldwin resulted from a mob action taken by a group of white residents of the city of Nicolaus, California against their Chinese counterparts. Charges were filed by Sing Lee, a Chinese resident of the city, against Thomas Baldwin, Bird Wilson, William Hays, and others, likewise residents of the same city, who had allegedly conspired to deprive Sing Lee of the equal protection of the laws, and of equal privileges and immunities under the laws.

The mob action in Nicolaus was part of the frequent anti-Chinese violence that swept through the Pacific Coast in the 1880s. A minor disturbance occurred in February 1885 in Eureka, California, that resulted in the expulsion of the Chinese residents of the city.[80] During the same year, major violence broke out at Rock Springs, Wyoming Territory, against Chinese miners on September 2. When the violence had subsided, a total of twenty-eight Chinese were found murdered, another fifteen wounded, and the rest of the Chinese residents were driven out of the city into the surrounding hills.[81] On November 3, 1885, a group of white citizens drove out of the city of Tacoma, Washington Territory, its Chinese residents, with the help of their mayor, J. Robert Weisbach; and an angry mob of Sinophobes of Tacoma's adjacent city, Seattle, took violent action against Chinese residents and also drove them out of the city.[82]

In response to the lawlessness that prevailed in the Western region, the Chinese government had addressed its concerns with the safety of its subjects through diplomatic channels in Washington and had requested the U.S. government to provide protection for its citizens. After the riot in Tacoma, the Chinese minister, representing his government in Washington, asked Secretary of State Thomas F. Bayard to bring the perpetrators to justice. However, the U.S. government, although sympathetic to the Chinese government's concern and the plight of the Chinese who had been targets of unruly white mob actions, refused to assume any legal responsibility to bring the perpetrators to justice.[83] Neither was it willing to assume any liability to compensate for the loss of life and property among the harassed and persecuted Chinese. The leaders of the Chinese community became frustrated with such passive attitudes of the federal government toward the lawlessness unleashed against the Chinese, and they decided to sponsor a legal action against Thomas Baldwin and his associates.

The criminal proceedings against Thomas Baldwin and some fifteen other local residents of Nicolaus, California began on March 8, 1886, when Sing Lee swore out a complaint charging the defendant and his associates of conspiring to expel him and other Chinese residents from the town. Sing Lee asserted that this constituted a violation of their right to equal protection of the law. On the basis of this complaint, a warrant was issued by B. N. Bugby, a Commissioner of the Circuit Court of the United States for the District of California, who directed the U.S. Marshal, J. C. Franks, to bring Thomas Baldwin and his associates into custody. Franks went to Nicolaus on March 12, arrested them, and brought them to Sacramento for trial.

The trial took place in the courtroom of the Circuit Court of the United States for the District of California before Circuit Judge Lorenzo Sawyer and District Judge George Sabin. A. L. Hart argued for the defendants, while the Chinese community retained Hall McAllister on behalf of Sing Lee. McAllister argued that the decision handed down by the Supreme Court on the case of *U.S. v. Harris*,[84] which ruled that Section 5519 of the Revised Statutes was unconstitutional, applied to actions of U.S. citizens against other U.S. citizens only. It should not be applied to actions of U.S. citizens against citizens of another nation, since the latter were under the jurisdiction of treaties that were equal to the Constitution, the supreme law of the land. In countering McAllister's point of view, A. L. Hart argued that the powers of a state over common criminal offenses could not be limited by Congress, even if it ratified the treaty. One of the implications of McAllister's argument, if it had prevailed, was that every offense against a Chinese, in any state, had to be tried in a federal court.

Justice Sawyer was persuaded by McAllister's argument that the federal government had treaty-making powers that were broad enough to secure a wide range of rights for Chinese residents in the United States. But he was faced with the question of whether Section 5519 of Revised Statutes was limited to the protection of Chinese rights or included rights of other classes of people. This was precisely the reason why the Supreme Court ruled Section 5519 unconstitutional in relation to the *U.S. v. Harris* case. Therefore, Justice Sawyer suggested that a certificate of division of opinion be made and a writ of error be forwarded to the Supreme Court for its authoritative ruling on the case. When his suggestion was accepted by both parties concerned, Baldwin was freed on his own recognizance.

The Supreme Court ruled on the case on March 7, 1887. Chief Justice Waite read the Court's majority opinion in favor of the plaintiff, Thomas Baldwin, in error, while Justice Harlan and Field dissented from their brethren. Chief Justice Waite noted that there were nine questions; the first six referred to Section 5519 of the Revised Statutes, while others were related to Sections 5508 and 5336. But Waite acknowledged that the fourth question in reference to Section 5519 summed up the case, as it questioned

whether a conspiracy of two or more persons in the state of California, for the purpose of depriving Chinese residents, lawfully residing in California, in pursuance of the provisions of the several treaties between the United States and the emperor of China, of the right to live and pursue their lawful vocations at the town of Nicolaus, in said state, and in pursuance of such conspiracy actually, forcibly, expelling such Chinese from said town, in the manner shown by the record, is (1) a violation of and an offense within the meaning of section 5519 of the Revised Statutes of the United States; (2) whether said section, so far as it applies to said state or facts and such Chinese residents, and makes the acts stated an offense against the United States, is constitutional and valid.[85]

Chief Justice Waite did not repudiate McAllister's claim that Congress had the treaty-making power. In fact, he acknowledged that the treaties made by the United States "are part of the supreme law of the land and that they are binding within the territorial limits of the states." The real question, however, insofar as the majority opinion of the Court was concerned, was whether Section 5519 could be so applied to Thomas Baldwin and his associates as to indict them, prosecute them, and put them on trial for conspiracy against the government of the United States. The Court ruled that unless Baldwin and his associates attempted to use or used force against the U.S. government, the first clause of Section 5519 could not become grounds for their arrest and prosecution.

Justice Harlan, in his dissenting opinion, stated that if the Chinese could be driven out of their homes when their rights were guaranteed by treaties between China and the United States, and if the government of the United States was without power to protect them against such violence, then "it must be equally true as to the citizens or subjects of every other foreign nation residing or doing business here under the sanction of treaties with their respective governments." Justice Harlan did not believe such was the case and stated that he had to dissent from the majority opinion. He asserted that the majority's interpretation of Section 5508 was wrong, because it was not only applicable to wrongs done against U.S. citizens by their counterparts, but also to wrongs done by U.S. citizens against foreigners. He declared,

I cannot think it possible that Congress, while providing for the punishment of two or more persons who go on the premises of a citizen with intent to prevent his free exercise or enjoyment of rights secured by the constitution or laws of the United States, purposely refrained from providing for the punishment of the same persons going on the premises of one not a citizen, with intent to prevent the enjoyment by the latter of rights secured by the same constitution and laws.[86]

INSULAR CASES

On December 2, 1901, the Supreme Court handed down a decision on the case of *Emil J. Pepke v. United States.*[87] This was commonly known as the Diamond Rings case, as it involved fourteen diamond rings brought by Pepke into the United States without paying import duties on the rings. This case was also part of the Insular Tariff Cases as designated by Justice Brown. Included among these cases were *Elias S. A. de Lima v. George R. Bidwell,*[88] *Henry W. Dooley v. United States,*[89] and *Samuel Downes v. George Bidwell.*[90] In appearance, the case of *Emil Pepke v. United States* had nothing to do with Asian Americans, as it involved an American soldier who had returned from his duty in the Philippines. However, the decision had a profound impact on the legal status of Filipinos both in their native land and in the United States.

Emil Pepke, a native of North Dakota, was a soldier attached to the First Regiment of the North Dakota United States Volunteer Infantry serving on the island of Luzon in the Philippine Islands. While stationed in the Philippines, he had purchased fourteen diamond rings, and he brought them with him when his unit was ordered to return to San Francisco, California, where he was discharged on September 25, 1899. Prior to this date, the Treaty of Paris was signed on December 10, 1898, between the United States and Spain, was ratified on February 6, 1899, and was proclaimed by the president of the United States on April 11, 1899. In May 1900, a customs officer in Chicago seized Pepke's diamond rings for violation of the tariff act of July 24, 1897, which required duties on all articles imported from foreign countries. Pepke filed a plea claiming that his rings were not subject to customs duties, but it was considered insufficient, and the government took action against Pepke for forfeiture and sale of the diamond rings.

This case reached the Supreme Court on a writ of error and was argued on December 17, 18, 19, and 20, 1900. It was decided almost a year later, on December 2, 1901. The question before the Court was whether the rings in question were imported from a foreign country. The Court decided by a narrow margin of five to four that the Philippine Islands were a territory of the United States, and therefore Pepke was not subject to customs duties. Justice Fuller, in delivering the majority opinion, declared that the case under review was not distinguishable from *De Lima v. George Bidwell,* which was decided on May 27, 1901. In *De Lima v. George Bidwell,* the essential question was whether territory acquired by the United States by cession from a foreign power remains a "foreign country" within the meaning of tariff laws. The Court decided by a narrow margin of five to four that Porto [Puerto] Rico was not a foreign country within the meaning of the tariff laws, and therefore duties levied on sugar imported from Puerto Rico to New York were charged illegally. In another insular case, namely *Downes v. George Bidwell,* the majority opinion of the Court delivered by Justice Brown declared that "Porto [Puerto] Rico is a territory appurtenant and belonging to the United States, but not a part of the United States within the revenue clauses of the Constitution."[91]

The three decisions by the Supreme Court placed the inhabitants of the Philippines and Puerto Rico in a strange legal status. The Philippine Islands and Puerto Rico were not foreign countries, in that they were not exclusively within the sovereignty of a foreign power, but they were foreign in the sense that they were without the sovereignty of the United States. In other words, the Court ruled that the Constitution did not apply to these territories directly, but the president and Congress could extend the Constitution to them through legislation. The Court rejected the commonly accepted notion that the Constitution follows the flag. Thus, the natives of the Philippine Islands and Puerto Rico were subject to American laws without their constitutional protection. What was more important for the future of Filipinos, both in their native land and in the United States, was that they could not become U.S. citizens, although they had to obey American laws. They were called nationals.

1907 IMMIGRATION LAW AND GENTLEMEN'S AGREEMENT

The Japanese were able to come to the United States as immigrants without severe legal restrictions imposed on them until 1907, in spite of two major Supreme Court decisions on *Nishimura v. U.S.* and *Yamataya v. Fisher.* The order by the San Francisco Board of Education on October 11, 1906 to segregate Japanese school children, however, set in motion a number of factors that contributed to the restriction on Japanese immigration.[92] The order fanned anti-Japanese fervor among California exclusionists, who were bent on preventing the Japanese from immigrating to the United States. The reaction to this segregation order from Tokyo alarmed the Roosevelt administration. To defuse the school crisis, the administration chose to deal with this international problem in three separate ways.

First, President Roosevelt sent his Secretary of Commerce and Labor, Victor Metcalf, a Californian, to San Francisco to investigate the incident. Metcalf met with school board members and tried to persuade them to rescind the order. But his effort failed. Second, the Roosevelt administration filed a suit against the board to test the constitutionality of its order on the grounds that it violated Article I of the 1895 Treaty signed between the United States and Japan. Third, a compromise was sought and reached between Washington and Tokyo. The Japanese government had been concerned about the possibility of a total exclusion of Japanese immigration to the United States, as the Chinese had been excluded. A total exclusion would be an unbearable humiliation to the nation, and Tokyo wanted to keep Japanese immigration open to Hawaii. Therefore, it agreed with Washington to prevent Japanese citizens carrying passports for Hawaii, Canada, or Mexico from entering the continental United States.

President Roosevelt sent his annual message to the Fifty-Ninth Congress at its beginning, urging them to pass an immigration law to protect the country from unwanted immigrants. He suggested that immigrants be sent to the countryside rather than to the cities. He recommended classes of people who should be excluded as follows:

There should be an increase in the stringency of the laws to keep out insane, idiotic, epileptic and pauper immigrants. But this is by no means enough. Not merely the anarchist, but every man of anarchistic tendencies, all violent and disorderly people, all people of bad character, the incompetent, the lazy, the vicious, and physically unfit, defective, or degenerate should be kept out.[93]

Congress responded to Roosevelt's call for more restrictions on immigration by passing the Immigration Act of February 20, 1907.[94] The law had forty-four sections. Section Two listed twenty different excluded classes of people, including contract laborers and any person whose ticket was paid for with the money of another person. Section One, however, had the most important provision as it authorized the president to exclude from admission into the continental United States Japanese and Koreans who were issued passports to go to Mexico, Canada, and Hawaii. The president exercised this authority on March 14, 1907, by issuing an executive order[95] one day after the San Francisco Board of Education had rescinded its segregation order. The federal suit against the board was dismissed, and Japanese children were allowed to go to school with their white counterparts, although Chinese and Korean children were still affected by the segregation order.

Section Thirty-Nine of the law also authorized the president to make international agreements to prevent the immigration of aliens who were excluded from admission into the United States. Accordingly, the Roosevelt administration instructed Thomas O'Brien, U.S. Ambassador to Japan, to exchange views on Japanese immigration with Japanese Foreign Minister Hayashi through correspondence in January 1908. Their correspondence continued until March 1908, when the two sides reached a series of understandings that constituted what is known as the Gentlemen's Agreement of 1908. Although the complete text of this agreement has never been made public, the U.S. government made available the following report in its annual immigration report of 1908:

This understanding contemplates that the Japanese government shall issue passports to the continental United States only to such of its subjects as are non-laborers or are laborers who, in coming to the continent, seek to resume a formerly acquired domicile, to join a parent, wife, or children residing there, or to assume active control of an already possessed interest in a farming enterprise in this country; so that the three classes of laborers entitled to receive passports have come to be designated as "relatives," "former residents," and "settled agriculturalists."[96]

This Gentlemen's Agreement had an immediate impact on the number of Japanese immigrants entering the United States. In 1907, the number of Japanese who entered the United States amounted to 12,888, but in the following two years their numbers were reduced to 8,340 and 1,596, respectively. In 1913, more Japanese resumed immigration to the United States, and Japanese women known as "picture brides," who were married by proxy in Japan to Japanese men already in the United States, began to come to the United States to join their husbands. As more Japanese immigrants were seen among them, anti-Japanese agitators in California felt that they had been betrayed by the Roosevelt administration, which was supposed to have eliminated the Japanese problem, and they mounted pressure on their legislature to pass legislation that would deprive Japanese residents of their source of livelihood. In 1913, the California legislature passed the so-called Webb-Henry bill over the Wilson administration's protest and sent it to the governor for his signature in May, but it was not signed into law until May 19, 1913. Although the law did not mention the Japanese, it was clearly directed against Japanese resident aliens in California, as they were aliens ineligible for naturalization. It had already been ruled that the Chinese alien residents could not become naturalized. Among the provisions made in the law, Section One was crucial in that it stated the following: "All aliens eligible to citizenship under the laws of the United States may acquire, possess, enjoy, transmit and inherit real property, or any interest therein, in this State, in the same manner and to the same extent as citizens of the United States, except as otherwise provided by the laws of this State."[97]

In accordance with the Alien Land Law of 1913, all Asian resident aliens ineligible for naturalization were excluded from the right to acquire, possess, enjoy, transmit, and inherit real property. Sections Two and Three of the law also prohibited Asian resident aliens from holding a majority interest in land. Leasing agricultural land to Asian resident aliens was limited to three years. Section Five allowed escheat to the state of property owned by aliens or corporations in violation of the law. The original Alien Land Act of 1913 was amended in 1920 to omit the leasing clause and to prevent aliens from acquiring stock in any corporations authorized to possess real property. The law was again amended in 1923 to prohibit aliens from entering into a cropping contract with a land owner. The constitutionality of these laws was tested in the Supreme Court in the early 1920s.

THE ASIATIC BARRED ZONE ACT OF 1917

With passage of the Immigration Act of February 20, 1907, two major sources of Asian immigration to America were dealt a severe blow. The Chinese exclusion had become permanent in 1904, and in 1908 the Gentlemen's Agreement put stringent restrictions on the Japanese wishing to come to Continental America. Congress then began to pay attention to other sources of Asian immigration to America. When the Immigration Act of February 20, 1907, went into effect, Congress also established a commission to study immigration, as required by Section Thirty-Nine of the law. A nine-member commission was created based on congressional appointment on February 22, 1907, with William Paul Dillingham chairing the commission. The commission developed a report in 1911, and the following year Dillingham introduced a bill in Congress. The bill was designed to require Asian immigrants to take a literacy test. The bill went through minor changes but was passed by Congress. President Taft vetoed it, however, because of its literacy proviso.

During the first session of the Sixty-Fourth Congress, a total of thirteen immigration bills were considered. Some of them proposed further restrictions on Chinese, Japanese, Hindus, and others. A total of ten bills were introduced, but only one bill, introduced by Representative John Burnett of Alabama, was reported out on January 31, 1916. The report increased the number of excluded classes of people, including chronic alcoholism, vagrancy, tuberculosis in any form, and constitutional psychopathic inferiority. Of all the measures proposed in the bill, the Asiatic Barred Zone and the literary test were most critical to Asian immigration, because they would virtually do away with it. The bill was debated for five days, during which numerous amendments were introduced, but only one amendment was accepted. The Senate worked on the Burnett bill and finally approved it on December 14, 1916. When it was sent to President Wilson for his signature, he vetoed it, again because of the literacy test proviso. Congress overrode his veto and passed the bill, making it the Immigration Act of February 5, 1917.[98]

The law entitled "An Act To regulate the immigration of aliens to, and the residence of aliens in the United States" had thirty-eight sections and was one of the most comprehensive immigration laws ever passed by Congress to date. Section Three enumerated more than thirty excluded classes of people. Included among these classes of people were the natives of a zone defined by latitude and longitude.[99] The geographic area commonly known as the Asiatic Barred Zone encompassed a vast area of the Asian continent and the Pacific Ocean. The countries included were India, Burma, Thailand, Afghanistan, most of the Polynesian islands, the area known then as Indochina, Indonesia, Malaysia, and the Asiatic parts of the former Soviet Union. Section Three also required of all immigrants a literacy test to be administered by immigrant inspectors.

By virtue of this law, the natives of Asia, with the exception of the Japanese and Filipinos, were excluded from the class of people allowed to immigrate to America. It took another seven years before Congress passed a law, in 1924, to exclude the Japanese. A decade after the Japanese exclusion had become a reality Congress decided to exclude the natives of the Philippine archipelago in 1934, thus completing the legislative work to keep out of America those who were considered undesirable.

SUMMARY

Our examination of numerous cases litigated by Chinese Americans goes against the commonly held belief that they were helpless victims of American racial antipathy and legislated discrimination. The American government was certainly opposed to Chinese emigration, and particularly Congress and the Supreme Court did their part to discourage the Chinese from coming to America. Congress continued to pass legislation that was discriminatory against the Chinese, Japanese, Hindus, and other Asian people. The Supreme Court did not hesitate to hand down questionable decisions against Asian American litigants. Some of its decisions differentiated between citizens and noncitizens, thereby legitimating and fortifying the People's Domain separate from the Plural Domain.

The period discussed in this chapter also marked an era in American history when Chinese Americans saw racial prejudice against them transformed into legislated discrimination under the auspices of Congress. When they turned to the Supreme Court for reason and justice, it used distorted logic and chauvinistic partiality. Chinese Americans were deprived of their civil rights, property rights, rights for education and employment, and, above all, their human dignity. Their underprivileged and underclassed status drove them into voluntary segregation in Chinatowns across the nation. Prejudice, discrimination, and segregation—ordinary solution stages in the escalation of racial conflict as hypothesized by Harry Kitano and Roger Daniels—were not sufficient in dealing with the Chinese problem, and Congress and the Supreme Court collaborated to exclude and expel Chinese.

The Chinese in America persisted with their legal battles, nevertheless, believing that reason and justice would prevail. By redressing racial discrimination against them through the judicial system, Chinese litigants forced justices in the federal courts to be more careful of and deliberate with their decision-making process. Most of all, they forced the powers to be in the government to see themselves as oppressors and examine what their decisions had wrought in the lives of the oppressed.

NOTES

1. David J. Vogler and Sidney R. Waldman, *Congress and Democracy* (Washington, D.C.: Congressional Quarterly, Inc., 1985), pp. 2–4.

2. Leroy N. Rieselbach, *Congressional Politics* (New York: McGraw-Hill, 1973), p. 30.

3. Claudia Frances Wright, "Legitimation by the Supreme Courts of Canada and the United States; A Case Study of Japanese Exclusion," an unpublished doctoral dissertation, Claremont Graduate School, 1973, pp. 90–123.

4. Joel B. Grossman, *Lawyers and Judges: The ABA and the Politics of Judicial Selection* (New York: John Wiley and Sons, 1965), pp. 19–20.

5. John B. Schmidhauser, *The Supreme Court: Its Politics, Personalities, and Procedures* (New York: Holt, Rinehart and Winston, 1960), pp. 32, 55.

6. Ibid., p. 58.

7. John Braeman, "Deportation and Expulsion," in *Asian Americans and the Supreme Court: A Documentary History,* Hyung-chan Kim (ed.) (Westport, Conn.: Greenwood Press, 1992), p. 77.

8. 112 U.S. 537 (1884).

9. 112 U.S. 526 (1884).

10. 112 U.S. 559–60 (1884).

11. Christian G. Fritz, "Due Process, Treaty Rights, and Chinese Exclusion, 1882–1891," in *Entry Denied: Exclusion and the Chinese Community in America, 1882–1943,* Sucheng Chan (ed.), (Philadelphia: Temple University Press, 1991), pp. 41–43.

12. 112 U.S. 562 (1884).

13. 112 U.S. 568 (1884).

14. 112 U.S. 569 (1884).

15. 112 U.S. 579 (1884).

16. 124 U.S. 621 (1888).

17. 124 U.S. 627–34 (1888).

18. 130 U.S. 581 (1889).

19. 25 Stat. 504.

20. S. W. Kung, *Chinese in American Life: Some Aspects of Their History, Status, Problems, and Contributions* (Seattle: University of Washington Press, 1961), pp. 63–64.

21. 112 U.S. 580 (1884).

22. Kermit L. Hall (ed.), *The Oxford Companion to the Supreme Court of the United States* (Oxford: Oxford University Press, 1992), p. 368.

23. 130 U.S. 607 (1889).

24. 130 U.S. 609 (1889).

25. 299 U.S. 304 (1936).

26. 140 U.S. 424 (1891).

27. 140 U.S. 417 (1891).

28. 140 U.S. 424 (1891).

29. 142 U.S. 651 (1892).

30. 22 Stat. 214.

31. Ibid.

32. 26 Stat. 1084.

33. 23 Stat. 332.

34. 142 U.S. 653–55 (1892).

35. 142 U.S. 664 (1892).

36. Roger Daniels (ed.), *Three Short Works on Japanese Americans* (New York: Arno Press, 1978).

37. 189 U.S. 186 (1903).

38. 144 U.S. 47 (1892).

39. 144 U.S. 52–53 (1892).

40. 144 U.S. 55 (1892).

41. Ibid.

42. 27 Stat. 25.

43. 149 U.S. 698 (1893).

44. 149 U.S. 707 (1893).

45. 149 U.S. 709 (1893).

46. 149 U.S. 737 (1893).

47. 149 U.S. 741 (1893).

48. 149 U.S. 760 (1893).

49. 158 U.S. 538 (1895).

50. 158 U.S. 540 (1895).

51. 32 Stat. 176.

52. 33 Stat. 428.

53. 185 U.S. 213 (1902).

54. 185 U.S. 296 (1902).

55. 186 U.S. 193 (1902).

56. 186 U.S. 200 (1902).

57. 189 U.S. 86 (1903).

58. 189 U.S. 101–2 (1903).

59. Ibid.

60. 193 U.S. 65 (1904).

61. 193 U.S. 517 (1904).

62. 194 U.S. 161 (1904).

63. 194 U.S. 178 (1904).

64. 198 U.S. 253 (1905).

65. 198 U.S. 273 (1905).

66. Delber L. McKee, *Chinese Exclusion versus the Open Door Policy, 1900–1906* (Detroit: Wayne State University Press, 1977), pp. 103–25.

67. 208 U.S. 8 (1908).

68. 223 U.S. 673 (1912).

69. 253 U.S. 454 (1920).

70. 253 U.S. 464 (1920).

71. 163 U.S. 233 (1896).

72. Ibid.

73. 169 U.S. 688 (1898).

74. 118 U.S. 356 (1886).

75. 118 U.S. 360 (1886).

76. 118 U.S. 362 (1886).

77. 118 U.S. 362–63 (1886).

78. 118 U.S. 373 (1886).

79. 120 U.S. 678 (1887).

80. Lynwood Carranco, "Chinese Expulsion from Humboldt County," *Pacific Historical Review,* 30 (November 1961), pp. 329–40.

81. Isaac Hill Bromley, *The Chinese Massacre at Rock Springs, Wyoming Territory, September 2, 1885* (Boston: Franklin Press, Rand Avery and Co., 1886). Also see Paul Crane and Alfred Larson, "The Chinese Massacre," *Annals of Wyoming,* 12 (January 1940), pp. 47–56, 153–61.

82. Jules Alexander Karlin, "The Anti-Chinese Outbreaks in Seattle, 1885–1886," *Pacific Northwest Quarterly,* 39 (April 1948), pp. 103–30. Also see Karlin's article, "The Anti-Chinese Outbreak in Tacoma, 1885," *Pacific Historical Review,* 23 (August 1954), pp. 271–83.

83. Alexander Saxton, *The Indispensable Enemy: Labor and the Anti-Chinese Movement in California* (Berkeley: University of California Press, 1971), pp. 203–4.

84. 106 U.S. 629 (1883).

85. Ibid. Section 5519 of the revised statute stated, "If two or more persons in any state or territory conspire, or go in disguise on the highway or on the premise of another, for the purpose of depriving, either directly or indirectly, any person or class of persons of the equal protection of the laws, or of equal privileges and immunities under the laws, or for the purpose of preventing or hindering the constituted authorities of any state or territory from giving or securing to all persons within such state or territory the equal protection of the laws, each of such persons shall be punished by a fine of not less than five hundred, nor more than five thousand dollars, or by imprisonment, with or without hard labor, not less than six months, nor more than six years, or by both such fine and imprisonment." See also Charles J. McClain, Jr., "The Chinese Struggle for Civil Rights in 19th-Century America: The Unusual Case of Baldwin v. Franks," *Law and History Review,* 3, 2 (1985), pp. 349–73.

86. 186 U.S. 629 (1883).

87. 182 U.S. 222 (1901). See also William J. Pomeroy, *American Neocolonialism: Its Emergence in the Philippines and Asia* (New York: International Publishers, 1970), pp. 121–24.

88. 182 U.S. 1 (1901).

89. 182 U.S. 222 (1901).

90. 182 U.S. 244 (1901).

91. Ibid.

92. Roger Daniels, *The Politics of Prejudice* (New York: Atheneum, 1972), pp. 31–45.

93. *Congressional Record,* 40 (1905): 101.

94. 34 Stat. 898.

95. The executive order read as follows:

Whereas, by the act entitled, "An Act to regulate the immigration of aliens into the United States," approved February 20, 1907, whenever the President is satisfied that passports issued by any foreign government to its citizens to go to any country other than the United States or to any insular possession of the United States or to the Canal Zone, are being used for the purpose of enabling the holders to come to the continental territory of the United States to the detriment of labor conditions therein, it is made the duty of the President to refuse to permit such citizens of the country issuing such passports to enter the continental territory of the United States from such country or from such insular possession or from the Canal Zone. . . .

I hereby order that such citizens of Japan and Korea, to wit: Japanese or Korean laborers, skilled or unskilled, who have received passports to go to Mexico, Canada, or Hawaii and come therefrom, be refused permission to enter the continental territory of the United States.

96. Frank F. Chuman, *The Bamboo People: The Law and Japanese Americans* (Del Mar, Calif.: Publishers' Inc., 1976), pp. 35–36.

97. 263 U.S. 232 (1923). For the complete text of the law, see Hyung-chan Kim (ed.), *Asian Americans and the Supreme Court: A Documentary History* (Westport, Conn.: Greenwood Press, 1992), pp. 624–25.

98. 39 Stat. 874.

99. The zone was defined in the act (39 Stat. 876) as

Continent of Asia, situate south of the twentieth parallel latitude north west of the one hundred and sixtieth meridian of longitude east from Greenwich, and north of the tenth parallel of latitude south . . . the Continent of Asia west of the one hundred and tenth meridian of longitude east from Greenwich and east of the fiftieth parallel of latitude north, except that portion of said territory situate between the fiftieth and the sixty-fourth meridian of longitude east from Greenwich and the twenty-fourth and thirty-eighth parallels of latitude north . . .

—6—

The Restriction and Exclusion
Period
(1921–1952)

The immigration of Asians to the United States was virtually halted by the end of World War I, particularly after Congress passed the Immigration Act of February 5, 1917 (which is also known as the Asiatic Barred Zone Act, because it excluded from admission into the United States all natives of Asia who lived in those regions defined by latitude and longitude). The two groups of people in Asia that were not excluded even after passage of the 1917 law were the natives of Japan and of the Philippine Islands.

Probably because of the literacy test required of incoming immigrants, the flow of immigration from southern and eastern Europe was reduced from 127,545 in 1917 to 27,991 in 1918, and the figure dropped to 17,628 in 1919. This drastic reduction of immigrants from Europe, however, did not stop white nationalistic exclusionists from wanting either to put more restrictions on existing laws or do away with immigration entirely. However, the clamor for more restrictions or total exclusion was qualitatively different from similar demands of the past. American immigration policies from the colonial period until 1920 had metamorphosed from open to restrictive immigration, with an emphasis on excluded classes of people on the basis of their qualifications, but there had never been an attempt to impose numerical limitations on potential immigrants on the basis of their nationality.

The impetus for such immigration policy came from many directions. As the nation began to settle into a period of isolationism during the 1920s, which John Higham rightly characterized as "the tribal twenties,"[1] there emerged from across the nation a legion of civic organizations interested in keeping America homogeneous. Their leaders believed that America had been misled into a period of international adventure, thus endangering the nation. What America now needed was to restore "normalcy"[2] by ridding itself of all sources of nonconformity and disloyalty.

The leaders of this movement believed that immigrants from southern and eastern Europe and Asia could not be trusted for their loyalty to America.

The Immigration Restriction League led the campaign for quantitative restriction. It was founded in 1894 in Boston by a small group of intellectuals who convinced the Massachusetts Senator Henry Cabot Lodge to work in Congress toward legislation to put such a policy into effect. The campaign was comprised of a coalition of strange bedfellows who each had their own targets of hatred. For instance, the Ku Klux Klan was against southern and eastern Europeans because they were considered Catholic, while the American Legion fanned the Red Scare, believing that Communists may slip into the country. The American Federation of Labor had its own axe to grind in this campaign. Its leaders insisted that immigrants drove down the wages of native American workers, and therefore they wanted to see them excluded as their competitors.[3]

Not all people against the immigration of southern and eastern Europeans and other groups were imbued with pure economic motives; some felt that they had yet a higher ground to reach in their aspired journey to a pure white America. They sincerely believed that the American democratic form of government would be imperiled by the presence of large numbers of foreigners who were unfamiliar with democracy. This was nothing new, however, as it had been used in many public debates against Chinese and Japanese immigration. What was new, however, was a plethora of "scientific studies" on race led by people such as Madison Grant, Lothrop Stoddard, Charles W. Gould, Kenneth Roberts, Henry Fairchild Osborn, Edward M. East, and Ellsworth Huntington. Although these people came from different educational and professional backgrounds, their ideas converged on a singular theory: the Nordic superiority over all other people. Thus, Gould declared, "Americanism is actually the racial thought of the Nordic race, evolved after a thousand years of experience."[4]

Congress was not free from people who had definite ideas about who should be considered one hundred percenters. In the House, Albert Johnson of Washington, John Burnett of Alabama, Pat Harrison of Mississippi, and Henry Lee Myers of Montana were all in favor of exclusion. In the Senate, exclusionists found their support in John Sharp Williams of Mississippi and Thomas Heflin of Alabama, among others. Ultimately, exclusionists found a strong supporter for their cause in the White House. Warren G. Harding, addressing the Republican National Convention that nominated him in 1920 said, "I believe in establishing standards for immigration which are concerned with the future citizenship of the Republic, not with mere man power in industry."[5] Vice-President Coolidge, who succeeded Harding after his death in office, was a man hewed out of the same cloth. While he was still serving as vice-president he said, "there is no room in our midst for those whose direct purpose is political, social, or economic mischief, and whose presence jeopardizes the physical or moral health of the community." He continued, "we should have no more aliens to cope with . . . than our institutions are able to handle."[6]

QUOTA IMMIGRATION ACTS OF 1921 AND 1924

Given the national mood for exclusion, it was politically expedient for Congress to pass in 1921 the first quota act in the history of the United States. The number of aliens to be admitted into the United States as immigrants was limited to 3 percent of the number of foreign-born persons of that national origin who were enumerated in the 1910 census. This system was devised because in 1909 and 1910 the United States had received its greatest number of immigrants from England, Ireland, Scotland, and the Scandinavian countries. It was believed that this system would keep America white.

During the first session of the Sixty-Eighth Congress, a total of fifteen immigration-related bills were introduced (as the Quota Immigration Act of 1921 was to expire), and the House began to work on the bill introduced by Albert Johnson of Washington. The Senate, however, decided to replace the Johnson bill with the Reed bill, which it had been debating. During the debate held on April 7, 8, and 9, Senator Lodge of Massachusetts spoke in favor of the Reed amendment, which would have set the national origin quota at the 1920 census level, because he believed that it would effectively check Japanese immigration without providing grounds for the accusation that it was discriminatory against the Japanese.

On April 10, 1924, Hanihara Masanao, Japanese Ambassador to the United States, sent a letter to Secretary of State Charles Evans Hughes expressing his strong feelings of reservation against the bill. He asked Congress "to refrain from resorting to a measure that would seriously wound the proper susceptibilities of the Japanese nation," and he suggested the "grave consequences" that the law "would bring upon the otherwise happy and mutually advantageous relations between our two countries."[7] The letter was transmitted to the Senate on April 11, and Senator Lodge seized the opportunity to criticize the Japanese government and characterized Hanihara's letter as "improper"; furthermore, he accused Hanihara of making a "veiled threat" to America. Lodge urged the Senate, which had been reluctant to legislate for a total exclusion of the Japanese, to abrogate the Gentlemen's Agreement (see Chapter 5) and approve the bill. Senator Lodge's appeal to his colleagues changed the mood of the Senate, as Senators George Pepper of Pennsylvania, David Reed of Pennsylvania, J. Thomas Heflin of Alabama, and Frank Willis of

Ohio decided to go along with Senator Lodge. The Senate finally approved the Reed bill.

Due to the differences in provisions in the bills approved by the House and the Senate a conference committee was created to work on a report acceptable to both chambers. The first conference report presented a revised bill, but some lawmakers objected to Section 13, which was then revised. Congress finally accepted the second conference report agreed on by the conference committee, and it was signed into law on May 26, 1924 and became the Immigration Act of 1924,[8] with the official title, "An Act to limit the immigration of aliens into the United States, and for other purposes." But it was commonly known as the Quota Immigration Law, Nationality Origins Act, or the Japanese Exclusion Act. The law had thirty-two sections, and it established two broad categories of people admissible into the United States: (1) nonquota immigrants and (2) quota immigrants. Within the category of quota immigrants a preference system was established by which visas were to be issued. The law imposed numerical limitations on the number of immigrants allowed to come to America. The annual quota of immigrants was set at 2 percent of the foreign-born U.S. citizens of that nationality residing in the continental United States as enumerated in the U.S. census of 1890, and the minimum quota of any nationality was set at 100 annually, as specified in Paragraph (a) of Section Eleven of the law. Congress adopted the 1890 census data as its basis for determining the number of aliens to be admitted because this census showed fewer people from eastern and southern European countries. Of course, not many people from Asian countries were enumerated in the 1890 census. However, Paragraph (b) of the same section stipulated that the annual quota of any nationality for the fiscal year starting July 1, 1927, and thereafter was to be based on the 1920 census. Furthermore, the law included in Paragraph (c) of Section Thirteen a statement to the effect that "no alien ineligible to citizenship shall be admitted to the United States." Since the Supreme Court had ruled in 1922 that the Japanese could not become eligible for citizenship, they were excluded from admission into the United States as immigrants. From 1910 to 1945 Korea remained a colony of Japan, and in 1924 Koreans were considered subjects of Japan. Therefore, Koreans were also excluded as the Japanese were. Congress had postponed implementation of the quota system twice, but it finally went into effect on July 1, 1929.

THE TYDINGS-MCDUFFIE ACT OF 1934

The natives of the Philippine Archipelago had a unique status due to their dubious state of being nationals of the United States between 1902 and 1946. As mentioned before, they acquired the status after the Supreme Court had ruled on a number of "Insular Cases," which dealt with American relations with Puerto Rico and the Philippines. The natives of the Philippine Islands were subject to American laws without equal protection of those laws. If they had one advantage over other people in Asia, it was their "privilege" of being able to come to America even after passage of the Nationality Origins Act of 1924.

Natives of the Philippine Islands came to Hawaii as early as 1906, when fifteen of them were brought to the islands. In the following year, 150 more Filipinos toiled on sugar plantations in Hawaii.[9] As Filipino workers were proven useful on sugar plantations, the Hawaiian Sugar Planters Association developed an active recruitment system, and in 1909 a large-scale importation of Filipino workers known as Sakadas began. Most of these plantation workers were used initially as strike breakers, but they were later organized by union activists such as Pablo Manlapit, who led the Higher Wage Movement in 1920. The Higher Wage Movement intensified its demands for a $2-per-day minimum wage, and on September 9, 1924, there was a confrontation between striking workers and the local police that resulted in the deaths of sixteen workers and four police officers. This confrontation is known as the Hanapepe Massacre in the history of the Hawaiian labor movement.[10]

Before World War II, two distinctly different groups of Filipinos were found on the U.S. mainland. The first known group of Filipinos who came to continental America were *pensionados,* who were sent to study at various institutions of higher learning. In 1907, there were 183 *pensionados* who were being trained in American democracy. They were expected to go back to the Philippines and transmit American ideals of democracy as well as its practices. *Pensionados* attracted other ambitious young people from the colony to American colleges and universities. Between 1910 and 1940 there were as many as 14,000 Filipino youth[11] enrolled in those institutions. The second group of Filipinos went through the experience of second immigration as they came to the West Coast from Hawaii. As Filipino sugar plantation workers completed their terms of contract, they looked for other opportunities elsewhere. Some came to work in central California to harvest various crops, while others went to Alaska to work at its canneries. The third group of Filipinos consisted of workers who were recruited to come to California directly from the Philippines. From 1923 to 1929, Filipinos came to California at an annual average of 4,077.

As large numbers of Filipino workers began to come into California, anti-Filipino sentiments began to develop among organized workers. They believed that they could not compete against Filipinos, who they felt were willing to work for less wages. Some white citizens in local communities where large numbers of Filipino workers lived felt that white women were not safe. This fear might have originated from the unbalanced importation of Filipino males, who outnumbered Filipino women. It was estimated that of every one hundred Filipinos (or Pinoys, as they were called) who came to California between 1910 and 1929, ninety-three were males and seven were females. Filipinos became targets of racial hatred, which frequently resulted in race riots. The riot that broke out on January 22, 1930, in Watsonville, California, showed the depth of white hatred against the Filipinos.[12]

The increasing demand for the exclusion of Filipinos, along with other political forces supporting the independence of the Philippines, found sympathizers in Congress, which passed the Hare-Hawes-Cutting Act in 1933. This law promised political independence of the Philippines from the United States ten years after its passage. A number of factors contributed to this turn of events. America was already in the throes of the Great Depression when the debate on Filipino exclusion began to receive public attention. Businesspeople and corporations feared great losses of their investments in the event of Philippine independence, and they lobbied heavily against any legislation giving or promising political independence to the natives of the Philippine Islands. Organizations and associations that were against Filipino immigration and duty-free importation of raw materials and goods made in the Philippines were diametrically opposed to these business interests. When the debates on the Hare bill in the House and the Hawes-Cutting bill in the Senate began, people were ideologically divided on the issue. Generally speaking, Democrats were for independence, while Republicans were interested in keeping the political status quo. Finally, the bill passed through Congress and was sent to President Hoover for his signature, but he vetoed it. Congress overrode his veto on January 17, 1933.

Political leaders in the Philippines were divided into two groups over the question of whether the law should be implemented. One group (led by Osmena, the majority leader of the Philippine Senate, and Roxas, speaker of the Philippine House) was supportive of the law. It wanted to see the act put into effect immediately. This group was opposed by a number of political groups led by Manuel L. Quezon, president of the Phlippine Senate, who had begun to work against the act even before its passage. He felt that the provision allowing the United States to maintain military bases in the Philippines after independence was a political mockery. He was not opposed to the presence of the American military bases per se, but he argued that the government of the Philippines should have the right to decide the issue rather than being told to accept the American decision to keep military bases. He was also opposed to the law because he believed that it would wreck the islands' economy. He led the opposition movement and had the act referred to the general populace, which voted against it. After his victorious opposition to the Hare-Hawes-Cutting Act, he came to America in December 1933 to lobby for legislation more favorable to the colony's economy. Upon arrival in Washington, D.C., he held a round of talks with President Roosevelt, Secretary of War George Dern, and Senator Millard E. Tydings. After much negotiation and maneuvering, Quezon agreed with Senator Tydings on a bill sponsored by the latter. The bill was approved by Congress on March 23, 1934, and was signed into law the following day.

This act, which was officially titled, "To provide for the complete independence of the Philippine Islands, to provide for the adoption of a constitution and a form of government for the Philippine Islands, and for other purposes,"[13] had seventeen sections. Section One authorized the Philippine legislature to call for a constitutional convention before October 1, 1934, to draft a constitution "for the government of the Commonwealth of the Philippines Islands." Section Two declared, "all citizens of the Philippine Islands shall owe allegiance to the United States," thus subjecting them to obedience to American laws without due process or equal protection of those laws. Section Six included crucial provisions related to the economic relations between the United States and its colony. It enumerated the items for export from the American colony to be taxed, including sugar, coconut oil, and hard fibers. Furthermore, the rate of duty to be imposed on the enumerated goods was fixed at 5 percent of the rates of duty imposed on articles imported from other foreign countries. This rate was to start during the sixth year of the inauguration of the new government, but it was to increase to 25 percent during the ninth year of government operation. After the independence, there was to be a 100 percent tariff on all Philippine products, according to Section Thirteen of the law. In Section Eleven, America proposed "the perpetual neutralization of the Philippine Islands," and the president was requested to enter into negotiations with foreign powers to accomplish this political goal. Section Eight of the act stated that "the citizens of the Philippine Islands who are not citizens of the United States shall be considered as if they were aliens" for the purposes of the Immigration Act of 1917 and the Immigration Act of 1924. Section Eight declared, "for such purposes the Philippine Islands shall be considered as a separate country and shall have for each fiscal year a quota of fifty." Thus, Filipinos were excluded.

While Congress was busy with its legislative agenda to establish "normalcy" and to get rid of the colonial liability by making laws against the immigration of hetereogenous people, the Supreme Court handed down some major decisions that affected adversely the lives of Asian Americans.

From the time of the Quota Immigration Act of 1921 to the passage of the McCarran-Walter Immigration Act of 1952, litigation cases that were brought by Asian Americans to the Supreme Court, with a few exceptions, concerned six areas of constitutionality of major significance for Asian Americans who were not born in the United States.

The first group of cases dealt with the question of whether persons claiming to be foreign-born U.S. citizens had the right to judicial hearings, while the second group of cases tested the constitutionality of naturalization laws that prohibited persons who were born in Asia and were now legal residents of the United States from becoming U.S. citizens. The Supreme Court also had to deal with the question of whether American citizens could be denaturalized without going through the judicial process. The fourth group of litigations dealt with the rights of Asian alien residents legally to own real property. The fifth group of cases concerned the language and education rights of Asian Americans, while the sixth group of cases resulted from the U.S. government's decision to intern persons of Japanese ancestry during World War II.

EXCLUSION OF U.S. CITIZENS

The case of *Ng Fung Ho et al. v. White*[14] was decided by the Supreme Court on May 29, 1922. Justice Brandeis delivered the opinion of the Court on the two questions raised before the Court. First, it was questioned if Chinese laborers found to be in the United States illegally before passage of the General Immigration Act of February 5, 1917, could be deported in accordance with that act. Second, it was asked if Chinese laborers, claiming to be foreign-born citizens of the United States, had the right to a judicial hearing before deportation. The answers to both questions were affirmative. Justice Brandeis stated that even foreign-born citizens of the United States had the right to a judicial hearing. It was ruled, however, that aliens claiming to be citizens could not be released from custody, but were to be held for trial on the question of their citizenship.

Paragraph (c) of Section Thirteen of the Immigration Act of 1924 was tested in the cases of *Cheung Sum Shee et al. v. Nagle, Commissioner of Immigration* and *Chang Chan, Wong Hung Kay, Yee Sin Jung et al. v. Nagle* in 1925.[15] Cheung Sum Shee and other wives and children of Chinese merchants, who were lawfully domiciled in the United States, requested permission to enter the United States. They were denied by the Secretary of Labor on the grounds that the Immigration Act of 1924 prohibited from admission aliens who were ineligible for citizenship. Justice McReynolds delivered the opinion of the Court on *Cheung Sum Shee v. Nagle* on May 25, 1925. In his opinion, the Immigration Act of 1924 did not mandatorily exclude Chinese wives and minor children of Chinese merchants who were lawfully domiciled, because Article II of the Treaty of Commerce and Navigation with China, dated November 17, 1880, stated that

Chinese subjects, whether proceeding to the United States as teachers, students, merchants or from curiosity, together with their body and household servants, and Chinese laborers who are now in the United States shall be allowed to go and come of their own free will and accord, and shall be accorded all the rights, privileges, immunities, and exemptions which are accorded to the citizens and subjects of the most favored nation.[16]

Justice McReynolds delivered the Court's opinion on the case of *Chang Chan et al. v. Nagle*[17] on the same day. The case involved Chang Chan and three persons of Chinese ancestry who claimed to be native-born citizens of the United States and who were married to Chinese women in China before July 1, 1924. Their wives arrived in San Francisco aboard the *President Lincoln* on July 11, 1924, and requested permission to enter the United States, but they were refused by the Secretary of Labor on the grounds that the 1924 Act excluded the wives of U.S. citizens of the Chinese race; therefore, the wives were ineligible for citizenship. According to the Court's opinion, Chinese wives who were ineligible for U.S. citizenship "remained incapable of naturalization" even though they were married to U.S. citizens of Chinese ancestry.

The case of *Quon Quon Poy v. Johnson, Commissioner*[18] was decided on February 21, 1927. Justice Sanford delivered the Court's opinion. The appellant, Quon Quon Poy, arrived at the port of Boston and requested permission to land, claiming to be a foreign-born son of a native-born citizen of Chinese ancestry. He was a minor, as he was only fifteen years of age. The appellant's attorney argued before the Court that his client received an unfair hearing because he was interviewed by only one examiner without the presence of a friend or a kinsman. The Court ruled that the appellant received a fair hearing because he waived his right to have someone with him during the hearing. The Court determined that the appellant was not entitled to a judicial hearing.

NATURALIZATION RIGHTS

The first case dealing with naturalization, *Takao Ozawa v. United States*,[19] which tested the legality of denying an Asian alien resident the right to naturalization, was argued before the Supreme Court on October 3 and 4, 1922. The Court handed down its decision against Ozawa on November 13, 1922. Ozawa, the appellant, was born in Japan but was educated in the United States, had graduated from a high school in Berkeley, California, and had finished three years at the University of California. He had lived continuously in the United States for twenty years before he applied for naturalization on October 16, 1914. His petition was, however, denied by the District Court for the Territory of Hawaii. It was concluded even by Justice Sutherland who delivered the unanimous opinion of the Court that Ozawa "was well qualified by character and education for citizenship." Then why was he refused U.S. citizenship?

Justice Sutherland dealt with the three questions raised before the Court by Ozawa's attorneys. In their brief, the appellant's attorneys asked whether the Act of June 29, 1906, providing for an uniform rule for naturalization, was complete in itself or was limited by Section 2169 of the Revised Statutes of the United States. They also asked if a person born in Japan, and of the Japanese race, was eligible for citizenship through naturalization. Finally, they raised the question of whether a person born of the Japanese race, and in Japan, could be eligible for citizenship even if naturalization were limited to aliens who were free white persons and to aliens of African nativity and of African descent. In their defense for their client, the attorneys insisted that the words *free white persons* inserted in the Act of March 26, 1790, which provided an uniform rule of naturalization, did not intend to exclude the Japanese. They argued that the words "neither in their common and popular meaning, nor in their scientific definition, define a race or races, or prescribe a nativity or locus of origin."[20] They claimed that the word *free* was meant to be used in opposition to slavery, while the word *white* signified a class of individuals who were considered superior and who did not have "negro blood." A person is an individual of the human race, as defined by the appellant's attorneys. This definition related to the attorneys' claim that the words *free white persons* were meant to deal with individuals, not with races. Finally, the attorneys insisted that the Japanese were assimilable.

Justice Sutherland conceded that the original intent of Congress that passed the Act of March 26, 1790, did not exclude the Japanese. But this was immaterial to him. What was important to him was that only "free white persons" were to be included in "that class of persons whom the fathers knew as white, and to deny it to all who could not be so classified." Justice Sutherland recognized the practical problem of differentiating persons in terms of skin color:

Manifestly, the test afforded by the mere color of the skin of each individual is impracticable as that differs greatly among persons of the same race, even among Anglo-Saxons, ranging by imperceptible gradation from the fair blond to the swarthy brunette, the latter being darker than many of the lighter hued persons of the brown or yellow races. Hence to adopt the color test alone would result in a confused overlapping of races and a gradual merging of one into the other, without any practical line of separation.[21]

Justice Sutherland, therefore, did not want to use any ethnological or scientific definition of race, but preferred to go for a "popularly known" concept of what a white person was at the time of his ruling. Of course, this popular version of race meant only a person of the Caucasian race. Justice Sutherland advanced the doctrine of "the gradual process of judicial inclusion and exclusion" in determining who should be ruled eligible for naturalization. To him, there was no clear-cut line of demarcation between those who were eligible for naturalization and those who were not, but "only a zone of more or less debatable ground outside of which, upon the one hand, are those clearly eligible, and outside of which, upon the other hand, are those clearly ineligible for citizenship." This was certainly judicial double talk. What Sutherland actually did was to establish three zones, one of which was "debatable ground," to borrow from his words. There was a zone of people who were definitely eligible for naturalization, whereas there was another zone of people who were clearly ineligible for citizenship. The middle zone consisted of people whose eligibility would be determined by "the gradual process of judicial inclusion and exclusion." Although Justice Sutherland claimed that there was no clear line of demarcation, he clearly differentiated the three zones from each other without explaining what criteria were established and how they were used. Justice Sutherland waded through the muddled pool of logic to reach his conclusion.

On the day of the Ozawa decision, the Court also handed down its ruling on *Takuji Yamashita et al. v. Hinkle, Secretary of State of the State of Washington*.[22] Yamashita had been naturalized sometime before 1906, in the state of Washington. As a U.S. citizen, he filed articles of incorporation for a real estate company, but Hinkle refused to receive them on the grounds that Yamashita had never had the right to be naturalized. Had he not been naturalized, he could not have filed articles of incorporation because he would be still an alien ineligible for citizenship, and under the laws of the state of Washington, no alien ineligible for citizenship was allowed to form a corporation. Justice Sutherland delivered the opinion of the unanimous Court upholding the decision of the Supreme Court of the State of Washington, which had ruled that the superior court that had admitted Yamashita to citizenship did not have jurisdiction, and therefore its judgment was null and void.

Having ruled Yamashita's citizenship null and void in 1922, the Court agreed to hear arguments on the case of *United States v. Bhagat Singh*

Thind[23] on January 11 and 12, 1923, and it made a decision on February 19, 1923. The appellee, Bhagat Singh Thind, had been naturalized by the District Court in Oregon over the objection of the officer examining naturalization cases. The Court's decision was challenged in a bill, but it was dismissed by the District Court, and the government then appealed to the Circuit Court of Appeals, which subsequently certified questions to be addressed by the Supreme Court. The attorneys for the appellee presented the following questions in their brief:

Question 1. Is a high caste Hindu of full Indian blood, born at Amrit Sar, Punjab, India, a white person within the meaning of section 2169, Revised Statutes?

Question 2. Does the act of February 5, 1917 disqualify from naturalization as citizens those Hindus, now barred by that act, who had lawfully entered the United States prior to the passage of said act?

Justice Sutherland, in delivering the Court's unanimous opinion, reiterated his point of view, stating that the privilege of citizenship was to go to the class of persons "whom the fathers [who enacted the Act of March 26, 1790] knew as white." Justice Sutherland had ruled on *Ozawa v. United States* that the word *white* meant a person of the Caucasian race, but he now changed his mind about that definition. In the case of Thind, Justice Sutherland argued that Thind fell outside that zone of debatable ground even if he was a person of the Caucasian race. One is hard pressed to find this ethereal ground that excludes from U.S. citizenship both a person who is neither white nor Caucasian and a person who is Caucasian. If one is to follow Sutherland's logic, every person should be excluded. But Sutherland insisted that the word *white* meant not Caucasian, but white as understood by the common person. According to Justice Sutherland's logic, Thind was not entitled to naturalization because he was not white. Thind was not qualified to be eligible for naturalization in accordance with the Act of February 5, 1917, because the law excluded all natives of Asia, including those of India, from admission into the United States. Although exclusion from immigration did not necessarily mean exclusion from naturalization, Justice Sutherland surmised that "it is not likely that Congress would be willing to accept, as citizen a class of persons whom it rejects as immigrants."

A rather strange case, *Toyota v. U.S.,*[24] involving a Japanese native who served in the United States Coast Guard from 1913 to 1923, went to the Supreme Court for its decision on May 25, 1925. On May 14, 1921, Toyota filed his petition for naturalization in the U.S. District Court for the District of Massachusetts. His petition was approved and a certificate of naturalization was issued, but the government wanted to have the certificate canceled because it considered that it was obtained illegally.

Justice Butler, who delivered an *obiter dictum* opinion for the Court, with which the Chief Justice dissented, ruled that the certificate should be canceled because the Act of May 9, 1918, and the Act of July 19, 1919, were not meant to include the natives of Japan in a class of people eligible for naturalization. The Act of May 9, 1918, allowed "any alien" serving in the United States forces during the First World War to file for naturalization without making the preliminary intention and without the required proof of five years' residence. The Act of July 19, 1919, extended the benefit of the Act of May 9, 1918, to "any person of foreign birth." Toyota had served in the U.S. Coast Guard, which was part of the U.S. naval force, during the First World War. Therefore, he was entitled to the right to naturalization, as provided in the said acts of Congress. However, Justice Butler ruled that nothing in these two acts was intended to eliminate from the qualifications for naturalization the distinction made in the Act of May 26, 1790, on the base of color and race.

The Court disagreed with the appellant's attorney, Laurence M. Lombard, who said that Filipinos and Puerto Ricans could be naturalized in accordance with the Act of June 29, 1906. The Court ruled that Filipinos were not eligible for naturalization until passage of the said two acts. According to Justice Butler, the Act of 1918 "was to make eligible, and to authorize the naturalization of native-born Filipinos of whatever color or race having the qualifications specified in the seventh subdivision of #4."

It is doubtful if Congress had intended to exclude from eligibility for naturalization any person on account of race or color when the acts of 1918 and 1919 were passed. These two acts specifically mentioned "any alien" and "any person of foreign birth." One would be inclined to give the benefit of the doubt to aliens who had served the United States through its armed forces. One can only state that Justice Butler must have been privy to the intention of Congress.

DENATURALIZATION

During the Pacific War, American citizens of Japanese ancestry lost their citizenship for a number of reasons. Some of them renounced their citizenship because they lost faith in America. After all, they were taught to believe in freedom, justice, and equality for all, as put forth in the Pledge of Allegiance. But they were incarcerated in concentration camps for no other reason than that they were born of Japanese parentage. Many of them felt that they were betrayed by their own country. Therefore, when they were given an opportunity to renounce their citizenship, a total of 5,766 Nisei decided to give it up, and 1,116 of them went to Japan voluntarily. By May 21, 1959, however, 4,978 of these people had their citizenship restored, and only 357 had not tried to restore it as of that date. Others lost their citizenship because the U.S. government took their citizenship away from them on the grounds that they had served in the enemy's armed forces during the war.

The case of *Acheson, Secretary of State v. Okimura*[25] involved such a person. Okimura Kiyokura was born in 1921 of Japanese parents in Kauai, Hawaii. He lived there until he was four years old, when he went to Japan for education, as many of his generation did to honor their parental wishes. These children were called Kibei. Many of them were stranded in Japan because of the sudden outbreak of hostility between Japan and the United States. In 1942, Okimura was inducted into the Japanese Army against his will, and he served in China before he was captured in 1945. In 1947, while Japan was still under American military rule, Okimura voted in an election. Two years later he wanted to come to Hawaii; he applied for a U.S. passport but was denied on the grounds that he had served in the Japanese Army and voted in a Japanese election. The government's decision was in conformity with Sections 801 (c) of Title Eight, United States Code, which reads as follows: "A person who is a national of the United States, whether by birth or naturalization, shall lose his nationality by: (c) Entering, or serving, in the armed forces of a foreign state unless expressly authorized by the laws of the United States, if he has or acquires the nationality of such foreign state."[26]

Okimura argued before the District Court that Congress did not have the power to revoke the citizenship of a native-born American, even if he had served in the armed forces of a foreign state and had voted in an election in a foreign country. The District Court ruled in Okimura's favor, stating that Congress could not take citizenship away from an American citizen. Secretary of State Acheson appealed directly to the Supreme Court, and the Court handed down a *per curiam* decision on January 2, 1952. Justice Douglas supported the District Court's decision on the grounds that evidence showed that Okimura served in the Japanese armed forces under compulsion.

This ruling was further buttressed by the Court's decision on the case of *Nishikawa v. Dulles, Secretary of State*[27] on March 31, 1958. The case involved a Kibei who had gone to Japan to study and was stranded there during the Pacific War. He was inducted into the Japanese armed forces and served in China as a mechanic against his will. After the war was over, he applied for an American passport, but he was given a certificate of loss of nationality. The Court's opinion, delivered by Chief Justice Warren, declared that expatriation of a native-born American citizen could not be considered complete and final unless it was done voluntarily. The Court further stated that the burden of proof was on the government to demonstrate by "clear, convincing, and unequivocal evidence" that Nishikawa renounced his citizenship.

Another Kibei was involved in the strange case of *Kawakita v. United States*.[28] The petitioner, Kawakita Tomoya, was eighteen years old in 1939 when he went to Japan on a U.S. passport. He stayed in Japan and went to Meiji University. He renewed his passport in 1941, taking the oath of allegiance to the United States. In 1943 he graduated from the university and entered his name in the family Koseki. This amounted to renunciation of his American citizenship.

During World War II, Kawakita served as an interpreter working for the Oeyama Nickel Industry Company, where American prisoners of war worked. After the war was over, he came back to the United States in 1946 on a U.S. passport, which he had obtained by stating that he had not done anything to renounce his citizenship. In September 1947, a former prisoner of war, William L. Bruce, recognized Kawakita in a Los Angeles department store and reported him to the Federal Bureau of Investigation. Kawakita was arrested, and a federal grand jury indicted him, charging him with fifteen counts in relation to his mistreatment of American prisoners at the Oeyama Nickel Industry Company. He was tried and convicted of treason, and Federal District Judge William C. Mathes imposed the death sentence on him. During his trial he insisted that he was a citizen of Japan at the time of his employment at the Oeyama Nickel Industry Company, because he had entered his name in the family Koseki or registry. Because of his expatriation at the time of the alleged crime, he further maintained, he could not be tried as an American citizen. He appealed to the Circuit Court of Appeals, but the original conviction was upheld. The case went to the Supreme Court on certiorari for the defendant.

On June 2, 1952, the Court upheld by a four to three decision the original conviction and death sentence imposed on Kawakita by the lower courts. Justice Douglas, in delivering the opinion of the majority (with which Justices Vinson, Black, and Burton dissented) stated the Court's main position:

If he can retain that freedom [to act against America voluntarily and willfully] and still remain an American citizen, there is not even a minimum of allegiance which he owes to the United States while he resides in the enemy country. That conclusion is hostile to the concept of citizenship as we know it, and it must be rejected. One who wants that freedom can get it by renouncing his American citizenship.

He cannot turn it into a fair-weather citizenship, retaining it for possible contingent benefits but meanwhile playing the part of the traitor. An American citizen owes allegiance to the United States wherever he may reside.[29]

Chief Justice Vinson dissented and filed a separate opinion, with which Justices Black and Burton concurred. Chief Justice Vinson contended that the defendant had already renounced his American citizenship at the time of his employment at Oeyama Nickel Industry Company. He traveled to China on a Japanese passport. This was another indication that he was not an American citizen. He also prayed for a Japanese victory and the Emperor's health. His mistreatment of American prisoners of war was also indicative of his loyalty to Japan, not to the United States. The fact that he obtained an American passport, Chief Justice Vinson further maintained, did not restore his American citizenship.

Kawakita was sent to the Alcatraz federal prison, where he spent sixteen years of his life in imprisonment. His death sentence was commuted on November 2, 1953. President Kennedy granted him a presidential pardon on the condition that he return to Japan and never come back to the United States. Thus ended a tragic chapter in the life of Kawakita, who was caught between loyalty to his country of birth and the impersonal conditions of war demanded of him.

ALIEN LAND ACTS AND THE SUPREME COURT

The California's Alien Land Act of 1913, as amended in 1920 and 1923, was challenged in the Supreme Court, which was asked to rule on the constitutionality of the act. The first two cases that reached the court were *Porterfield v. Webb*[30] and *Terrace v. Thompson*.[31] Both cases were argued on April 23 and 24, 1923, and were decided on November 12, 1923. The former dealt with the Alien Land Act of California, while the latter dealt with the Anti-Alien Land Act of 1921 of the State of Washington.

Porterfield, a citizen of the United States, had eighty acres of land in the county of Los Angeles, which he wanted to lease to Mizuno, a Japanese resident alien who was not eligible for citizenship. Under provisions made in the Alien Land Act of 1913, such a lease was in violation of the law because Mizuno was an alien ineligible for citizenship, and the state had the right to take an escheat action against Porterfield. Porterfield filed suit to stop Webb, Attorney General of the state of California, from enforcing the said law.

Before the Court, the appellant's attorney, Louis Marshall, argued that the law was in violation of the treaty of February 21, 1911, and the Fourteenth Amendment of the Constitution. Justice Butler, in delivering the

Court's opinion, stated that the case was similar to that of *Terrace v. Thompson,* and the decision on the latter "controls the decision of all questions raised here." In the case of *Terrace v. Thompson,* Terrace wanted to lease land to Nakatsuka, a Japanese resident alien who was not eligible for citizenship. The appellant Terrace claimed that Thompson, as Attorney General of the state of Washington, threatened to enforce the Anti-Alien Land Act and to prosecute. The appellants, Terrace and Nakatsuka, filed suit to determine if the said law was constitutional. Two questions raised before the Court asked if the Washington law was in violation of the treaty of February 21, 1911, between the U.S. and Japan and of the Fourteenth Amendment of the Constitution. Justice Butler ruled that the Washington law was neither in violation of the Fourteenth Amendment of the Constitution or of the 1911 treaty. According to Butler, the treaty did not exempt the Japanese from the requirement of declaring their intention to become U.S. citizens in order to have any interest in land, as required by the Washington law. The law did not discriminate against those eligible aliens who had not filed their intention to become U.S. citizens or those ineligible aliens who had failed to file their intention to become U.S. citizens, according to Justice Butler. One of the implications of Justice Butler's ruling was that even if the Japanese were ineligible, they should have filed their intention to become U.S. citizens. But this could not be done because they were ineligible. Thus, the Japanese resident aliens found themselves in a Catch-22 situation.

On November 19, 1923, the Supreme Court handed down its decisions on two more cases related to the Alien Land Act of 1913. The case of *Webb v. O'Brien*[32] involved two appellees, O'Brien and Inouye, who were prevented from concluding a cropping contract by Ulysses S. Webb, attorney general of the state of California. Webb threatened them with an escheat action to take land away from O'Brien. O'Brien owned ten acres of agricultural land in Santa Clara County. He wanted to enter into a cropping contract with Inouye, whose ability as a farmer was conceded by the Court. The appellees' attorney, Louis Marshall, argued before the Court that the cropping contract was not in violation of the law because it did not involve a transfer of real property. He further argued that prohibiting any aliens from concluding a contract to work on agricultural land would be in violation of the Fourteenth Amendment of the Constitution. Justice Butler, in delivering the Court's opinion, disagreed with the appellees' attorney and ruled that the Alien Land Act of 1913 was constitutional.

On the same day, the case of *Frick et al. v. Webb*[33] was decided in favor of the state of California, thus upholding the constitutionality of the state's Alien Land Act of 1913, which was approved by the electors of California on November 2, 1920. Frick owned twenty-eight shares of the capital stock of the Merced Farm Company and wanted to sell them to Satow, a Japanese resident alien who was therefore ineligible for citizenship. Because the state threatened to take an escheat action against the appellants, Frick and Satow, they applied for an interlocutory injunction to enjoin the state from enforcing the Alien Land Act of 1913. A lower court ruled against the appellants, and the case went to the Supreme Court on appeal. The appellants' attorney, Louis Marshall, argued that the law was in violation of the Fourteenth Amendment of the Constitution and of the Treaty of Commerce and Navigation of 1911 between Japan and the United States. Particularly, since the treaty allowed citizens of both nations to carry on trade, wholesale and retail, in their respective territories, any law that would prevent Satow from purchasing the stocks would be in contravention of the treaty. Justice Butler ruled that the right "to carry on trade" did not allow Japanese resident aliens to purchase stocks owned by an agricultural corporation.

On May 11, 1925, the Supreme Court ruled in favor of the state of California on the case of *Cockrill et al. v. People of California*,[34] again upholding the constitutionality of the Alien Land Act of 1913. Cockrill and Ikada, plaintiffs in the case, went into an agreement to purchase land. Ikada was to provide money and Cockrill was to take out a title on the purchased land under his name. The plaintiffs planned to transfer the title to Ikada's children as their property. Because of their intention, they were convicted of conspiracy to violate the Alien Land Act of 1913 in the superior court of Sonoma County, California. They filed a petition, which was subsequently denied, and the case went to the Supreme Court. The attorneys for the plaintiffs, Algernon Crofton and Charles A. Wetmore, argued against Section Nine of the said law, which stated that "a *prima facie* presumption that the conveyance is made with such intent [to prevent, evade, or avoid escheat to the state] shall arise upon proof" (268 U.S. 260). They also contended that the law was in violation of the Treaty of Commerce and Navigation of 1911. Justice Butler delivered the opinion of the Court, stating that "the inference that payment of the purchase price by one from whom the privilege of acquisition is withheld and the taking of the land in the name of one of another class are for the purpose of getting the control of the land for the ineligible alien is not fanciful, arbitrary, or unreasonable." He brushed aside the contention that the Alien Land Act violated the Fourteenth Amendment, and he declared the law constitutional because the treaty did not provide "any protection to Japanese subjects in this country against application of a rule of evidence created by state enactment that is not given them by the due process and equal protection clause of the Fourteenth Amendment" (268 U.S. 262-63).

The Supreme Court ruled that the detention of persons of Japanese ancestry in America against their will during World War II was unconstitutional, when the case of *Endo Ex Parte* came to the Court for its decision. In compliance with this decision, General H. C. Pratt, who replaced General DeWitt, revoked the West Coast mass evacuation order effective as of January 2, 1945. The Japanese Americans who had been detained for three years were now allowed to go home. Many of them returned to their homes and farmland to face threats of violence against them. Some were shot at, while others saw their homes set on fire. Secretary of Interior Harold Ickes reported that there had been twenty-four incidents of violence and terrorism against Japanese Americans by May 14, 1945. Residents on the West Coast were not willing to accept Japanese Americans into their communities, and the state of California attempted to take land away from Japanese Americans by enforcing the Alien Land Act of 1913, as amended in 1920 and 1923. Armed with $200,000 appropriated by the California legislature, the California Attorney General's office went rigorously after agricultural land to be escheated to the state of California. Escheat actions were taken against the Nisei and their parents, particularly if it could be proven that land was purchased illegally by Issei parents to hand it over to their children. One of these escheat actions was against Fred Oyama and Oyama Kajiro.

The escheat action involved two parcels of land Oyama Kajiro had purchased in 1934 and 1937. The purchase price for the first parcel was $4,000, while the second parcel was sold for $1,500. Oyama Kajiro had a deed executed under his son's name, Fred Oyama, who was six years old at the time of the first purchase. He then petitioned to the Superior Court that he be appointed as his son's guardian, and this was approved by the Court. In 1942, the Oyamas were evacuated from the place of their residence and were detained in a relocation camp. While they were in detention, the state of California took an escheat action against the two parcels of land, claiming that the Oyamas violated the Alien Land Act of 1913.

The case of *Oyama v. California*[35] reached the Supreme Court on a writ of certiorari to the Supreme Court of California, which had ruled that the Alien Land Act was constitutional. Chief Justice Vinson delivered the majority opinion of the Court on January 19, 1948. Justices Jackson, Burton, and Reed dissented, filing separate opinions. The petitioners argued against the Alien Land Act as it applied to them on the following three grounds: First, Fred Oyama was deprived of the equal protection of the laws and of his privileges as an American citizen; second, Oyama Kajiro was denied equal protection of the laws; and third, the due process clause was violated because the law approved escheat action after expiration of the application limitations period. The Court ruled against California, upholding "the right of American citizens to own land anywhere in the

United States." Although the Court agreed with the first point of the petitioners' argument, it did not support the rest of the argument. The concurring opinion of Justice Murphy attacked the racist nature of the said law. Murphy stated that "the California statute in question, as I view it, is nothing more than an outright racial discrimination." Justice Black, with whom Justice Douglas concurred, filed a separate opinion in support of the petitioners. One of his reasons for support concerned the American commitment to cooperate with the United Nations "to promote . . . universal respect for, and observance of, human rights and fundamental freedoms for all, without distinction as to race, sex, language, or religion."

Soon after the Supreme Court had struck down the Alien Land Act of 1913, it also ruled against a California law that had prohibited aliens ineligible for U.S. citizenship from fishing in the ocean waters off the coast of California. The case of *Takahashi v. Fish and Game Commission et al.*[36] reached the Supreme Court on a writ of certiorari to the Supreme Court of California that had reversed a superior court order to issue a fishing license to the petitioner, Takahashi Torao, a person ineligible for U.S. citizenship. The petitioner had fished in ocean waters off the California coast from 1915 to 1942, when he was relocated and was detained in accordance with Executive Order 9066. Prior to 1943, California had issued commercial fishing licenses to any person qualified, regardless of alienage or ineligibility for citizenship. In 1943 the California Fish and Game Code was changed to include "alien Japanese" in a class of people who could not receive commercial fishing licenses. This 1945 code was again changed to include all aliens ineligible for U.S. citizenship. This was done to head off any court challenges that would have the code ruled unconstitutional on the grounds that it singled out only "alien Japanese."

Before the Court, Ralph W. Scott, Deputy Attorney General of California, argued that the state had the right to exclude all aliens, and particularly aliens ineligible for citizenship, from "catching fish within or without the three-mile coastal belt and bringing them to California for commercial purposes," because the state had a "proprietary interest in fish." He further argued that the state's code was within the rationale of "the special public interest," for the code was part of a fish conservation measure. The Court's majority opinion, delivered on June 7, 1948, by Justice Black, repudiated the state's claim of special public interest and ruled that California was not justified in excluding aliens "who are lawful residents of the State from making a living by fishing . . . while permitting all others to do so." The concurring opinion that Justice Murphy filed separately from the majority opinion (with which Justices Reed and Jackson dissented) went to the heart of the code:

We should not blink at the fact that #990 (California Fish and Game Code), as now written, is a discriminatory piece of legislation having no relation whatever to any constitutionally cognizable interest of California. It was drawn against a background of racial and economic tension. It is directed in spirit and in effect solely against aliens of Japanese birth. It denies them commercial fishing rights not because they threaten the success of any conservation program, not because their fishing activities constitute a clear and present danger to the welfare of California or of the nation, but only because they are of Japanese stock, a stock which has had the misfortune to arouse antagonism among certain powerful interests. We need but unbutton the seemingly innocent words of #990 to discover beneath them the very negation of all the ideals of the equal protection clause.[37]

RIGHTS FOR LANGUAGE AND EDUCATION

In 1927 the Supreme Court handed down two decisions that sent a conflicting signal on the cultural and educational rights of Asian Americans. The first case, *Farrington, Governor et al. v. T. Tokushige et al.,*[38] had to do with Japanese language programs carried out by Japanese language schools in Hawaii. In 1927 there were 163 foreign language schools in Hawaii, and 157 of them taught Japanese, while 9 and 7 taught Korean and Chinese, respectively. A total of 20,000 pupils were enrolled at these schools, which were staffed with 300 teachers. The property value of these schools was estimated at $250,000. The Hawaiian legislature passed a law, "An Act Relating to Foreign Language Schools and Teachers Thereof," which was amended by Act 171 of 1923 and by Act 1952 of 1925. According to this law, no foreign language school was allowed to operate unless it received written permission from the Department of Public Instruction and unless a fee of $1 per pupil had been paid. The petitioners, represented by their attorney William B. Lymer, argued in favor of enforcing the law passed by the Hawaiian legislature, claiming that the law did not violate the Constitution. The respondents, including T. Tokushige, argued that enforcement of the law would deprive them of their liberty and property without due process of law, which is guaranteed by the Fifth Amendment. Justice McReynolds, in delivering the Court's unanimous opinion, ruled in favor of T. Tokushige, grounding the Court's reasoning on the *Meyer v. Nebraska, Bartels v. Iowa,* and *Pierce v. Society of Sisters* decisions.[39] The court's decision read in part,

Enforcement of the Act probably would destroy most, if not all, of them; and, certainly, it would deprive parents of fair opportunity to procure for their children instruction which they think important and we cannot say is harmful. The Japanese parent has the right to direct the education of his own child without unreasonable restrictions; the Constitution protects him as well as those who speak another tongue.[40]

While the Court ruled in favor of the right of T. Tokushige to teach Japanese to his children, determining that the enforcement of the said law would be in violation of the Fifth Amendment, the same court decided on the case of *Gong Lum et al. v. Rice et al.*[41] against the plaintiff, Gong Lum. Martha, the plaintiff's daughter, was sent to a segregated school for "the colored races" in the state of Mississippi. The plaintiff claimed that the state deprived his daughter of equal protection of law. He asked the Court to order the State Superintendent of Education to cease discrimination against Martha and to admit her into the high school that was "assigned to white children exclusively." Justice Taft, in delivering the Court's unanimous decision on the case, upheld the "separate but equal doctrine" established by the Court in the case of *Plessy v. Ferguson*[42] in 1896 and stated as follows:

The question here is whether a Chinese citizen of the United States is denied equal protection of the laws when he is classified among the colored races and furnished facilities for education equal to that offered to all, whether white, brown, yellow or black. Were this a new question, it would call for very full argument and consideration, but we think that it is the same question which has been many times decided to be within the constitutional power of the state legislature to settle without intervention of the federal courts under the Federal Constitution.[43]

JAPANESE INTERNMENT CASES

There were no major cases of litigation involving American citizens of Asian ancestry or Asian resident aliens between 1927 and 1943, when Executive Order 9066, issued by the president on February 19, 1942, was challenged in the Supreme Court. In 1934 the Court reaffirmed the ineligibility of a Japanese person, Doi, for U.S. citizenship in the case of *Morrison et al. v. California.*[44] After the Japanese surprise attack on Pearl Harbor on December 7, 1941, the case of *Ex parte Kumezo Kawato*[45] reached the Court. The case was argued on October 12, 1942, and was decided on November 9 of the same year. The case involved Kumezo Kawato, a person born in Japan, who came to the United States in 1905. He filed a libel suit against the vessel *Rally* in order to claim wages to which he was entitled, for he worked on the ship as a seaman and fisherman. However, the claimants of the ship filed a motion in the District Court for the Southern District of California to dismiss the libel action on the grounds that the petitioner became an enemy alien and therefore had no right to prosecute any action, in any court of the United States, during the war. The District Court granted the motion, and the petitioner appealed to the Circuit Court of Appeals to compel the District Court to vacate its judgment, but his appeal was denied without opinion. Justice Black, in delivering the Court's opinion, stated that the Trading with the Enemy Act was not intended "to affect resident aliens at all" without presidential proclamation. Furthermore, according to Justice Black, the Attorney General responsible for the administration of alien affairs interpreted "existing statutes and proclamations as not barring this petitioner from our courts." In closing, Justice Black stated that "the doors of our courts have not been shut to peaceful, law-abiding aliens seeking to enforce rights growing out of legal occupations."

Immediately after the bombing of Pearl Harbor, the U.S. government took measures to impose various restrictions on resident enemy aliens or citizens of Germany, Italy, and Japan. They became more stringent when applied to aliens of Japanese birth and American citizens of Japanese ancestry. Some of these restrictions on German and Italian citizens in the United States were relaxed. Because of security concerns, the military wanted to exclude all Japanese resident enemy aliens and U.S. citizens of Japanese ancestry from the militarily sensitive areas on the West Coast. Finally, General John Lesesne DeWitt, Commanding General of the Western Defense Command, sent to the Department of Justice his final recommendation that requested evacuation of 112,000 persons of Japanese ancestry, regardless of their citizenship status. Various government agencies, including the War Department, approved DeWitt's recommendation, and Justice Department officials drafted the order on February 18, 1942. The following day, the order was presented to the president for his signature and became Executive Order 9066.

Executive Order 9066 authorized the secretary of war, or the military commander whom he might designate, "to prescribe military areas in such places and of such extent as he . . . may determine, from which any or all persons may be excluded" (320 U.S. 86). To give force of law to provisions included in Executive Order 9066, Congress passed Public Law 503 and sent it to the president for his signature on March 21, 1942. The law made it a misdemeanor to violate the orders of a military commander in a designated military area, and such a violation was punishable by a fine and imprisonment. General DeWitt, authorized by Executive Order 9066, issued a number of Public Proclamations: Public Proclamation No. 1, issued on March 2, 1942, established Military Area No. 1; Public Proclamation No. 2, issued on March 16, 1942, required that enemy aliens and persons of Japanese ancestry notify government authorities of a change of residence; and Public Proclamation No. 3, issued on March 24, 1942, established military curfew and travel regulations on enemy aliens and persons of Japanese ancestry. The curfew was to be enforced between 8:00 P.M. and 6:00 A.M., to begin on March 27, in Military Area No. 1. General DeWitt also issued a number of Civilian Exclusion Orders to control and exclude persons of Japanese ancestry: Civilian Exclusion Order No. 1 of March 24, 1942, excluded all persons of Japanese ancestry from Bainbridge Island on Puget Sound to the Bremerton Naval Yard, regardless of their citizenship status, and required them to assemble at the Puyallup Army Assembly Center; Civilian Exclusion Order Nos. 2 and 3 excluded all persons of Japanese ancestry from San Pedro, Long Beach, and other areas in Los Angeles County, California; Civilian Exclusion Order No. 4 ordered all persons of Japanese ancestry removed from the city and county of San Diego; and Civilian Exclusion Order No. 5 had all persons of Japanese ancestry excluded from most dock areas and the waterfront of San Francisco.

After the U.S. government had 112,000 persons of Japanese ancestry removed from their place of residence, it transported them to ten different relocation camps, where they were detained against their will. These camps were administered by the War Relocation Authority that was created by Executive Order No. 9102 on March 18, 1942. These relocation camps, commonly known as internment camps, were located in seven different states: Tule Lake and Manzanar in California, Poston and Gila River in Arizona, Rohwer and Jerome in Arkansas, Heart Mountain in Wyoming, Granada in Coloroda, Topaz in Utah, and Minidoka in Idaho.

Resulting from the government's decision to remove, relocate, and detain Japanese Americans were four major cases of litigation that challenged the constitutionality of the Act of March 21, 1942, that Congress passed to execute Executive Order 9066. The first two cases, *Hirabayashi v. U.S.*[46] and *Yasui v. U.S.*,[47] were decided on June 21, 1943, against both defendants. The defendant Hirabayashi, an American citizen of Japanese ancestry, was a senior in the University of Washington at the time of his conviction for violation of the Act of March 21, 1942. Gordon Hirabayashi was charged with two counts of misdemeanor and was convicted of both. The first charge against him was that he violated a curfew law, as specified in Public Proclamation No. 3, while the second charge was his failure to remain in his residence in the designated military area. The District Court gave the defendant two sentences of three months each on two counts that were to run concurrently. Through his attorneys, Hirabayashi claimed that the Act of March 21, 1942, was unconstitutional because Congress unconstitutionally delegated its legislative power to the military commander to impose a curfew. He further argued that even if the curfew law was legal, in all other respects, it was still unconstitutional because it violated the Fifth Amendment, which guarantees nondiscrimination. He appealed to the Ninth Circuit Court of Appeals, which certified questions to be answered by the court. Chief Justice Stone delivered the Court's unanimous opinion, stating that the curfew law in question did not unconstitutionally discriminate against citizens of Japanese ancestry. The Court also ruled that the defendant's Fifth Amendment rights were not violated because the Fifth Amendment guarantees due process of law against discriminatory legislation by Congress, and not equal protection of law.

The Court based its decision on the idea that the war power of the government was to wage war successfully. To wage war and to wage it successfully, according to the Court, meant that the war power should be extended beyond the battlefields to include every phase of the national defense, including protecting the nation against sabotage and espionage. In his opinion for the Court, Chief Justice Stone pointed to the danger of Japanese "fifth column" activities possibly engaged in by persons of Japanese ancestry; he claimed that "espionage by persons in sympathy with the Japanese Government had been found to have been particularly effective in the surprise attack on Pearl Harbor." Chief Justice Stone made a damaging statement against persons of Japanese ancestry in America: "Whatever views we may entertain regarding the loyalty to this country of the citizens of Japanese ancestry, we cannot reject as unfounded the judgement of the military authorities and of Congress that there were disloyal members of that population, whose number and strength could not be precisely and quickly ascertained." [48]

Justices Douglas, Murphy, and Rutledge filed separate concurring opinions. Justice Murphy's opinion was particularly interesting in that it was originally written as a dissenting opinion. It was suggested that Justice Murphy changed it to make the Court's decision unanimous after he was pressured by his colleagues, particularly by Justice Frankfurter. Justice Murphy indirectly chastised his colleagues by stating that "the great American experiment has failed" if they admitted that a certain group (i.e., Japanese Americans) could not be assimilated. Justice Murphy strongly expressed his disagreement with his colleagues:

Today is the first time, so far as I am aware, that we have sustained a substantial restriction of the personal liberty of citizens of the United States based upon the accident of race or ancestry. Under the curfew order here challenged no less than 70,000 American citizens have been placed under a special ban and deprived of their liberty because of their particular racial inheritance. [49]

The case of *Yasui v. U.S.* did not fare better with the Court. Yasui Minoru was born and educated in Portland, Oregon. He was a member of the bar of Oregon and a second lieutenant in the U.S. Army Infantry Reserve. He also worked for the Japanese Consulate Office in Chicago, but he resigned after the bombing of Pearl Harbor. After Public Proclamation No. 3 was issued, he wanted to test its constitutionality. He discussed his intention with an FBI agent and carried it out to violate the curfew order. He was brought to the District Court in Oregon, and it was ruled that the Act of March 21, 1942, was unconstitutional. However, in the case of Yasui, the law was ruled constitutional because it was thought that Yasui had renounced his citizenship when he went to work for the Japanese Consulate Office in Chicago. The Supreme Court, however, ruled that the decision on the case of *Hirabayashi v. U.S.* had authority on *Yasui v. U.S.*

Two other cases involving the question of constitutionality of the Act of March 21, 1942, *Korematsu v. U.S.*[50] and *Ex parte Mitsuye Endo,*[51] were decided on December 18, 1944. By this time the outcome of the Pacific War had already been conclusively decided in favor of the United States. Fred Korematsu, a citizen of the United States by birth, was found in violation of Civilian Exclusion Order No. 34, which prohibited him from remaining in San Leandro, California, a military area designated by the order. He was arrested, indicted, and convicted by a federal district court. He appealed to the Circuit Court of Appeals, which certified the constitutional question to be responded to by the Supreme Court. Through his attorneys, Wayne M. Collins and Charles A. Horsky, Korematsu challenged the assumptions the Court made when it decided on the case of *Hirabayashi v. U.S.* He further argued that when Civilian Exclusion Order No. 34 was issued, the threat of Japanese invasion of the West Coast had disappeared.

Justice Black, who delivered the Court's majority opinion (with which Justices Roberts, Jackson, and Murphy dissented), brushed aside the contention made by the petitioner and ruled that the Act of March 21, 1942, was constitutional because of "military necessity." Justice Black conceded that exclusion from one's own residence put more hardship on one than the curfew did. But he declared that "exclusion from a threatened area, no less than curfew, has a definite and close relationship to the prevention of espionage and sabotage." Justice Black assumed that Japanese Americans, had they not been excluded from military areas, would have engaged in sabotage and espionage activities. He further assumed a collective guilt of Japanese Americans:

Like curfew, exclusion of those Japanese origin was deemed necessary because of the presence of an unascertained number of disloyal members of the group. . . . It was because we could not reject the finding of the military authorities that it was impossible to bring about an immediate segregation of the disloyal from the loyal that we sustained the validity of the curfew order as applying to the whole group. . . . The judgement that exclusion of the whole group was for the same reason a military imperative answers the contention that the exclusion was in the nature of group punishment based on antagonism to those of Japanese origin.[52]

Justice Roberts's dissenting opinion pointed to the conflict between Public Proclamation No. 4 and Civilian Exclusion Order No. 34 and stated that the petitioner was placed in an impossible situation as he was ordered to remain in the area of his residence by the former, while he was required to leave by the latter. Roberts said that "the two conflicting orders, one which commanded him to stay and the other which commanded him to go, were nothing but a cleverly devised trap to accomplish the real purpose of the military authority, which was to lock him up in a concentration camp." Justice Murphy, in his dissenting opinion, went one step further to point to racism against Japanese Americans as a possible motive, stating that "exclusion goes over 'the very brink of constitutional power' and falls into the ugly abyss of racism." He found racism in General DeWitt's Final Report as being responsible for the forced exclusion:

That this forced exclusion was the result in good measure of this erroneous assumption of racial guilt rather than bona fide military necessity is evidenced by the Commanding General's Final Report on the evacuation from the Pacific Coast area. In it he refers to all individuals of Japanese descent as "subversive," as belonging to "an enemy race" whose "racial strains are undiluted," and as constituting "over 112,000 potential enemies . . . at large today," along the Pacific coast.[53]

The case of *Ex parte Mitsuye Endo* challenged the leave procedure of the War Relocation Authority. The appellant, Endo, was evacuated from Sacramento, California, and was sent to the Tule Lake Relocation Center. In 1942 she filed a petition for a writ of habeas corpus, requesting that she be discharged from the center and that she be freed from detention. She claimed through her attorneys, Wayne M. Collins and James C. Purcell, that she was a loyal citizen who was detained against her own will. Her petition was denied in 1943, when she was transferred from Tule Lake to the Central Utah Relocation Center in Topaz, Utah, where she was detained at the time of the Court's decision. Justice Douglas delivered the Court's unanimous decision, although Justices Murphy and Roberts filed separate concurring opinions, stating that they concurred with the decision, but not with the reasons given for it.

The Court ruled that a citizen who was loyal was not a spy or saboteur by definition, and therefore he or she did not present any problem related to sabotage or espionage. If a law was passed to authorize detention to protect war efforts against sabotage and espionage, "detention which has no relationship to that objective is unauthorized," according to the Court's opinion. Although Justice Roberts concurred with the Court's opinion, he objected to the idea that detention in Relocation Centers was not originally planned when Congress made appropriations to the War Relocation Authority, but it was later developed by the officials in charge to deal with community hostility directed against the evacuees. Justice Roberts was of the opinion that a loyal citizen had been deprived of her liberty for a period of years. Justice Murphy was of the opinion that loyalty was not the issue, because detention was not authorized by either Congress or the Executive. Detention of persons of Japanese ancestry, from Justice Murphy's point of view, was "another example of the unconstitutional resort to racism inherent in the entire evacuation program."

REPEAL OF EXCLUSION LAWS

During World War II, thoughtful people were forced to examine their troubled conscience and nation. They were brought to the inescapable realization that their nation was fighting to preserve democracy abroad on the one hand, but was practicing racial discrimination against its minority people at home, on the other. Particularly, discriminatory immigration policies aimed at persons of Chinese descent were considered contrary to the best national interest, as the Chinese were fighting shoulder to shoulder with American soldiers in the battlefields in Asia against the Japanese forces. The Japanese government was also using American immigration policy as its propaganda in an attempt to fan anti-American sentiments among the people in Asia.

While Congress considered a number of bills that proposed repeal of Chinese exclusion laws, a number of organizations opposed such a change in American immigration policy. The American Federation of Labor, for instance, went on record opposing any change in Chinese exclusion laws. Some veterans' groups joined the labor group in support of America's traditional exclusion policy. Campaigning against these traditional exclusionist organizations was Richard J. Walsh, a New York publisher and husband of Pearl S. Buck. He was primarily responsible for organizing the Citizens Committee to Repeal Chinese Exclusion and Place Immigration on a Quota Basis. The committee had a broad membership of 150 prominent Americans with a wide political spectrum that included Roger Baldwin of the American Civil Liberties Union on the left, and Henry Luce of *Time, Life,* and *Fortune* on the right. The committee put pressure on Congress to repeal all Chinese exclusion laws,[54] and Congress was motivated into legislative action with strong words of encouragement from President Roosevelt, who characterized such legislation as "important in the cause of winning the war and of establishing a secure peace."[55] It was fitting that Warren Magnuson of Washington, where violent anti-Chinese riots had occurred more than half a century earlier, introduced a bill to repeal some fifteen different Chinese exclusion laws. During the first day of debate on the bill there was a minor change of wording, but all amendments were rejected, and during the second day of debate the House passed the bill. The Senate committee reported out the same bill, which was passed by the Senate. The bill was signed into law by President Roosevelt and became the Act of December 17, 1943, with the official title, "To repeal the Chinese Exclusions Acts, to establish quotas, and for other purposes."[56]

The law had three sections. Section One enumerated all the Chinese exclusion laws repealed. Section Two assigned an annual quota of 105 to the Chinese, and 75 percent of the quota was allocated to Chinese born and resident in China. Section Three made Chinese, or persons of Chinese descent, eligible for naturalization. Thus ended the trail of discriminatory legislation that had continuously maintained the separation of the People's Domain from the Plural Domain.

During the second session of the Seventy-Eighth Congress, which lasted from January 10 to December 19, 1944, Representatives Clare Boothe Luce of Connecticut and Emanuel Celler of New York introduced separate bills designed to give natives and descendants of natives of India the privileges of immigration and naturalization, but no action was taken during the session. During the second session of the Seventy-Ninth Congress the Celler Bill, which had been considered during the first session, was reported out and was debated. While Congress was considering the bill, President Roosevelt wrote a letter to Representative Samuel Dickstein, Chairman of the House Committee on Immigration and Naturalization. In the letter, dated March 5, 1945, the President wrote, "I regard this legislation as important and desirable, and I believe that its enactment will help us to win the war and to establish a secure peace."[57]

In his letter, President Roosevelt characterized the existing provisions as being discriminatory against persons of East India and "incongruous and inconsistent with the dignity of both of our peoples." Then he appeased Congress by stating that 100 immigrants per year, from India, would present no real danger in the search for jobs. He urged Congress to take positive steps to remove the existing provisions. After the death of President Roosevelt, his successor considered the bill important enough to warrant immediate attention. He asked William D. Hassett, his secretary, to write a letter to Representative Dickstein reminding him of the letter his predecessor had written and informing him that he was in agreement with President Roosevelt.[58]

While the bill was debated, a number of government officials were asked to testify on its behalf. One of them, William Philips, then special assistant to the secretary of state, stated that India was leaning toward Russia as "her best hope." He believed that Russia had "the natural magnetic power" that "pulls neighboring countries into its sphere." He claimed that one of the major reasons why India was attracted to Russia was because "the Soviets have made great success in obtaining unity among different peoples. India has the same problem in that respect." Continuing his comments as he compared Russia with India, he stated, "there are mutual problems of different languages, different customs, and different religions, and the Soviet have, in a sense, solved those problems."[59] He urged Congress to approve the bill because he believed it was "a very cheap way of holding the Indian people facing West."

In her testimony in Congress on behalf of the bill, Representative Luce used the same line of reasoning. She stated that she had made a statement to the effect that Indian intellectuals were leaning toward Russia for guidance in the "techniques of revolution." She was on the radio when she made the statement. Less than two days after she had made the statement, four major Communist newspapers in India responded to her statement by characterizing her as an American imperialist. They also claimed that "Russia was the natural ally of India because Russia was the one country that made no discrimination on racial or pigmentation grounds."[60] Luce concluded her testimony as follows: "I think we should pass the bill first because the principle of no discrimination is the right one. . . . We will have far more friendly relations with the whole Far East, and therefore probably more trade with India. If we pass this legislation it will help to counter Communist ambitions in India, which are serious and grave and very effective at this moment."[61]

Ethnic strife in the former Soviet Union between 1989 and the present has strongly demonstrated that the Soviet Union had not solved its ethnic problems, as Philips suggested. The Soviet propaganda machine was successful in convincing American government officials that the Soviet nationality policies were working to bring peace and social harmony to the Soviet Union. History has proven Philips wrong, but he probably fell victim to the Cold War mentality. Philips and Luce were perhaps justified in their assessment of the effectiveness of Soviet propaganda, which was aimed at pitting the people of Asia against the United States. From their vantage points in 1945, they were led to believe that America could not afford to maintain a discriminatory immigration policy against Indians and other colored people if it were to combat the Russian propaganda. Congress took their advice in earnest and passed the Luce Bill, which became the Act of July 2, 1946.[62]

The law had five sections. Section One gave persons of Chinese, Indian, and Filipino descent the privilege of becoming U.S. citizens through naturalization. Section Four brought the natives of India under Section Eleven of the 1924 Immigration Act and allowed persons indigenous to India to come to America as immigrants. As much as 75 percent of the annual quota allocated to India could be used by people born and resident in India. Persons of Japanese and Korean descent were still excluded from classes of people admissible to the United States as immigrants.

WONG YANG SUNG v. MCGRATH

On February 20, 1950, the case of *Wong Yang Sung v. McGrath, Attorney General, et al.*[63] was decided by the Supreme Court, which was asked to rule if administrative hearings in deportation cases were to comply with provisions made in the Administrative Procedure Act of June 11, 1946. The law was enacted basically to prevent an immigration officer from performing the duties of prosecutor and judge simultaneously. The Immigration and Naturalization Service had long been under criticism because its officers had not only assumed investigative and prosecutorial duties, but also adjudicatory functions, when illegal immigrants were apprehended and questioned.

Wong Yang Sung was arrested because he was in the United States unlawfully. He was ordered deported after a hearing before an immigration inspector, and the deportation order was approved by the Acting Commissioner (whose action was affirmed by the Board of Immigration). The petitioner Wong sought release from custody on the grounds that the hearing was not conducted in accordance with Paragraphs 5 and 11 of the Administrative Procedure Act of 1946. Justice Jackson, in delivering the Court's majority opinion, ruled that deportation proceedings, because of their importance, had to conform to the requirements of the Act.

SUMMARY

The long trail of discriminatory laws passed by Congress demonstrated that government officials elected to represent the American people were not immune from prejudice. Because they were elected to represent their electorate, they may have approved discriminatory laws out of a sense of duty, not out of personal prejudice. But it did not make any difference to those who were adversely affected by exclusion laws. Such laws kept members of families long separated from each other; they kept various

Asian American communities deprived of a generation of young people who could have provided them with new human resources; and they denied Asian Americans their rights for education, employment, and social services. It was not until after 1943, during the middle of the Pacific War, that Congress began to tear down the wall of discrimination in immigration laws. It did so, however, not because it was morally wrong for America to have discriminatory laws, but because America was in need of allies, which happened to be China, India, and the Philippines.

The Supreme Court handed down a number of ill-considered decisions that supported institutionalized discrimination. Asian community leaders relied desperately on the Court as their last resort. They saw the Court as the final place where the wrongs could be made right. But they were proven wrong. Justices of the Court were willing supporters of the American brand of justice, an aberration of justice.

Between the passage of the 1921 Quota Immigration Act and the acts of 1943 and 1946, institutionalized discrimination escalated from discrimination to expulsion. Persons of Japanese ancestry were expelled from their homes and were incarcerated in concentration camps without trial. The expulsion or removal phase of the government's decision against Japanese Americans was supported by the Supreme Court decision on *Korematsu v. U.S.* in 1944. One wonders what would have happened if the Japanese armed forces had landed on the West Coast. According to Kitano and Daniels, the last hypothesized stage of solution of the race problem is extermination of the undesirables.

NOTES

1. John Higham, *Strangers in the Land: Patterns of American Nativism 1860–1925* (New York: Atheneum, 1985), pp. 264–99.

2. Peter Heywood Wang, "Legislating 'Normalcy': The Immigration Act of 1924," an unpublished doctoral dissertation, University of California, Riverside, 1971.

3. Higham, *Strangers in the Land,* pp. 286–307.

4. Ibid., p. 273.

5. *New York Times,* July 23, 1920, p. 4.

6. Calvin Coolidge, "Whose Country Is This?" *Good Housekeeping Magazine,* 72 (February 1921), pp. 14, 106.

7. Wang, "Legislating 'Normalcy,' " p. 178.

8. 43 Stat. 153.

9. Luis V. Teodoro, Jr., *Out of This Struggle: The Filipinos in Hawaii* (Honolulu: The University of Hawaii Press, 1981), pp. 6–18.

10. Sister Mary Dorita Clifford, "The Hawaiian Sugar Planters Association and Filipino Exclusion," in *Letters in Exile,* edited by UCLA Asian American Studies Center (Berkeley: University of California Press, 1976), pp. 74–89.

11. Lorraine Jacobs Crouchett, *Filipinos in California: From the Days of the Galleons to the Present* (El Cerrito, Calif.: Downey Place Publishing House, 1982), pp. 31–34.

12. Howard A. DeWitt, "The Watsonville Anti-Filipino Riot of 1930: A Case Study of the Great Depression and Ethnic Conflict in California," *Southern California Quarterly,* 61, 3 (1979), pp. 291–302.

13. 48 Stat. 456.

14. 259 U.S. 276 (1922).

15. 268 U.S. 336 (1925).

16. 268 U.S. 345 (1925).

17. 268 U.S. 346 (1925).

18. 273 U.S. 352 (1927).

19. 260 U.S. 178 (1922).

20. 260 U.S. 183–84 (1922).

21. 260 U.S. 197 (1922).

22. 260 U.S. 199 (1922).

23. 261 U.S. 204 (1923).

24. 268 U.S. 402 (1925).

25. 342 U.S. 899 (1952).

26. 343 U.S. 721 (1952).

27. 356 U.S. 129 (1958).

28. 343 U.S. 717 (1952).

29. 343 U.S. 733–36 (1952).

30. 263 U.S. 225 (1923).

31. 263 U.S. 197 (1923).

32. 263 U.S. 313 (1923).

33. 263 U.S. 326 (1923).

34. 268 U.S. 258 (1925).

35. 332 U.S. 633 (1948).

36. 334 U.S. 410 (1948).

37. 334 U.S. 427 (1948).

38. 273 U.S. 284 (1927).

39. 268 U.S. 510 (1925). See also Nicholas Appleton, *Cultural Pluralism in Education* (New York: Longman, 1983), pp. 97–99.

40. 273 U.S. 298 (1927).

41. 275 U.S. 78 (1927).

42. 163 U.S. 537 (1896). See also Roy L. Brooks, *Rethinking the American Race Problem* (Berkeley: University of California Press, 1990), p. 76.

43. 275 U.S. 85 (1927).

44. 291 U.S. 82 (1934).

45. 317 U.S. 69 (1942).

46. 320 U.S. 81 (1943).

47. 320 U.S. 115 (1943).

48. 320 U.S. 99 (1943).

49. 320 U.S. 111 (1943).

50. 323 U.S. 214 (1944).

51. 323 U.S. 283 (1944).

52. 323 U.S. 218–19 (1944).

53. 323 U.S. 235–36 (1944).

54. Fred W. Riggs, *Pressures on Congress: A Study of the Repeal of Chinese Exclusion* (Westport, Conn.: Greenwood Press, 1972).

55. Harry H. L. Kitano and Roger Daniels, *Asian Americans* (Englewood Cliffs, N.J.: Prentice Hall, 1988), p. 38.

56. 57 Stat. 600.

57. Seventy-Ninth Congress, Records of the U.S. House of Representatives, Received Group 233. (Deposited in the National Archives and recently declassified.)

58. Dated May 18, 1945, and signed by William D. Hassett, secretary to the president.

59. Records of the Executive Session, HR 2609 (Thursday, June 14, 1945). Typewritten manuscript, p. 10.

60. Ibid., p. 22.

61. Ibid., p. 23.

62. 60 Stat. 416.

63. 339 U.S. 33 (1950).

—7—

The Partial Liberalization Period (1952–1965)

America emerged from World War II as a superpower confident in its industrial and military power. However, this self-confidence was quickly shaken by the fear of communism as the Cold War began to set in between the United States and the Soviet Union. Taking advantage of the national fear of anything that had the semblance of communism, frequent labor strikes that crippled the national economy, and the retention of wartime price controls, a number of conservative political opportunitists in Congress attempted to derail the New Deal. They had long harbored a deep sense of distrust in the principles and programs of the New Deal. As a means of restoring America to the status quo before the New Deal, they relied on two major legislative tactics: (1) limiting or reducing appropriations for various New Deal programs, and (2) launching investigations of New Deal personnel. Part of their investigations resulted in the hearings of the House Committee on Un-American Activities.[1]

Commonly known as the Dies Committee, the Committee on Un-American Activities was originally established in 1938 with an appropriation of $25,000 under the leadership of the Committee chairman Martin Dies of Texas. As a headline-seeking sensational politician, Dies saw Reds anywhere along a wide spectrum of political ideology. He accused many organizations of having been infiltrated by the Nazis and Communists. Among the organizations investigated by his committee were the Department of Labor, the Works Progress Administration, the Federal Theater and Writers' Project, the National Labor Relations Board, the Wages and Hours Board, the American League for Peace and Democracy, and the Workers' Alliance, many of which were byproducts of the New Deal. During the hearings held between 1947 and 1948, charges were made that the New Deal had been infiltrated by Communists.[2]

Conservative Republican Congressmen tried to orchestrate these hearings with their presidential campaign in 1948, but they failed to have their man elected to the White House. After Truman was elected the thirty-third president, he openly attacked the Committee and issued an executive order limiting congressional access to the federal personnel loyalty files, which had been created as a result of President Truman's Executive Order 9835 (which had set up a loyalty procedure within the government to investigate loyalty of government officials).[3] Truman was determined to terminate the Committee. This aggressive policy of the Truman administration was met with the Committee's renewed attack on the Roosevelt-Truman administration for its foreign policy toward Eastern Europe and China. The committee claimed that because the administration was soft toward communism, it contributed to the military and territorial expansion of the Soviet Union. In particular, after the Soviet Union was successful in exploding an atomic bomb in 1949, Joseph McCarthy, speaking in Wheeling, West Virginia, in February 1950, launched the first of his many charges and accusations against the Truman administration. He charged that the Department of State was heavily infiltrated by Communists and their sympathizers.[4] He and his associates pointed their accusing fingers at federal employees who were considered disloyal enough to sell atomic secrecy to the Soviet Union. McCarthyism, an American brand of ideological purity spawned in the heat of the Cold War, engulfed the nation in a reign of terror. It ruined the careers of many decent people and drove some to suicide.

Thus, the issue of internal security against the imagined threat of communism became a major issue in American politics, even before the outbreak of the Korean War on June 25, 1950. The Truman administration, given the domestic political dissension and ideological conflict, decided to intervene in the war, which lasted until July 1953. The American intervention invited Chinese entry into the war, thus converting a police action into a potential global war. The imagined Communist threat, against which McCarthy and his associates had forewarned the American public, became an American reality. President Truman, to appease and ward off any more ideological attacks on his administration, asked for antisubversive legislation on August 8, 1950, with an emphasis on strengthening the existing sabotage and espionage laws.

INTERNAL SECURITY ACT OF 1950

Congress had already been working on a number of bills that were designed to put subversive individuals and organizations under government control when a bill was introduced to the House by the House Committee on Un-American Activities. This bill was designed to control subversive organizations by requiring them to register with the attorney general, and it was approved by the House with little debate on August 29, 1950. The Senate worked on its own bill, which was introduced by Senator McCarran of Nevada (who was characterized as a person "silver tongued, and silver haired" for his aggressive representation of Nevada's silver interest). This bill incorporated parts of other bills debated in the Senate, and it was approved with minor changes. The Senate then considered the House bill, which was substituted for the Senate bill. The bill went to conference for compromise and was reported out, retaining much of the features found in the Senate's original bill. Both chambers of Congress approved the bill and sent it to the president. President Truman vetoed the bill with a strong message, but his veto was crushed by an overwhelming majority in both chambers. Thus America, well known for its Bill of Rights, came to possess the Internal Security Act of September 23, 1950,[5] a law that was antithetical to the principles embodied in the U.S. Constitution.

The law had 116 sections, which were grouped into two titles: (1) subversive activities control and (2) emergency detention. Section Two gave the rationale for the law, which was grounded on congressional findings. One of the claims made by Congress was that there was a world Communist movement, the purpose of which was to establish a Communist totalitarian dictatorship throughout the world. Congress also asserted that individuals in the United States who participated in the world Communist movement repudiated their allegiance to the United States and transferred their allegiance to a foreign country. Congressional findings enumerated in fifteen paragraphs in Section Two concluded that the Communist movement in the United States, and "the nature and control of the world Communist movement itself, present a clear and present danger to the security of the United States."

Section Seven required Communist-action organizations to register every year with the attorney general. It also mandated annual registration of Communist-front organizations with the attorney general. Section Ten prohibited these registered organizations from transmitting, by U.S. mail or through interstate or foreign commerce, any publication for the purpose of dissemination among two or more persons without specifying their names. The container, envelope, or wrapper for such a publication was to be clearly marked with a label, "Disseminated by_____, a Communist organization." Section Twelve established the Subversive Activities Control Board, which was assigned the duty of determining whether an organization was Communist.

Provisions in the law pertinent to aliens, either already in the United States or wishing to enter the country, were found in Sections Twenty-

Two to Twenty-Nine. Section Twenty-Two amended the Act of October 1, 1918, to make aliens excludable if they belonged to a subversive organization. Section Twenty-Three amended Section Twenty of the Immigration Act of February 5, 1917, to authorize the attorney general to exercise discretionary power to deport aliens. Section Twenty-Four amended the Alien Registration Act of 1940, requiring all alien residents in the United States to report in writing to the attorney general their current address within ten days after January 1 of each year. Section Twenty-Five amended Section 305 of the Nationality Act of 1940, denying the right of naturalization to any person advocating or teaching opposition to all organized government. Any alien who was either affiliated with or a member of any Communist-action organization was denied the right of naturalization. Paragraph (d) of Section Twenty-Five stated that for any alien who obtained U.S. citizenship after January 1, 1951, but who became a member of a subversive organization within five years after naturalization, such membership was to be considered prima facie evidence that he or she was not loyal to the United States, and citizenship could be revoked.

Section 100, and all other sections following it, pertained to emergency detention measures. Section 101 enumerated congressional findings about the world Communist movement and presented the rationale for authorizing the government to detain potential dangerous people. Paragraph 14 of this section stated that people may be detained if there was reasonable ground to believe that they "probably will commit or conspire with others to commit espionage or sabotage."

THE MCCARRAN-WALTER IMMIGRATION ACT OF 1952

World War II created a number of social conditions, both in America and in other parts of the world, that compelled Congress to reconsider America's traditional immigration policy. Virulent nativism and fear of foreigners during the 1920s had helped to bring into existence an extreme form of exclusionist immigration policy. But America could no longer close its doors to the outside world and still retain world leadership. The destruction of Europe created refugees and displaced people who were eager to come to America. But the existing immigration laws could not allow them to emigrate. There soon developed a national debate on what roles America should play in helping refugees and others. In addition, American industries, which had been expanded during the war to produce war materiel, began to focus on producing consumer goods. They needed skilled laborers and trained personnel. Many social organizations in America, including social welfare agencies, came together to form the National Committee on Postwar Immigration, which began to put pressure on Congress to reconsider American policies for immigration and naturalization in light of changed international situations.

In 1947 there were senators in Congress who were in favor of changing immigration laws to allow displaced persons and political refugees to emigrate. But they were opposed by some powerful people in the Senate, including Senators Chapman Revercomb and Patrick McCarran, who were opposed to any major changes in the present immigration laws because they felt that such changes would undo basic immigration policy. Revercomb, then Chairman of the Judiciary Committee, and McCarran, the ranking Democrat on the committee, suggested that a study be made of the existing immigration and naturalization system. To accomplish this goal they introduced a resolution, which the Senate passed on July 26, 1947.[6] The resolution called for an investigation into five areas of concern: (1) the history and development of immigration policy, (2) the administration of laws concerning immigration and deportation, (3) the extent of violation of these laws, (4) the problem of displaced persons, and (5) the impact of changes in immigration policy on the nation.

A special subcommittee was appointed to conduct the investigation for more than two years, but no major legislative efforts were made to overhaul America's traditional immigration policy for racial and ethnic discrimination, national origin quota, and exclusion based on the personal character of the individual immigrant. Congress did not take immediate action to change American immigration policy because it had other urgent matters such as the Korean War and the works of the Dies Committee with which its members were preoccupied. However, Congress did approve a number of bills that eventually led to the McCarran-Walter Act of 1952: (1) the Act of June 28, 1947,[7] allowing alien fiancees and fiances of veterans to come to America as temporary visitors; (2) the Act of July 22, 1947,[8] admitting the alien spouse of an American citizen, regardless of race; (3) the Displaced Persons Act of June 25, 1948,[9] bringing to America, during the two years after passage of the Act, displaced persons who lost their country as a result of annexation by a foreign power; (4) the Act of April 21, 1949,[10] extending the expiration date of the GI Fiancees Act of June 29, 1946; (5) the Act of June 16, 1950,[11] amending the original Displaced Persons Act; and finally (6) the Internal Security Act of September 23, 1950.[12]

These pieces of legislation became forerunners of what was to be included in the McCarran-Walter omnibus bill. On April 20, 1950, the Senate Judiciary Committee submitted Senate Report 1515, called "The Immigration and Naturalization Systems of the United States." This report was the embodiment of hearings, testimonies, and research as mandated by the Senate. The tenor of the report was, however, restrictionist. As one scholar succinctly put it, the report included "a mountain of facts" but "consisted of prejudice and fear."[13] However, this prejudicial report became the catalyst for comprehensive legislation introduced by Senator McCarran and Representative Walter. Both chambers of Congress engaged in much debate on the bill, and it was finally voted for approval, but the president vetoed the bill because he believed that it did not go far enough to eliminate existing restrictions. His veto was, however, overridden by Congress, and the Immigration and Nationality Act of June 27, 1952,[14] became law.

This act, also known as the McCarran-Walter Immigration Act of 1952, was the most comprehensive immigration act passed by Congress as of 1952. It codified all existing immigration laws and organized them under different classifications. The law had 306 sections, starting with Section One, 101, and ending with Section 407. These sections were grouped into four titles, and each title was organized into chapters. For instance, under Title I, Chapter One dealt with the quota system. Chapter Two specified the qualifications of admissible aliens. Issuance of entry documents was explained in Chapter Three, and Chapter Four elaborated on provisions for entry and exclusion. Procedures for deportation and adjustment of status were specified in Chapter Five.

All aliens admissible to the United States were classified into two categories: (1) quota immigrants and (2) nonquota immigrants. The nonquota system was established in Section 205, and it stated that spouses and unmarried children of American citizens were entitled to a nonquota immigrant status. The quota system, particularly as specified in Sections 201 and 202, allowed one hundred immigrants per annum from each independent nation that was included in the so-called Asiatic Pacific triangle region. This was defined as "wholly east of the meridian sixty degrees east of Greenwich, wholly west of the meridian one hundred and sixty-five degrees, and wholly north of the parallel twenty-five degrees south latitude." This region, which included twenty independent countries with more than half of the world's population, encompassed all of Asia and the Pacific islands.

This effort to restrict immigration of Asians to the United States was in accordance with America's traditional policy established in 1921 and 1924. However, the law made all races eligible for U.S. citizenship and admissible to the United States as immigrants. One of the provisions included in the law expanded the grounds for exclusion and deportation of aliens, although another provision gave aliens safeguards against deportation by specifying procedures to be followed by the government. Particularly, Section 212 enumerated excluded classes of people who were ruled ineligible for immigration for a variety of reasons. Among these were provisions that were already included in the Internal Security Act of 1950, thus retaining much of the concerns with Communist subversive activities.

A preference system was established within the numerical quota in order to establish priority as well as the percentage of the total number of immigrants based on different family relations. For instance, first preference went to highly skilled immigrants, whose services the United States needed urgently, and to the spouses and children of such immigrants. Fifty percent per annum, per quota area, was assigned to this category. The second preference included the parents of U.S. citizens over age twenty-one and unmarried adult children of U.S. citizens. Thirty percent was assigned to this category. The third preference consisted of spouses and unmarried adult children of permanent resident aliens. This category was given 20 percent. The fourth preference went to the brothers, sisters, and married children of U.S. citizens and accompanying spouses and children.

REFUGEE RELIEF ACT OF 1953

From the moment of its passage, the McCarran-Walter Act of 1952 was destined to go through major changes. President Truman, who had vetoed the bill, issued Executive Order 10392 on September 4, 1952, to establish a presidential Commission on Immigration and Naturalization. Its task was to study and evaluate the immigration and naturalization policies of the United States. The commission was charged to complete its investigation and report by January 1, 1953. It issued a well-documented report, *Whom We Shall Welcome,* which supported President Truman's position on the need of a more liberal immigration policy. The report recommended a number of radical changes in immigration laws that would overhaul American immigration policy. It recommended abolition of the national origin quota system, and it urged Congress to do away with immigration laws discriminating against people of color. Congress was unable or unwilling to take up the commission's challenge, as it was still controlled by conservatives who had pushed the McCarran-Walter bill through Congress. But the commission's recommendations became the basis for passage of a more liberal law in 1965.

Congress was, however, more prone to do something about the plight of European refugees who were escaping from countries occupied by the Soviet Union. In addition, there were large numbers of Greek, Italian, and Turkish refugees. When the Graham bill was debated in the House, some expressed their fear that the United States would be infiltrated by Communists who would come in with refugees. But the voice of reason prevailed, and Congress passed the Graham bill, which was signed into law on August 7, 1953.[15]

The law had twenty sections. Section One defined in Paragraph (a) the term *refugee* to mean "any person in a country, or area, which is neither Communist nor Communist-dominated, who because of persecution, fear of persecution, natural calamity or military operation is out of his usual place of abode, and unable to return thereto, who has not been firmly resettled, and who is in urgent need of assistance for the essentials of life, or for transportation." Many a refugee, thus defined, was European. The number of refugees allowed to come into the United States with nonquota immigrant visa status was set at 205,000. Paragraph 13 of Section Four set aside no more than 2,000 nonquota immigrant visas for refugees of Chinese ethnic origin. Section Six granted permission to aliens to adjust their status if they had entered the country as a lawful alien but could not return to their native country due to events that occurred after their arrival in America. The attorney general was authorized to use discretionary power to grant such an alien a permanent resident status, provided that the alien had been of good moral character during the preceding five years.

THE U.S. GOVERNMENT AND CHINESE INTELLECTUALS IN AMERICA

Chinese students eager to learn modern science and technology came to America to attend its most prestigious institutions of higher learning. In 1847, Yung Wing arrived in America to study at Yale University. He graduated from Yale, thus becoming the first Chinese person with an American university degree. He went home with his American wife and later returned to lead the Chinese Education Mission, which was organized in 1872 and was responsible for bringing young ambitious Chinese students to America for their study. The American government made the Boxer indemnity* available for Chinese students at American colleges and universities. By the time the Pacific War broke out, there were approximately 5,000 Chinese students studying in America. After the end of the Pacific War, they were unable to return to China, as China was engulfed in another war between Communists and Nationalists.

Among these students were a handful of brilliant scientists who were trained in the fields of nuclear science and rocket propulsion. Included in

---

*Money received by the U.S. government from China which was required to pay for the damages done against Americans during the Boxer Rebellion.

this small group were Tsien Hsue-shen, Wang Kan-chang, Chien San-chiang, Chao Chung-yao, and others. Tsien Hsue-shen, who was also known as Ch'ien Hsueh-shen, was a native of Wuhsi, Kiangsu and was born either in 1912[16] or 1913,[17] although another source gave his birthday as September 2, 1909.[18] He came to America in September 1935 to study at the Massachusetts Institute of Technology. After completing his Master's degree in one year, he decided to go to the California Institute of Technology, where a renowned Hungarian rocket scientist, Dr. Theodore von Karman, was teaching in the aeronautics department. Karman got Tsien interested in supersonic aircraft design and jet propulsion. Tsien later transferred to MIT, where he completed his doctorate in 1938. He was appointed to teach and conduct research at the California Institute of Technology as Goddard Professor of Jet Propulsion at the age of thirty-nine, the youngest person to occupy such a prestigious position in the history of that institution.

During World War II, Tsien worked as Director of Rocket Section, United States National Defense Scientific Advisory Board, and was given the rank of United States Air Force colonel when he was sent to Germany as head of a scientist delegation to study German rocket development. Because of his outstanding service to the United States, he was awarded a commendation for Meritorious Civil Service by the War Department and Army Air Force. His work as group supervisor of the Jet Propulsion Laboratory at the California Institute of Technology between 1939 and 1945 was praised as an outstanding performance. James B. Conant and Vannevar Bush of the Office of Scientific Research and Development sent a certificate that stated, "On behalf of the Government of the United States of America this certificate is awarded in appreciation of effective service."[19]

The U.S. government, however, turned hostile toward Chinese students after China fell into the hands of Communists in 1949. Feeling the hostility directed against them, Chao Chung-yao, Wang Kan-chang, and other students trained in nuclear science and rocket propulsion left the United States for Mao's China. Because of his knowledge of nuclear physics, Chao was once dispatched by Generalissimo Chiang Kai-shek as China's representative from the United States to observe the detonation of an atomic bomb off Bikini Atoll in the Pacific. Chao had attended the California Institute of Technology, where he received a Ph.D. in nuclear physics in 1930 at the age of twenty-eight. He was respected by America's top nuclear scientists for his expertise. Chao did not feel comfortable with life in America, as McCarthy and associates went on their Red Scare campaign of terror. He decided to go back to mainland China aboard the *Presi-*

dent Wilson, but on his way, when the ship was docked at Yokohama, Japan, Chao was detained for investigation by American authorities for a few weeks before he was allowed to continue his journey to Hong Kong.

Tsien wanted to stay in America with his family. Although he had entertained the idea of going home, he decided against it because of his work and particularly his son, who was born in America. While teaching in Pasadena, California, he had associated with a small group of intellectuals who formed a small discussion group. They had discussions on many topics and issues ranging from the ideas of Marx to current problems relating to the Japanese aggression against China. Tsien attended these meetings because he appreciated the members of the group, who were sympathetic toward China. He did not know at the time that some in the group were affiliated with a Communist organization. His innocent association with these Communists gave the government an excuse to investigate him. Later, with the Chinese entry into the Korean War, the government decided to charge him with violation of the International Security Act of 1950. He was detained for questioning for two days and was sent home on $15,000 bail. Finally, the government deported him on September 17, 1955.[20]

Upon return to Mao's China, Tsien became the Director of the Institute of Mechanics. His friend, Chao Chung-yao, was appointed Director of the Institute of Atomic Energy and later had direct involvement in the Chinese atomic bomb project. Wang Kan-chang served as Deputy Director under Chao. During the era of McCarthy witch hunting, there were unsubstantiated charges that liberals in the State Department had sold atomic secrecy to the Soviet Union, thereby contributing to the development of the Soviet atomic bomb. It may be said in the same vein that conservatives during the McCarthy era forced Chinese scientists out of the country against their will, thus enabling China to build an atomic bomb that was tested on October 16, 1964.

THE MCCARRAN-WALTER ACT AND THE SUPREME COURT

Part of the Immigration and Nationality Act of June 27, 1952, was tested in the case of *Brownell, Attorney General v. Tom We Shung.*[21] The case involved a Chinese alien who requested admission into the United States, claiming that he was a son of an American citizen who served in the United States armed forces during World War II. He was denied admission by the Boards of Special Inquiry on the grounds that he was unable to establish the alleged relationship. The decision was affirmed by the

Board of Immigration, and Sung asked for judicial review of the decision through a declaratory judgment action before the passage of the Immigration and Nationality Act of 1952, but his request was again denied. After the 1952 law was passed, he filed a suit to ask for review of the decision to exclude him by a declaratory judgment action created in the said law. He argued that if deportation orders could be challenged by a declaratory judgment action under the 1952 law, then exclusion orders should be reviewed through the same procedure. Justice Clark delivered the Court's unanimous decision on December 17, 1956, declaring that "the safeguard of judicial procedure is afforded the alien in both exclusion and deportation proceedings," and thus deciding in favor of Shung.

Section 243 (h) of the Immigration and Nationality Act of June 27, 1952, was tested in the case of *Leng May Ma v. Barber.*[22] The petitioner was a native of China who claimed that she was a citizen. This claim was proven false, and she was ordered excluded from the United States. She then applied for a stay of deportation, claiming that she would be subject to physical punishment, if not death, upon returning to her native land. This application was in accordance with Section 243 (h) of the 1952 law, which stated that "the Attorney General is authorized to withhold deportation of any alien within the United States to any country in which in his opinion the alien would be subject to physical persecution and for such period of time as he deems to be necessary for such reason."[23]

Leng May Ha's application was denied, and she petitioned for a habeas corpus, arguing that because of her parole status she was already in the United States, and therefore Section 243 (h) was applicable to her. The Court decided on June 16, 1958, by a six to three decision, that the petitioner was not "within the United States" within the meaning of Section 243 (h), and that she was to be excluded. Justice Douglas filed a separate dissenting opinion, with which Justices Black and Brennan concurred. Justice Douglas contended that the attorney general had the authority to "save a human being from persecution in a Communist land."

On the same day, the Supreme Court handed down its decision on a similar case, *William P. Rogers, Attorney General v. Jimmie Quan, Jow Mun Yow, Yow Kwong Yeong, Yen Mok and Lam Wing.*[24] Four of the appellants arrived in the United States before passage of the McCarran-Walter Immigration Act. They were paroled and ordered excluded. Therefore, they applied for a stay of deportation under Section 243 (h) of the 1952 law. They filed complaints in the U.S. District Court for the District of Columbia to seek judgment of nondeportability. The decision of the District Court was to deport them to China, but that decision was reversed by the Court of Appeals, which ruled that they were "within the United States" for the purpose of Section 243 (h) of the said law. The case was sent to the Supreme Court on certiorari, which reversed the decision of the Court of Appeals.

Justice Clark, in delivering the Court's opinion (supported by four of his colleagues), stated that immigrants wishing to come to America were becoming more "litigious and contested departures often involving long delays." The Court seemed to have wanted to send a warning to immigrants wishing to enter the United States not to build great hopes on staying in America by delaying their deportation. Chief Justice Warren and Justices Black, Douglas, and Brennan dissented based on the same reasons they had given in the case of *Leng May Ma v. Bruce Barber.*

THE FIFTH AMENDMENT RIGHTS

Another case, *Kimm v. Rosenberg, District Director, Immigration and Naturalization Service,*[25] involving a Korean student who was ordered deported because of his suspected affiliation with a Communist organization, reached the Supreme Court, where it was argued on May 16 and 17, 1960. The case involved a native of Korea who came to America to study in 1928 and continued to pursue his study until 1938, when he planned to return to Korea. But the outbreak of war between China and Japan in 1937 changed his mind. Since 1938 he had been engaged in various jobs, including the job of editing a newspaper called *Korean Independence,* which was published by a political organization known as the Korean National Revolutionary Party of America, whose main office was in Los Angeles, California. Although Justice Douglas stated in his dissenting opinion that Kimm was ordered deported because of his employment, that was probably not the only reason for his arrest. Kimm came to work for the Korean National Revolutionary Party of America (a branch of the Korean National Revolutionary Party established in China), which began to publish its weekly newspaper, both in Korean and English, on October 6, 1943. During the Pacific War this organization worked toward the political goal of achieving Korea's independence, and the newspaper published frequent editorials supporting America's war efforts against Japan. After the end of the Pacific War in August 1945, the newspaper began to publish editorials against the American military government in Korea. It is possible that Kimm was arrested because of his political views expressed through the newspaper. Editorials of the newspaper often expressed political views that went against the American military government in South Korea. For instance, *Korean Independence* ran an editorial on July 16, 1947, criticizing pro-Japanese reactionary politicians supported by the American military government:

Of course, for those Americans in Southern Korea who are practicing ABCs of imperialism—divide and rule—the collapse of the U.S.-U.S.S.R. Joint Commission must be tantamount to scratching one's itching back. For they know success of the Joint Commission work in establishing a democratic Korean provisional government based on the Moscow Decision will mean the dawn of a new Korea for the Korean people, by the Korean people. . . . And it will mean the death knell to those pro-Japanese Korean collaborators, national traitors, pro-fascists, reactionaries, blood-sucking profiteers who are the proteges of the AMG (American Military Government) in Southern Korea and through whom the hounds of American monopoly capitalists are conspiring converting Korea into the Second Philippines and Greece.[26]

When Kimm was under investigation, the hearing officer asked Kimm if he was ever a member of the Communist Party. Kimm refused to answer the question, claiming the Fifth Amendment rights against self-incrimination. He was denied suspension of his deportation on the grounds that he failed to prove that he was a person of good moral character and that he was not either a member of or affiliated with the Communist Party. The hearing officer's decision was upheld by the Board of Immigration Appeals, and the Court of Appeals approved the decision.

Before the Court, Kimm argued that the burden of proof of his affiliation with the Communist Party was on the government. He further contended that Section 19 (c) of the Immigration Act of 1917 made him eligible for suspension of deportation. However, the government maintained that the law in question was amended by the Internal Security Act of 1950, which excluded from admission aliens who were members of the Communist Party. The Court handed down a *per curiam* decision against the petitioner on June 13, 1960. The Court shifted the burden of proof from the government to the petitioner, declaring that the petitioner was required by the regulations to present clear evidence that he was eligible for suspension of deportation.

Justice Douglas filed a dissenting opinion, with which Justice Black concurred. In his opinion, Justice Douglas stated that the government had not proven that Kimm was a person of bad moral character, unless the Court considered invoking the Fifth Amendment right by Kimm as its evidence. Douglas declared, "It seems to me indefensible for courts which act under the Constitution to draw an inference of bad moral character from the invocation of a privilege which was deemed so important to this free society that it was embedded in the Bill of Rights."[27]

SUMMARY

America emerged from World War II victorious, but it was engulfed by the ideological conflict between conservatives and liberals in American politics. Unfortunately for both America and the natives of Asian countries, who had long been inadmissible to America, McCarthy, his associates, and conservative politicians kept the door closed. The Cold War drove certain irrational elements of American society into witch hunting, destroying the lives of many decent people. Aliens were suspected of their loyalty to America and were driven out of the country. Expulsion of suspected aliens was considered crucial for the nation's security. The psychology of fear of anything foreign and un-American was veneered in the chauvinistic slogan "Love America, or leave it," a sign of fear-stricken people in a mean-spirited era of mass hysteria.

NOTES

1. Athan Theoharis, *Seeds of Repression: Harry S. Truman and the Origins of McCarthysim* (Chicago: Quadrangle Books, 1971), pp. 13–27.
2. Walter Goodman, *The Committee: The Extraordinary Career of the House Committee on Un-American Activities* (New York: Farrar, Straus and Giroux, 1968), pp. 190–271.
3. Theoharis, *Seeds of Repression,* p. 104.
4. Ibid., pp. 68–97.
5. 64 Stat. 987.
6. *Congressional Record,* 93 (1947):10,352.
7. 61 Stat. 190.
8. 61 Stat. 401.
9. 62 Stat. 1009.
10. 63 Stat. 56.
11. 64 Stat. 219.
12. 64 Stat. 987.
13. Erwin Alan Jaffe, "Passage of the McCarran-Walter Act: The Reiteration of American Immigration Policy," an unpublished doctoral dissertation, Rutgers University, 1962, p. 104.
14. 66 Stat. 163.
15. 67 Stat. 400.
16. *Who's Who in Communist China,* Vol. 1 (Hong Kong: Union Research Institute, 1969), p. 147.
17. *Chinese Communist Who's Who* (Taipei: Institute of International Relations, 1970), p. 153.
18. William Ryan and Sam Summerlin, *The China Cloud: America's Tragic Blunder and China's Rise to Nuclear Power* (Boston: Little, Brown and Company, 1967), p. 110.

19. Ibid., p. 66.
20. Ibid., p. 153.
21. 352 U.S. 180 (1956).
22. 357 U.S. 185 (1958).
23. 66 Stat. 214 (1952).
24. 357 U.S. 193 (1958).
25. 363 U.S. 405 (1960).
26. *Korean Independence,* July 16, 1947.
27. 363 U.S. 411 (1960).

—8—

The Liberalized Policy Period
(1965–Present)

As mentioned in the preceding chapter, the Commission on Immigration and Naturalization was appointed by President Truman, and it later issued a report, *Whom We Shall Welcome,* that recommended radical measures to reform America's racially discriminatory immigration policies. Among the measures recommended for legislation was the elimination of the national origins quota system, which had been part of America's immigration policy since 1924; an overall ceiling on quota immigration of 250,000 per annum; and consideration of need and overpopulation of countries sending their people to the United States for the allocation of immigration visas within the quota.

Before the Eighty-Eighth Congress undertook the task of revising American immigration policies, President Kennedy held a news conference on January 24, 1963, in which he expressed his support of a liberal immigration policy. Six months later, on July 23, 1963, Congress received a presidential message that recommended a sweeping reform of existing immigration policies. Encouraged by the administration's initiative, a liberal Congressman from New York, Emanuel Celler, Chairman of the House Judiciary Committee, introduced on the same day a bill that embraced much of the measures recommended by the administration. On the following day, the Senate received a counterpart bill introduced by Senator Philip Hart of Michigan, and some fifty odd bills followed his in the Senate. The bills introduced by Celler and Hart were drafted to reflect the administration's recommended guidelines, which included elimination of the Asiatic Pacific Triangle proviso. With the assassination of President Kennedy and the strong opposition of senators from southern states, Congress failed to overhaul U.S. immigration policies.

THE ACT OF OCTOBER 3, 1965

President Johnson sent a message to the Eighty-Ninth Congress on January 13, 1965, recommending that the McCarran-Walter Act of 1952 be amended for a more liberal legislation on immigration. On the same day Congressman Celler introduced a bill in the House, while Senator Hart submitted an identical bill to the Senate that was supported by thirty-two sponsors in the Senate. The bill included similar measures provided in the previous bill submitted to the Eighty-Eighth Congress. The Celler-Hart Bill called for the elimination of the Asiatic Pacific Triangle proviso and the establishment of new admission standards based on the personal qualifications of the immigrant rather than national origin.

After extensive hearings, the Celler Bill was reported out of the House Committee, which recommended that the bill be approved by the House. The bill was passed through the House by a vote of 318 to 95, with 19 not voting. The Senate approved its bill by a vote of 76 to 18, with 6 abstaining. Differences between the House and Senate versions of the bill were worked out by a conference committee, which submitted its report a week later for approval by both chambers. The conference draft was approved and was sent to the president for his signature, and President Johnson signed it on October 3, 1965, making it the Immigration Act of October 3, 1965.[1]

The law had twenty-four sections. Section One amended Section 201 of the McCarran-Walter Immigration Act of 1952, and Paragraph (c) of the section retained the annual quota of the 1952 act until June 30, 1968. The unused annual quotas from June 30, 1965 through June 30, 1967 were to be put into the immigration pool for redistribution purposes. Section Two amended Section 202 of the 1952 law, and it read, "No person shall receive any preference or priority or be discriminated against in the issuance of an immigration visa because of his race, sex, nationality, place of birth, or place of residence." This section did away with the Asiatic Pacific Triangle proviso of the 1952 law, which had discriminated against natives of Asian countries since 1924.

The law made spouses, unmarried minor children, and parents of U.S. citizens exempt from the numerical quota and established a preference system with eight categories:

First preference: Unmarried adult children of U.S. citizens (20 percent)

Second preference: Spouses and unmarried adult children of permanent resident aliens (20 percent and 26 percent after 1980)

Third preference: Members of the professions, scientists, and artists of exceptional ability (10 percent)

Fourth preference: Married sons and daughters of U.S. citizens (10 percent)

Fifth preference: Brothers and sisters of U.S. citizens over twenty-one years of age

Sixth preference: Skilled and unskilled workers in occupations for which labor is in short supply (10 percent)

Seventh preference: Refugees from Communist and Communist-dominated countries (6 percent)

Eighth preference: Nonpreference, which included applicants ineligible under the preceding categories.

Although the Act of October 3, 1965, officially known as "An Act To amend the Immigration and Nationality Act, and for other purposes," did away with the quota system based on national origins, it established a numerical ceiling of 290,000 immigrants allowed to come in on the preference system. The ceiling was divided into two areas: (1) 170,000 for the Eastern Hemisphere, and (2) 120,000 for the Western Hemisphere. There was also a cap of 20,000 on each country. Asian Americans who had long been denied the right to bring their immediate family members to the country quickly filed relative visa petitions, thus exhausting the 20,000 visas allowed to each country. Soon there developed a serious problem of backlog of cases waiting for petitions to be granted. By 1980, Filipino Americans who petitioned for visas for their relatives falling within the third and fifth categories had to wait eleven years before their petitions were approved.

THE ACT OF MAY 23, 1975

The American involvement in the Vietnam War became a catalyst that brought hundreds of thousands of refugees to the United States. With the American debacle in the war in the early months of 1975, Congress enacted a law known as "The Indochina Migration and Refugee Assistance Act" on May 23, 1975.[2] The law had four sections. Section Two authorized an appropriation of $455 million for the purpose of administering, accommodating, and settling Indochinese refugees. The same section stipulated that no funds could be spent for this purpose after September 30, 1977. But the original law was amended three times, with the last amendment on October 30, 1978. Section Three defined *refugee* to mean aliens who "(A) because of persecution or fear of persecution on account of race, religion, or political opinion, fled from Cambodia or Vietnam, (B) cannot return there because of fear of persecution on account of race, religion, or political opinion, and (C) are in urgent need of assistance for the essentials of life." Section Four required the president to report to Congress through appropriate committees on the status of refugees no later than thirty days after passage of the law.

The law initially aimed at assisting no more than 140,000 Indochinese refugees who began to evacuate from their homeland immediately after the American defeat in Vietnam. But waves of refugees risked their lives on the high seas in an attempt to flee from the repressive government in Vietnam during subsequent years. Many lost their lives in the process, and thus the refugees gained the sympathy of nations around the world, which decided to take them in. Between 1975 and 1984 the United States admitted 700,000 Indochinese refugees, while China took in more than 250,000. France and Canada received more than 80,000 each, and Australia admitted 60,000.

THE SUPREME COURT ON STAY OF DEPORTATION

On June 10, 1968, the case of *Cheng Fan Kwok v. Immigration and Naturalization Service*[3] was decided by the Supreme Court. The petitioner, a native and citizen of China, stayed in the United States illegally after he deserted his ship. He was legally allowed to stay in the United States for twenty-nine days if his ship was in port. He was arrested and the government undertook deportation proceedings against him in accordance with Section 242 (b) of the Immigration and Nationality Act of 1952. He requested that he be permitted to leave voluntarily and received permission. However, he did not leave, and therefore the government ordered him to surrender for deportation. Cheng Fan Kwok then petitioned for a stay of deportation and prepared to apply for adjustment of status. But the district director of immigration denied the petitioner a stay of deportation after he decided that the petitioner was not eligible for a status adjustment. The petitioner then requested a review of the denial of a stay. The Circuit Court of Appeals dismissed his petition, however, on the grounds that it did not have proper jurisdiction. The Supreme Court issued a writ of certiorari to review the case. Justice Harlan delivered the Court's opinion (with which Justice White dissented, filing a separate opinion). The Court affirmed the decision of the Circuit Court of Appeals, declaring that courts of appeals do not exclusively have jurisdiction to review the denials of a stay of deportation.

The case of *Immigration and Naturalization Service v. Bagamasbad*[4] came to the Supreme Court on a writ of certiorari petitioned by Immigration and Naturalization Service. The respondent Bagamasbad came to the United States on a tourist visa and stayed four years more than her visa allowed. She applied for adjustment of her tourist status to that of permanent resident alien in accordance with 8 U.S.C. Section 1255 (a), which authorized the Attorney General to grant such a status change to an alien, particularly if the alien was already in the United States.

The District Director of Immigration denied Bagamasbad's application on the grounds that she had misrepresented herself to the U.S. consul at the time when she was issued a visa. This decision was upheld by the Board of Immigration Appeals, but the Circuit Court of Appeals reversed the decision, stating that the law required the judge "to make findings and reach conclusions with respect to respondent's eligibility for admission into this country as a permanent resident." The Supreme Court disagreed with the Court of Appeals and agreed to review the case.

The Court handed down a *per curiam* decision on November 1, 1976, reversing the Appeals Court's decision. The Court ruled that since the respondent's application would have been denied, there was no reason for the judge "to arrive at purely advisory findings and conclusions as to statutory eligibility."

Another case dealing with deportation, *Immigration and Naturalization v. Jong Ha Wang,*[5] was decided on March 2, 1981. The case involved a deportation order of two natives of Korea, husband and wife, who came to the United States as nonimmigrant treaty traders. They were to leave America on January 10, 1972, but they did not depart; and therefore they were ordered deported. They applied for permission to depart voluntarily, and permission was granted. But they did not depart. Instead, they applied for adjustment of status in accordance with 8 U.S.C. Section 1255. They were, however, found ineligible for status adjustment, and the Board of Immigration Appeals denied their application in October 1977. The respondents claimed that deportation would result in severe educational hardship for their children, because they did not know Korean. They also argued that they would suffer economically. It was found, however, that they had a dry-cleaning business valued at $75,000, a house valued at $60,000, $24,000 in a savings account, and $20,000 in other assets. Their liabilities were assessed at $81,000. On appeal, the Court of Appeals reversed the decision by the Board of Immigration Appeals on the grounds that educational hardship on the respondents' children and their economic interests required a hearing in which the total potential effect of deportation could be studied thoroughly.

The Supreme Court reversed the decision of the Court of Appeals on two grounds: First, the Court of Appeals made an error in that it ignored the regulations that required the alien to support his claim of "extreme hardship" by evidentiary material and particular facts; and second, the Court of Appeals erred in that it encroached on the Attorney General's authority to consider what really constitutes "extreme hardship." It was up to the Attorney General and those who were delegated by him to construct standards by which "extreme hardship" could be interpreted. Then the Court declared that the Court of Appeals "erred in ordering that the case be reopened."

A major constitutional question was raised in relation to the case of *Immigration and Naturalization Service v. Chadha et al.*[6] The case reached the Supreme Court on certiorari as an appeal from the U.S. Court of Appeals for the Ninth Circuit. It involved an Asian Indian student, Jagdish Rai Chadha, who was born in Kenya but carried a British passport. He came to the United States to study in 1966 on a nonimmigrant student visa, but his visa expired on June 30, 1972. He was ordered to appear before the District Director of Immigration and Naturalization Service on October 11, 1973, when he was asked to show cause for not being deportable. He conceded that he was deportable, but he said he wanted to file an application for suspension of deportation in accordance with Section 244 (a) (1) of the McCarran-Walter Immigration Act of 1952 and 8 U.S.C. 1254(a) (1). His deportation hearing was held on February 7, 1974, when it was decided that his deportation should be suspended because he was a man of good moral character and would suffer extreme hardship if deported. A report prepared by the Immigration Judge was then transmitted to Congress in accordance to Section 244(c) (1) of the McCarran-Walter Act of 1952. Chadha thought he was given permission to stay in America since there was no further legal action taken against him for more than a year. In the meantime, he was married to an American citizen.

During the first session of the Ninety-Fourth Congress, Representative Eilberg, Chairman of the Judiciary Subcommittee on Immigration, Citizenship, and International Law, introduced a resolution on December 12, 1975. He was opposed to giving permanent residence status to six aliens, including Chadha. The resolution was passed without debate, vetoing the attorney general's decision to allow Chadha to stay in the country. When the immigration judge reopened the deportation proceedings against Chadha, he responded by moving to terminate the proceedings on the grounds that Section 244(c) (2) of the 1952 immigration law was unconstitutional. The judge ruled that he had no power to rule on the constitutionality of the law in question and ordered Chadha deported. Chadha then appealed his case to the Board of Immigration Appeals, but it too ruled that it had no authority to rule on the constitutionality of the law in question. Out of desperation, Chadha then filed a petition to have his case reviewed by the U.S. Court of Appeals for the Ninth District. The Court of Appeals ruled in favor of Chadha, declaring that the House did not have the power of legislative veto and, therefore, did not have constitutional authority to enforce Chadha's deportation. Thus, an obscure deportation case involving a powerless foreign student developed into a constitutional battle between the legislative and executive branches of the government.

This case involved the doctrine of separation of powers. Congress had asserted its legislative veto over power delegated to the President during the 1930s to gain control over reorganization of executive branches of the government. The legislative veto power was considered more necessary than ever before in light of American involvement in the Vietnam War and the Watergate scandal of the 1970s. During the 1970s and 1980s, many consumer protection agencies had worked hard to push legislation to regulate big corporations. Corporations responded to these various regulations by lobbying Congress to use its legislative veto power. Consumer protection agencies viewed this as a major threat to their legislative interests and decided to challenge the constitutionality of the legislative veto. Alan B. Morrison, chief litigator representing Ralph Nader, seized the opportunity to take over Chadha's case. Joining him were the Department of Justice as well as the American Bar Association, which filed an amicus curiae brief represented by Antonin Scala (who later became a justice of the Supreme Court).

Chief Justice Burger delivered the Court's majority opinion on June 23, 1983, in which Justices Brennan, Marshall, Blackmun, Stevens, and O'Connor joined. Justice Powell filed a separate concurring opinion. Justice White filed a dissenting opinion, and Justice Rehnquist also filed his dissenting opinion, in which Justice White joined. The Court's ruling repudiated a number of legal points raised by the attorneys representing both houses of Congress. It brushed aside the argument that the Court did not have jurisdiction on the basis of the decision made on the case of *Parker v. Levy*[7] in 1974. There was also a finer legal point of the severability of Section 244(c) (2) from Section 244. The House asserted that they could not be separated, while the Court ruled that they should be separated. The House also claimed that the present case would advance the interests of the executive branch of the government, were Chadha to prevail. Since the case had to do with a separation-of-powers dispute, rather than with Chadha's private interest, he did not have standing. The Court argued against such assertion and stated that Chadha had standing because he would suffer if deported. The House also maintained that Chadha had other alternative reliefs since he was married to an American citizen. The Court brushed aside this argument and stated that "a person threatened with deportation cannot be denied the right to challenge the unconstitutional validity of the process which led to his status merely on the basis of speculation over the availability of other forms of relief."

Of all the legal points raised in relation to the case, the doctrine of political question perhaps had the most cogency. The House claimed that the case dealt with a political question that was not judiciable, because Chadha was simply challenging the authority of Congress over immigration and naturalization. Congress was granted authority over regulation and control of aliens under Article I of the Constitution. This authority was nonreviewable, according to the House. The Court conceded that Congress had "a plenary authority in all cases in which it has substantive legislative jurisdiction." The Court then enumerated situations to which the doctrine of political question may be applicable. This had been done by the Court in its decision on *Baker v. Carr*[8] in 1962. Basing the majority's argument on three precedents—*Marbury v. Madison*,[9] *Field v. Clark*,[10] and *Cohens v. Virginia*[11]—the Court declared that the doctrine of political question should not deter the Court from making a decision on the case.

The majority opinion then presented its own rationale grounded on the presentment clauses and bicameralism. According to the Court, the Founding Fathers framed the Constitution in such a way that all legislation was to be presented to the president so he could exercise his veto power, if he so chose. This authority could not be circumvented or denied. Then it repeated part of the opinion handed down in the case of *Myers v. United States*,[12] which stated "that the President elected by all the people is rather more representative of them all than are the members of either body of the Legislature whose constituencies are local and not countrywide."

The Founding Fathers were as much concerned with the bicameral nature of the legislative branch of the government as they were with the presentment clause, according to the Court. Although the framers of the Constitution granted special powers to one House, independent of the president or of the other House, such one-House powers were explicit and clear. One House may engage in legislative action that may not be reviewable or subject to the presidential veto on the following four grounds: (1) to initiate impeachment by the House, (2) to conduct trial by the Senate after the impeachment, (3) to approve presidential appointments by the Senate, and (4) to ratify treaties. The Court handed down its decision in favor of Chadha, declaring that "the congressional veto provision in 244(c) (2) is severable from the Act and that it is unconstitutional."

Justice Powell, although agreeing with the majority opinion, wanted to have his decision based on much narrower grounds. Since Congress decided that Chadha did not meet the legal requirements for him to remain in the country, it assumed a judicial function. This was in violation of the separation of powers. Justices White and Rehnquist dissented from the majority and filed separate opinions. Justice White reasoned that without the legislative veto power, Congress would either "refrain from delegating the necessary authority . . . or . . . abdicate its law-making function to the Executive Branch and Independent agencies." According to White, a complex modern bureaucracy necessitates the legislative veto power as a means of balancing the power of Congress and of the president.

RIGHTS FOR EQUAL EDUCATION

In 1927, the Court ruled against Gong Lum, who petitioned to order the State Superintendent of Education of Mississippi to stop discrimination against his daughter, Martha, who could not attend an all-white public school in her community because of her race. This was certainly in conformity with the "separate but equal" doctrine, established in 1896 in the case of *Plessy v. Ferguson,*[13] as declared by Justice Taft. In 1971, the San Francisco Unified School District submitted a comprehensive desegregation plan that was approved by the District Court. This plan was in conformity with the decisions on *Brown v. Board of Education*[14] and *Swann v. Charlotte-Mecklenburg Board of Education.*[15] This plan called for reassigning Chinese children attending neighborhood schools. It was found that 456 children out of a total school population of 482 in one school were Chinese, while another school reported 1,074 Chinese students out of 1,111 students. However, Guey Heung Lee and other Chinese parents in San Francisco applied for a stay of District Court's order on the grounds that the Chinese culture could not be preserved if children attending neighborhood schools were dispersed. They also contended that the Chinese language could not be maintained if children were sent away from their community.

Justice Douglas, acting as Circuit Justice, delivered the opinion on the case of *Guey Heung Lee v. Johnson*[16] on August 25, 1971, declaring that the decision on *Brown v. Board of Education* in 1954 was not for blacks alone, but it was grounded on the equal protection clause of the Fourteenth Amendment of the Constitution. He reminded the Chinese in San Francisco that they were once beneficiaries of the Fourteenth Amendment, when the Court ruled on the case of *Yick Wo v. Hopkins.* According to Justice Douglas, California practiced segregation in education as it established by law separate schools for Chinese children. Schools thus segregated by state action must be desegregated by state action, until the effect of the earlier segregation was made ineffective. In conclusion Douglas stated, "I see no reason to take contrary action. So far as the overriding questions of law are concerned the decision of the District Court seems well within bounds. It would take some intervening event or some novel question of law to induce me as Circuit Justice to overrule the considered action of my Brethren of the Ninth Circuit."[17]

Justice Douglas had another chance to deliver the Court's opinion in relation to a litigation involving Chinese students and their parents in San Francisco in 1974. This case, known as *Lau et al. v. Nichols et al.,*[18] was argued on December 10, 1973, and was decided on January 21, 1974. The decision on the case has had a far-reaching impact on the language education of children whose primary language is not English. It could be suggested that Justice Douglas was partially responsible for the state of educational affairs prevailing then in the San Francisco Unified School District. After the desegregation order of 1971, which Justice Douglas ruled legal, the school district had an enrollment of 2,856 Chinese students whose primary language was not English. Of these, approximately 1,000 students received help with their English, while the rest did not receive either bilingual or supplemental English instruction.

The case involved thirteen non-English-speaking Chinese students in the San Francisco Unified School District who claimed that they had been denied an equal education because of their inability to comprehend the language of instruction. They argued that they were denied equal protection of the law under the Fourteenth Amendment and under the Civil Rights Act of 1964, because the school district failed either to instruct them bilingually or to teach them English. This class action suit, however, did not ask for any specific remedies to be instituted by the school district. The District Court decided in favor of the school district, and the Circuit Court of Appeals upheld the lower court's decision. The Court of Appeals declared that "every student brings to the starting line of his educational career different advantages and disadvantages caused in part by social, economic, and cultural background, created and continued completely apart from any contribution by the school system." The Supreme Court agreed to review the decision by the Court of Appeals because it had public importance.

Justice Douglas delivered the unanimous opinion of the Court, which reversed the ruling of the Court of Appeals. The Court was of the opinion that within the public system of education in California there was no equality of treatment even if students were provided with the same teachers, textbooks, curriculum, and facilities. If students cannot understand English, which is "the basic language of instruction in all schools" in California, as stated in the California Education Code, then they are unable to receive any meaningful education. Justice Douglas, however, refused to ground his decision on the Fourteenth Amendment. Instead, he applied Section 601 of the Civil Rights Act of 1964 in order to reverse the decision of the Court of Appeals. The reasoning behind this was that Section 601 prohibits discrimination based "on the ground of race, color, or national origin." This ban was later buttressed by Health, Education and Welfare

(HEW) regulations issued in conformity with Section 601, which states that the recipients of federal financial assistance may not

(ii) Provide any service, financial aid, or other benefit to an individual which is different, or is provided in a different manner, from that provided to others under the program; . . . [or]
(iv) Restrict an individual in any way in the enjoyment of any advantage or privilege enjoyed by others receiving any service, financial aid, or other benefit under the program.[19]

Justice Douglas brushed aside the argument that children should acquire basic skills before they can participate in educational programs, and he said that such an argument makes a mockery out of public education. Then he agreed with the thirteen students: "We know that those who do not understand English are certain to find their classroom experiences wholly incomprehensible and in no way meaningful."

EQUAL RIGHTS FOR CIVIL SERVICE EMPLOYMENT

On June 1, 1976, the Supreme Court of the United States handed down a major decision that has influenced the economic lives of countless Asian Americans. The case of *Hampton, Chairman, U.S. Civil Service Commission, et al. v. Mow Sun Wong, et al.*[20] reached the Court on a writ of certiorari petitioned by the chairman and the commissioners of the Civil Service Commission. The case involved five persons of Chinese ancestry who were denied employment because of their nationality, although they were all lawful residents: Kae Cheong Lui, a respondent in this class action suit, lost his employment with the Post Office Department because he was not a U.S. citizen; Mow Sun Wong could not work as a janitor for the General Services Administration because he was not a citizen; Siu Hung Mok lost his job as a file clerk because of his alien status; Frances Lum could not take an examination for a civil service position because of her alien status; and finally, Anna Yu could not take a typing test, although she wanted to work as a clerk-typist. These five people began their class action suit on December 22, 1970, charging that the chairman and the commissioners of the Civil Service Commission and the heads of the three agencies (the General Services Administration, the Department of HEW, and the U.S. Post Office Department) denied the plaintiffs employment. The five individuals contended in their litigation that there were 4 million aliens in the United States who could not apply for 300,000 federal jobs made available each year because of their alien status. They argued that the advantage received by citizens in their search for federal civil service violates the due process clause of the Fifth Amendment of the Constitution and Executive Order No. 11,478.

The District Court ruled in favor of the defendants, stating that discrimination among citizens, not discrimination between citizens and noncitizens, was prohibited by Executive Order No. 11,478. It ruled that the commission's discrimination against aliens was constitutional. The decision was, however, reversed by the Circuit Court of Appeals, which ruled that the Civil Service Commission's regulation was in violation of the Fifth Amendment of the Constitution. Thus, the chairman and commissioners of the Civil Service Commission petitioned for certiorari, which was granted by the Supreme Court. The Court was asked to decide "whether a regulation of the United States Civil Service Commission that bars resident aliens from employment in the federal competitive civil service is constitutional."[21]

The Court ruled by a five to four decision against the petitioners, declaring that "Section 338.101 (a) of the Civil Service Commission Regulations has deprived these respondents of liberty without due process of law, and is therefore invalid." Justice Stevens, who delivered the Court's majority opinion, conceded that overriding national interests may justify a citizenship requirement in the federal service, but he flatly rejected the idea that all aliens could be subjected to different rules from those applicable to citizens because the federal government has power over aliens. Justice Stevens recognized the power of the federal government over immigration and naturalization, but he insisted that there are countervailing forces that compelled him to reject the position that supported the commission's regulation. As countervailing forces that would require special consideration for aliens, Justice Stevens listed, among others, a lack of familiarity with language and customs and the disfranchised status of aliens. Justice Stevens declared,

The added disadvantage resulting from the enforcement of the rule—ineligibility for employment in a major sector of the economy—is of sufficient significance to be characterized as a deprivation of an interest in liberty. Indeed, we deal with a rule which deprives a discrete class of persons of an interest in liberty on a wholesale basis. By reason of the Fifth Amendment, such a deprivation must be accompanied by due process. It follows that some judicial scrutiny of the deprivation is mandated by the Constitution.[22]

Justice Rehnquist dissented and filed a separate opinion, with which Justices Burger, White, and Blackmun concurred. Justice Rehnquist argued that Congress has exclusive power to set conditions for entry of aliens, including regulations to control their employment. He supported the petitioners' position that special national interests may exclude aliens from the federal service. However, he went one step further to declare that the special interests claimed by the petitioners were not really special but instead general, because they concerned the formulation of policies toward aliens.

JAPANESE INTERNMENT CASES REVISITED

The Supreme Court's decisions on *Hirabayashi v. U.S., Yasui v. U.S.,* and *Korematsu v. U.S.* went unchallenged for almost forty years, validating the wholesale evacuation and incarceration of lawful resident aliens, as well as citizens of the United States, without charges or trials. In 1981, Gordon Hirabayashi and Fred Korematsu were informed by Peter Irons, a Harvard-trained lawyer, that the government had suppressed evidence at the time of the evacuation decision (authorized by Executive Order 9066), which suggested that the government manipulated information presented to the Supreme Court and that the entire unfortunate affair was of government making. Armed with new evidence, they petitioned for a writ of error coram nobis to have their case reviewed and their convictions overturned.

They were represented by young, aggressive, and competent lawyers of Japanese descent, including Dale Minami of San Francisco. There were negotiations between the Japanese lawyers and government lawyers, who wanted to have these cases dismissed after the original convictions were vacated. On November 10, 1983, the lawyers representing Fred Korematsu agreed with the government to have his case dismissed with the understanding that his original conviction was to be vacated. Yasui followed suit in January of the following year. On May 18, 1984, U.S. District Court Judge Donald Voorhees denied the plea of Justice Department Assistant Attorney Victor Smith, who had moved that the case be dismissed if the original conviction was vacated. Gordon Hirabayashi, encouraged by the Japanese American community's support and Judge Voorhees's ruling, pushed ahead with his struggle to have his original conviction overturned and the entire sordid legal episode reexamined through a judicial review.

Judge Voorhees handed down his decision on February 10, 1986. He found the government guilty of concealing information from the Supreme Court, as well as from the lawyer who represented Gordon Hirabayashi in 1943. According to the judge, the War Department altered General DeWitt's original report to mislead the government into making decisions to evacuate more than 110,000 persons of Japanese ancestry. The report had stated that the evacuation was necessary because it was impossible to determine which Japanese were loyal to the United States. But it was changed to read that the evacuation was necessary because there was a lack of time to determine the loyalty of Japanese Americans. Judge Voorhees was of the opinion that had the Court received this information, it might have drawn different conclusions on these cases.[23] The judge vacated Hirabayashi's original conviction on violation of the exclusion order, but refused to vacate his curfew violation conviction because he believed the DeWitt report would not have affected the Court's ruling. Both Hirabayashi and the government filed appeals. The Ninth Circuit Court of Appeals handed down its decision on September 24, 1987. In its decision it was ruled that Hirabayahsi's curfew violation conviction should have been vacated since the two convictions were based on a single theory of military necessity.

While the coram nobis cases were going through the courts, another case, *United States v. Hohri et al.*,[24] also known as a class action redress suit, was filed to challenge the validity of the government decision to evacuate and intern persons of Japanese descent. Nineteen persons of Japanese ancestry, including William Hohri, and the National Council for Japanese American Redress filed a suit in March 1983 in the District Court of Washington, D.C., listing twenty-one legal injuries inflicted on all evacuees of Japanese descent during World War II. The suit sought "damages and declaratory relief for the tangible and intangible injuries" suffered by the 120,000 evacuees. The damage award asked for was $10,000 for every evacuee for each of the legal injuries mentioned in the suit.

The case was heard in the District Court of Washington, D.C., which ruled that "all claims were barred." When the decision was appealed, the Court of Appeals reversed the dismissal of certain claims related to the Little Tucker Act. It also asserted its jurisdiction over the case. The case went to the Supreme Court on certiorari to the U.S. Court of Appeals for the District of Columbia Circuit when the government petitioned for a writ of certiorari. The Court made a decision on June 1, 1987. Justice Powell delivered the Court's opinion (Justice Scala did not take part in the decision). All other justices joined in the decision.

On behalf of the government, Solicitor General Charles Fried, a Harvard Law School Professor on leave, presented his argument that the Federal Circuit Court of Appeals had jurisdiction on this case, not the Court of Appeals for the District of Columbia. The Court agreed with the solicitor general and decided to remand the case to the Court of Appeals, which was instructed to transfer the case to the Federal Circuit. The case was heard again in March of the following year, but it was dismissed. The plaintiffs then petitioned the Supreme Court to review the ruling, but the Court denied a writ of certiorari on October 31, 1988, thus putting an end to the Japanese American quest for justice. Before the Court made the decision, Congress had already passed a redress bill authorizing the government to pay $20,000 to each surviving evacuee. President Reagan signed the Civil Liberties Act of 1988 into law on August 10, 1988, and issued a national apology for the injustice the government had committed against Japanese Americans.[25] The government was slow in issuing checks to the surviving internees, perhaps it was aware that they were dying at a rate of 200 a month. The government must have considered paying internees not as important as other projects. Finally, the first checks were issued in 1990.

THE IMMIGRATION REFORM AND CONTROL ACT OF 1986

The impetus for another attempt to reform existing immigration laws originated from the Select Commission on Immigration and Refugee Policy, which President Carter had created in 1978 to protect national interests (which were frequently articulated in American history as the peculiar national obsession with protecting American workers against illegal aliens). The bipartisan commission made a number of recommendations, including sanction against employers who knowingly hired undocumented aliens, amnesty for all illegal aliens who came to the country before January 1, 1980, and an increase of the worldwide immigration quota from 270,000 to 350,000 per annum.

An overview of the problem related to the presence of large numbers of undocumented aliens in the United States may help the reader appreciate its magnitude. According to one study, there were as many as 6 to 12 million undocumented aliens in the United States when Congress contemplated legislative measures to deal with the problem.[26] Another study that is rather conservative in its estimation reports 2 million (2,093,000) undocumented aliens of fourteen years of age or older in the country as of April 1983.[27] It was estimated that about 68 percent of them were from Mexico, with another 20 percent from other Latin American countries. The same report did not give the number of undocumented aliens of Asian descent, but the 1980 Census Report estimated that there were 187,000 undocumented aliens of Asian ancestry.[28] Therefore, one may assume that the number of undocumented aliens of Asian ancestry in the country constituted less than 10 percent of the total undocumented population.

America has been dependent on immigrant labor for its industrial and agricultural development since the beginning of the nation. Millions of immigrants came to live in dark and crowded urban tenements. They worked in the mines and on the railroads to eke out a meager living. They bore the brunt of the industrialization of America. The history of exploitation of immigrant labor is not new. It is as old as America. What is new, however, is that today's immigrant labor, particularly undocumented labor, comes by and large from Third World countries whose economic infra- structure is inseparably intertwined with the American economic interest. It has been suggested that for every legal alien admitted to the United States, there are three who are entering the country illegally. One of the implications of entry into the United States of large numbers of illegal aliens is that their native countries' economic systems, which are tailored to meet export cash crops and other export-oriented manufactured goods for American consumers, have failed to provide them with economic opportunity. The export economies of these countries are so elastic to the whimsical nature of American consumers and their degree of affluence that the boom and bust business cycles of these countries perform like a roller coaster. In view of the fact that the major flow of undocumented aliens is from Mexico into the United States, the fiscal crisis of that coun- try seems to have contributed to the worsening situation of the illegal entry of aliens.

In response to the Commission's recommendations, Senator Alan Simp- son, a former member of the Select Commission, and Representative Romano Mazzoli, Chairperson of the House Subcommitee on Immigration, Refugees, and International Law, teamed up to introduce their first bill in 1982. But the bill was received in Congress with mixed response. The bill proposed, among other things, to eliminate the fifth preference from the Immigration Act of 1965. Simpson even played on the nativistic sentiments of unemployed workers as economic recession began to set in during the early 1980s. If the bill was approved, brothers and sisters of U.S. citizens could no longer come to the country. Asian American groups strongly lobbied against the bill, characterizing it as a measured attempt to stop Asian immigration. The bill failed in Congress in 1982, but it was reintro- duced in 1983. In 1984, the Mazzoli bill was approved by the House, but the conference committee could not reach a compromise between the Mazzoli bill and Simpson bill, and Congress did not act further due to congressional and presidential elections.

In 1985, Simpson chose to work with Representative Peter Rodino, Chairperson of the House Judiciary Committee, and they introduced an immigration bill that did not propose the elimination of the preference system. The strategy used by Senator Simpson was to deal with the prob- lem of illegal aliens and then to work toward eliminating or reducing the preference system. The Simpson-Rodino bill was approved by the House and the Senate and was signed into law[29] on November 6, 1986, by Presi- dent Reagan.

The law was designed primarily to deal with the problem of illegal immigration. The law had provisions in three areas. First, it included employer sanctions. The law made it unlawful for employers to hire knowingly or willfully an alien not authorized to work in the United States. Varying fines were to be imposed on the employer depending on whether the violation was a first, second, or third offense. A fine ranging from $3,000 to $10,000 was to be assessed against violators of a third offense for each alien illegally employed. Second, the law included antidiscrimination provisions. Third, it granted temporary residence status to aliens who entered the country prior to January 1, 1982, and continued to live in the country thereafter. This status could be changed into permanent residence after eighteen months, provided that the aliens acquired a basic understanding of English and a fundamental knowledge of U.S. history and government.

Although the Act of 1986 was put into effect to curb entry of undocumented aliens into the country, there are a number of studies suggesting that the act was headed for trouble due to legislative flaws inherent in the immigration law-making process. Calvavita studied employer sactions violations of 103 employers in three southern California counties and found that the "three-day notice" and "voluntary employer compliance" provisions[30] created loopholes for employers to continue to hire undocumented alien workers in restaurants, food-processing plants, and garment industries, which are labor-intensive, low-paying jobs.

The act also has a nondiscrimination provision to ensure that employers do not discriminate against aliens, particularly nonwhite aliens, on the basis of national origin, color, and citizenship. However, employers have been so discriminating against Latinos that there were as many as 350 complaints reported to branch offices of California, Illinois, and Texas of the Mexican Legal Defense and Education during the early months of the law's enforcement.[31] By the end of the second year of the law's implementation, 286 cases of discrimination had been filed with the Office of Special Counsel, and 148 had been filed with the Equal Employment Opportunity Commission. Discrimination is practiced by employers not only against nonwhite alien workers, but also against Anglo workers because ethnic employers prefer to hire workers of their ethnic background.[32]

Illegal immigration continues today in spite of the 1986 law that was designed to control it. During the first year of the law's enforcement, a total of 1,670,000 illegal aliens were apprehended,[33] and the number of illegal aliens entering the country has been increasing since the passage of the law. The entire nation was made aware of the shady side of illegal immigration when a freighter carrying 300 illegal Chinese aliens ran aground off Queens on June 6, 1993.[34] Once again the tragic drama of poor and downtrodden Chinese willing to risk their lives to come to America (long known to them as *Gumshan,* a mountain of gold) has triggered a national debate on what to do with immigration in general, and illegal immigration in particular.

Four days after the Immigration Reform and Control Act became law, Congress enacted another law, known as the "Immigration Marriage Fraud Amendments of 1986."[35] The major purpose of the law was to make conditional permanent residence status obtained by alien spouses, sons, and daughters of U.S. citizens. This measure was considered necessary because of fraudulent claims of foreign birth, adoption, or marriage. The attorney general was authorized to terminate the permanent status of aliens if he or she determined, before the second anniversary of the alien obtaining the status, that such status was fraudulently obtained. This law continues to have adverse affects on a large number of Asian spouses, who are often kept separated from their loved ones for two years.

THE IMMIGRATION ACT OF 1990

In 1987, Simpson introduced a bill that proposed to change the post-1965 liberal immigration policy by eliminating the fifth preference. But the bill was not acted on further by Congress. In 1989, Senators Alan Simpson and Edward Kennedy introduced a bill with three goals in mind. First, since there were too many Asian and Latin immigrants coming into America through family preference and the immediate relative system, family reunification should no longer serve as the principal basis for American immigration policy. After all, these people were considered a burden to the American economy. Second, since the family reunification had not attracted skilled and professional workers to America, a new system should be devised to bring people who were needed to meet the market demands. Third, the existing immigration laws had worked to exclude Western Europeans, and therefore they should be changed. Their bill was met with stiff resistance from a number of people in both Houses. Senator Paul Simon refused to go along with the bill unless the second and fifth preferences were preserved. Representative Bruce Morrison introduced a bill in the House that proposed not only to retain the second and fifth preferences, but also increase the number of visas in order to reduce the backlog of petitions.

Both Houses approved their bills, and a conference committee was organized to iron out their differences. After much negotiations the committee reached a compromise, and the House and the Senate passed the Immigration Act of 1990,[36] which was signed into law on November 29, 1990. The law is perhaps the second longest in the history of congressional legislation on immigration in American history. It is organized into eight different titles. The law was an improvement over the 1965 Immigration Act, as it increased the number of immigrants allowed to come from 290,000 to an unprecedented 700,000. Of this number, 465,000 were set aside for family-sponsored immigrants, while 140,000 were designated for employment-based immigration; 55,000 were for the spouses and children of new legalized aliens. The rest was for transition programs. The law also ensured that the number of family preference visas could not drop below 226,000 per annum. One special provision, known as diversity visas, was included in the law to allow 40,000 Western Europeans to come into the country between 1992 and 1994, because they had not been able to take advantage of the family preference system. Of these 40,000, 16,000 were set aside for the natives of Ireland. This was obviously done to accommodate Senator Kennedy's wishes.

The law also had a provision that allocated annual visas of 55,000 (beginning in 1995) to natives of so-called low admission countries to immigrate to the United States. However, countries such as India, Korea, the People's Republic of China, the Philippines, and Taiwan were excluded from this category. Although the family preference system was retained to allow Asian Americans to bring their immediate relatives, the diversity visa provisions went against natives of Asian countries. In spite of the 1990 Immigration Act, which increased the total number of visas, there are still heavy backlogs of petitions filed by Asian Americans for their immediate family members. For instance, petitions by Filipino Americans being processed as of February 1993 on behalf of their brothers and sisters had been filed in May 1977. Petitions by Asian Indians being processed as of February 1993 for fourth preference (the former fifth preference that included brothers and sisters of U.S. citizens, changed by the Immigration Act of 1990) had been filed in November 1982.[37]

SUMMARY

The traditional American immigration policy founded on racial discrimination has given way to a more liberal policy that has done away with the numerical quota system imposed on each country in Asia prior to passage of the 1965 Immigration Act. However, the post-1965 immigration policy has failed to establish affirmative action measures to give Asian Americans more visas to compensate for their past deprivation, a byproduct of discriminatory immigration laws. In view of the tremendous backlogs mentioned earlier, there is a need for another piece of legislation or an executive order to clear the existing backlogs that still keep members of Asian American families separated from each other.

The nature of society is often revealed by how its constituent members conceptualize justice. It is also revealed by how people in the position of power put justice into practice. The greatness of a people may be shown by how they treat powerless minorities in times of social and economic difficulties. White America, as a community of decent people, could have embraced its racial minorities as its members. On the contrary, minorities were often targeted as easy scapegoats for problems among members of the majority. The Asian American experience with the American system of justice is a vivid testimony to America's treatment of its powerless minorities.

During the last 150 years, the people of Asian ancestry in America have been viewed in ways that contributed to the deprivation of their fundamental rights. They have long been considered incapable of becoming American citizens. This was clearly demonstrated in a number of major decisions handed down by the Supreme Court of the United States, the ultimate political organ of justice among us. They have been also considered incapable of assimilating into American society. Given these assumptions, it was considered natural to deny persons of Asian ancestry their rights to come to America as immigrants, to become citizens, to marry outside their community, to purchase land, or to find employment. Insofar as Asian Americans are concerned, justice has failed to prevail over prejudice; rather, prejudice has prevailed over justice.

As we face the end of this century of scientific and technological miracles, it is fitting for us to reflect on whether race relations in America have been improved. It is true that immigration laws can no longer be used as criteria for judging if there is a two-category system in America (a device used in the past to separate the members of the community from those who were considered outsiders) because all discriminating clauses or provisions have been repealed. Perhaps the narrow conceptual and legal terrain of the community membership drawn up by America's Founding Fathers was partially responsible for the legal discrimination suffered by Asian Americans. As one author pointed out, it is a most common form of injustice when a group of people claims "territorial jurisdiction and rule over another group of people with whom they share the territory."[38] Asian Americans were outside the American political community for a long time, as they were denied the right to share the social goods that communal life makes available for all of its constituents.

It is too early to declare that the dominant American society considers Asian Americans as community members with equal standing. The narrow legal conception of community membership is no longer with us. But in the absence of values and beliefs shared in common by members of society, of life based on reciprocity, and of face-to-face direct contact (which are prerequisites of any meaningful community), the abstract notion of interest has become a dominant mode of social life. Since individuals are considered nothing but the carriers of interest, it is no wonder that we live in a social world in which interests constantly come into conflict with other interests. We no longer live in a community of people; we live in a world fragmented by conflicts of interest. In this sense, we are all separate individuals outside a genuine community, regardless of our racial or ethnic membership. Perhaps we have reached a point in American history wherein blatant racial discrimination of a person by another may be misconstrued as nothing but a conflict of interest. One wonders if conflict resolution would be handled only in favor of those who have power.

NOTES

1. 79 Stat. 911.
2. 89 Stat. 87.
3. 392 U.S. 206 (1968).
4. 429 U.S. 24 (1976).
5. 450 U.S. 139 (1981).
6. 462 U.S. 919 (1983).
7. 417 U.S. 733 (1974).
8. 369 U.S. 186 (1962).
9. 1 Cranch 137 (1803).
10. 143 U.S. 649 (1892).
11. 6 Wheat 264, 404 (1821).
12. 272 U.S. 52, 123 (1926).
13. 163 U.S. 537 (1896).
14. 347 U.S. 483 (1954).
15. 402 U.S. 1 (1970).
16. 404 U.S. 1215 (1971).
17. 404 U.S. 1218 (1971).
18. 414 U.S. 563 (1974).
19. 414 U.S. 567 (1974).
20. 426 U.S. 88 (1976).
21. 426 U.S. 98–99 (1976).
22. 426 U.S. 102 (1976).

23. *Seattle Post-Intelligence,* February 11, 1986, pp. 1, 5. See also Peter Irons, *Justice Delayed: The Record of the Japanese American Internment Cases* (Middletown, Conn.: Wesleyan University Press, 1989), pp. 3–46.

24. 482 U.S. 64 (1987).

25. Irons, *Justice Delayed,* p. 46.

26. Wilbur A. Finch, Jr., "The Immigration Reform and Control Act of 1986: A Preliminary Assessment," *Social Service Review,* 64, 2 (June 1990), p. 245.

27. Jeffrey S. Passel and Karen A. Woodrow, "Change in the Undocumented Alien Population in the United States, 1979–1983," *International Migration Review,* 21, 4 (Winter 1987), p. 1315.

28. Ibid., p. 1314.

29. 100 Stat. 3359.

30. Kitty Calavita, "Employer Sanctions Violations: Toward a Dialectical Model of White-Collar Crime," *Law & Society Review,* 24, 4 (1990), pp. 1061–64.

31. Finch, "Immigration Reform," p. 253.

32. Vernon M. Briggs, Jr., "Employer Sanctions and the Question of Discrimination: The GAO Study in Perspective," *International Migration Review,* 24, 4 (Winter 1990), pp. 812–13.

33. Finch, "Immigration Reform," p. 248.

34. *New York Times,* June 9, 1993, p. A15.

35. 100 Stat. 3537.

36. 104 Stat. 4978.

37. *Visa Bulletin,* January 1993.

38. Michael Walzer, *Spheres of Justice: A Defense of Pluralism and Equality* (New York: Basic Books, 1983), pp. 31–63.

Select Bibliography

Abbott, James Francis. *Japanese Expansion and American Politics.* New York: Macmillan Co., 1916.

Abrams, Bruce A. "A Muted Cry: White Opposition to the Japanese Exclusion Movement, 1911–1924." Ph.D. dissertation, City University of New York, 1987.

Alcantra, Ruben R. *Sakada: Filipino Adaptation in Hawaii.* Washington, D.C.: University Press of America, 1981.

Auerbach, Frank. *Immigration Laws of the United States.* Indianapolis: Bobbs-Merrill Co., 1955.

Bailey, Thomas A. *Theodore Roosevelt and the Japanese-American Crisis.* Stanford, Calif.: Stanford University Press, 1934.

Baldwin, S. L. *Must the Chinese Go? An Examination of the Chinese Question.* Boston: Rand, Avery and Co., 1886.

Barth, Gunther. *Bitter Strength: A History of the Chinese in the United States, 1850–1870.* Cambridge, Mass.: Harvard University Press, 1964.

Bean, Frank D., Georges Vernez, and Charles B. Keeley. *Opening and Closing the Doors: Evaluating Immigration Reform and Control.* Washington, D.C.: Urban Institute Press, 1990.

Bennett, Marion T. *American Immigration Policies.* Washington, D.C.: Public Affairs Press, 1963.

Bernard, William S. *American Immigration Policy: A Reappraisal.* New York: Harper and Brothers, 1950.

Bogardus, Emory S. *Immigration and Race Attitudes.* Boston: D. C. Heath, 1928.

Bonacich, Edna, and John Modell. *The Economic Basis of Ethnic Solidarity: Small Business in the Japanese American Community.* Berkeley: University of California Press, 1980.

Bosworth, Allan R. *America's Concentration Camps.* New York: W. W. Norton and Co., 1967.

California State Senate. *Chinese Immigration: Its Social, Moral, and Political Effect.* Sacramento, Calif.: State Office, 1878.

Campbell, Persia Crawford. *Chinese Coolie Emigration to Countries within the British Empire*. London: P. S. King and Sons, Ltd., 1923.

Chan, Sucheng, ed. *Entry Denied: Exclusion and the Chinese Community in America, 1882–1943*. Philadelphia, Pa.: Temple University Press, 1991.

Chandrasekhar, S. *From India to America*. La Jolla, Calif.: A Population Review Book, 1982.

Chen, Jack. *The Chinese of America*. New York: Harper & Row, 1980.

Cheng, Lucie, and Edna Bonacich, eds. *Labor Immigration under Capitalism: Asian Workers in the United States before World War II*. Berkeley: University of California Press, 1984.

Choy, Bong-Youn. *Koreans in America*. Chicago: Nelson Hall, 1979.

Chui, Ping. *Chinese Labor in California, 1850–1880*. Madison: State Historical Society of Wisconsin, 1963.

Chuman, Frank F. *The Bamboo People: The Law and Japanese-Americans*. Del Mar, Calif.: Publisher's Inc., 1976.

Consulate-General of Japan. *Documental History of Law Cases Affecting Japanese in the United States, 1916–1924*. 2 vols. San Francisco, 1925.

Coolidge, Mary R. *Chinese Immigration*. New York: Henry Holt, 1909.

Crouchett, Lorraine Jacobs. *Filipinos in California: From the Days of the Galleons to the Present*. El Cerrito, Calif.: Downey Place Publishing House, 1982.

Daniels, Roger. *Asian Americans: Chinese and Japanese in the United States since 1950*. Seattle: University of Washington Press, 1988.

———. *Coming to America: A History of Immigration and Ethnicity in American Life*. New York: HarperCollins, 1990.

———. *The Politics of Prejudice: The Anti-Japanese Movement in California and the Struggle for Japanese Exclusion*. New York: Atheneum, 1972.

Divine, Robert A. *American Immigration Policy, 1924–1952*. New Haven, Conn.: Yale University Press, 1957.

Dudley, W., ed. *Immigration: Opposing Viewpoints*. San Diego, Calif.: Greenhaven Press, Inc., 1990.

Esthus, Raymond A. *Theodore Roosevelt and Japan*. Seattle: University of Washington Press, 1966.

Fairbank, John King. *The United States and China*. Rev. ed. New York: Viking Press, 1955.

Fitzgerald, Keith A. "Immigration, the State, and the National Identity: The Development of United States Immigration Policy, 1880–1965." Ph.D. dissertation, Indiana University, 1987.

Garis, Roy L. *Immigration Restriction*. New York: Macmillan, 1927.

Gibson, Otis. *The Chinese in America*. Cincinnati: Hitchock and Walden, 1877.

Glick, Clarence E. *Sojourners and Settlers: Chinese Migrants in Hawaii*. Honolulu: University Press of Hawaii, 1980.

Hatamiya, Leslie T. *Righting a Wrong: Japanese Americans and the Passage of the Civil Liberties Act of 1988*. Stanford, Calif.: Stanford University Press, 1993.

Higham, John. *Strangers in the Land: Patterns of American Nativism, 1860–1925*. New Brunswick, N.J.: Rutgers University, 1955.

Hing, Bill Ong. *Making and Remaking Asian America Through Immigration Policy, 1850-1990*. Stanford, Calif.: Stanford University Press, 1993.

Hosokawa, Bill. *Nisei: The Quiet Americans*. New York: William Morrow and Co., 1969.

Huang, Tsen-ming. *The Legal Status of the Chinese Abroad*. Taipei, Taiwan: China Cultural Service, 1954.

Hundley, Norris, ed. *The Asian American: The Historical Experience*. Santa Barbara, Calif.: ABC-Clio Press, 1976.

Hune, Shirley. "The Issue of Chinese Immigration in the Federal Government, 1875–1882." Ph.D. dissertation, George Washington University, 1979.

Hutchinson, E. P. *Legislative History of American Immigration Policy, 1798–1965*. Philadelphia: University of Pennsylvania Press, 1981.

Ichihashi, Yamato. *Japanese in the United States: A Critical Study of the Problems of the Japanese Immigrants and Their Children*. Stanford, Calif.: Stanford University Press, 1932.

Irick, Robert L. *Ch'ing Policy toward the Coolie Trade, 1847–1878*. San Francisco: Chinese Materials Center, 1982.

Jaffe, E. A. "Passage of the McCarran-Walter Act in the Reiteration of American Immigration Policy." Ph.D. dissertation, Rutgers University, 1962.

Jensen, Joan M. *Passage from India; Asian Indian Immigrants in North America*. New Haven, Conn.: Yale University Press, 1988.

Kachi, Teruko Okada. *The Treaty of 1911 and the Immigration and Alien Land Law Issue between the United States and Japan, 1911–1913*. New York: Arno Press, 1978.

Kansas, Sidney. *Immigration and the Nationality Act*. New York: Immigration Publications, 1953.

Keely, Charles B. "The Immigration Act of 1965: A Study of the Relationship of Social Science Theory to Group Interest and Legislation." Ph.D. dissertation, Fordham University, 1970.

Kessler, J. B. "The Political Factors in California's Anti-Alien Land Legislation, 1912–1913." Ph.D. dissertation, Stanford University, 1958.

Kim, Hyung-chan, ed. *Asian Americans and the Supreme Court*. Westport, Conn.: Greenwood Press, 1992.

———, ed. *Dictionary of Asian American History*. Westport, Conn.: Greenwood Press, 1986.

———, ed. *The Korean Diaspora: Historical and Sociological Studies of Korean Immigration and Assimilation in North America*. Santa Barbara, Calif.: ABC-Clio Press, 1977.

Kimura, Yukiko. *Issei: Japanese Immigrants in Hawaii*. Honolulu: University of Hawaii Press, 1988.

Kitano, Harry H. L. *Japanese Americans: The Evolution of a Subculture*. Englewood Cliffs, N.J.: Prentice Hall, 1969.

Knoll, Tricia. *Becoming Americans: Asian Sojourners, Immigrants, and Refugees in the Western United States*. Portland, Ore.: Coast to Coast Books, 1982.

Konvitz, Milton R. *The Alien and the Asiatic in American Law*. Ithaca, N.Y.: Cornell University Press, 1946.

Kung, S. W. *Chinese in American Life*. Seattle: University of Washington Press, 1962.

LaBrack, B. *The Sikhs of Northern California, 1904–1975*. New York: AMS Press, 1988.

Lasker, Bruno. *Filipino Immigration*. Chicago: University of Chicago Press, 1931.

Lawyers Committee for Human Rights. *The Alien Blacklist: A Dangerous Legacy of the McCarthy Era*. New York: Lawyers Committee for Human Rights, 1990.

———. *The Implementation of the Refugee Acts of 1980: A Decade of Experience*. New York: Lawyers Committee for Human Rights, 1990.

Lee, Rose Hum. *The Chinese in the United States of America*. Hong Kong: Hong Kong University Press, 1960.

Lepore, H. "Exclusion by Prejudice: Anti-Japanese Discrimination in California and the Immigration Act of 1924." Ph.D. dissertation, Brigham Young University, 1973.

Li, Tien-Lu. *Congressional Policy of Chinese Immigration*. Nashville, Tenn.: Publishing House of the Methodist Episcopal Church, South, 1916.

Light, Ivan H. *Ethnic Enterprise in America: Business and Welfare among Chinese, Japanese and Blacks*. Berkeley: University of California Press, 1972.

McClellan, Robert. *The Heathen Chinese: A Study of American Attitudes toward China, 1890–1905*. Columbus: Ohio State University Press, 1971.

McKee, Delber L. *Chinese Exclusion versus the Open Door Policy, 1900–1906*. Detroit: Wayne State University, 1977.

McKenzie, R. D. *Oriental Exclusion*. Chicago: University of Chicago Press, 1928.

McLeod, W. H. *The Sikhs: History, Religion, and Society*. New York: Columbia University Press, 1991.

Melendy, H. Brett. *Asians in America: Filipinos, Koreans, and East Indians*. Boston: Twanye Publishers, 1977.

———. *The Oriental Americans*. Boston: Twayne Publishers, 1972.

Miller, Stuart Creighton. *The Unwelcome Immigrant: The American Image of the Chinese, 1785–1882*. Berkeley: University of California Press, 1965.

Misrow, Jogesh C. *East Indian Immigration on the Pacific Coast*. San Francisco: R&E Research Associates, 1971.

Montero, Darrel. *Vietnamese Americans: Patterns of Resettlement and Socioeconomic Adaptation in the United States*. Boulder, Colo.: Westview Press, 1979.

Nizami, Saeed Ahmad. "The Law of Immigration in the United States." Ph.D. dissertation, Southern Illinois University, 1968.

Patterson, Wayne. *The Korean Frontier in America: Immigration to Korea, 1896–1910*. Honolulu: University of Hawaii Press, 1988.

Pearlmutter, Philip. *Divided We Fall: A History of Ethnic, Religious, and Racial Prejudice in America*. Ames: Iowa State University Press, 1990.

Petersen, William. *Japanese Americans: Oppression and Success*. New York: Random House, 1971.

Riggs, Fred W. *Pressures on Congress: A Study of the Repeal of Chinese Exclusion*. New York: King's Crown Press, 1950.

Sandmeyer, Elmer Clarence. *The Anti-Chinese Movement in California.* Urbana: University of Illinois Press, 1939.

Saran, Paramatma, and Edwin Eames. *Asian Indian Experience in the United States.* Cambridge, Mass.: Schenkman Publishing Corp., 1985.

Saxton, Alexander. *The Indispensable Enemy: Labor and the Anti-Chinese Movement in California.* Berkeley: University of California Press, 1971.

Seward, George F. *Chinese Immigration: Its Social and Economic Aspects.* New York: Charles Scribner's Sons, 1881.

Simcox, David E. *U.S. Immigration in the 1980s.* Boulder, Colo.: Westview Press, 1988.

Stephenson, George M. *A History of American Immigration, 1820–1924.* New York: Russell and Russell, 1964.

Storti, Craig. *Incident at Bitter Creek: The Story of the Rock Springs Chinese Massacre.* Ames: Iowa State University Press, 1990.

Takaki, Ronald. *Strangers from a Different Shore: A History of Asian Americans.* Boston: Little, Brown and Company, 1989.

Tsai, Shih-shan, Henry. *China and the Overseas Chinese in the United States, 1868–1911.* Fayetteville: University of Arkansas Press, 1983.

Tsuneyoshi, Azusa. "Meiji Pioneers: The Early Japanese Immigrants to the American Far West and Southwest, 1880–1930." Ph.D. dissertation, Northern Arizona University, 1989.

Varma, Premdatta. "The Asian Indian Community's Struggle for Legal Equality in the United States, 1900–1946." Ph.D. dissertation, University of Cincinnati, 1989.

Waldinger, Roger D. *Through the Eye of a Needle: Immigrants and Enterprise in New York's Garment Trades.* New York: New York University Press, 1986.

Wang, Peter Heywood. "Legislating 'Normalcy': The Immigration Act of 1924." Ph.D. dissertation, University of California, Riverside, 1971.

Williams, Frederick Wells. *Anson Burlingame and the First Chinese Mission to Foreign Powers.* New York: Charles Scribner's Sons, 1912.

Wilson, Robert A., and Bill Hosokawa. *East to America: A History of the Japanese in the United States.* New York: William Morrow and Co., 1980.

Wollenberg, Charles. *All Deliberate Speed: Segregation and Exclusion in California Schools, 1855–1975.* Berkeley: University of California Press, 1976.

Wright, Claudia F. A. "Legitimation by the Supreme Courts of Canada and the United States: A Case Study of Japanese Exclusion." Ph.D. dissertation, Claremont Graduate School, 1973.

Yans-McLaughlin, Virginia, ed. *Immigration Reconsidered.* New York: Oxford University Press, 1990.

Zo, Kil Young. *Chinese Emigration into the United States, 1850–1880.* New York: Arno Press, 1978.

Index

judicial conservation, 68; political orientation of Justices, 68; social background of Justices, 69; socialization of Justices, 68
Suspension of Chinese immigration, 61
Sutherland, George, 120, 121, 122
Swann v. Charlotte-Mecklenburg Board of Education, 169

Taft, William H., 132, 169
Takahashi Torao, 130
Takahashi v. Fish and Game Commission et al., 130
Tang Tun v. Edsell, Chinese-Inspector, 91
Tenth Amendment, delegation of powers to the government, 84
Terrace v. Thompson, 126, 127
Theories: of Nordic superiority, 112; of the power of a sovereign nation, 82; racial conflict, 60; of sovereignty, 83
Thesis, California, 3, 41
Thompson, Smith, 38
Thornley, William H., 76, 77
Tobacco: British market, 18; as cash crop, 18; cultivation, 18, 24
Toyota v. U.S., 122
Trading with Enemy Act, 133
Treaties: of 1895, violation of, 102; of February 21, 1911, violation of, 127; of Tientsin, June 18, 1858, 52
Treaty of Commerce and Navigation: of November 17, 1880, 119; of 1894, 78; of February 11, 1911, violation of, 128
Truman, Harry S., 146, 151, 161; administration, 146
Tseng Shao-ching, 90
Tsien Hsue-shen, 153
Turner, Frederick Jackson, 2
Two-category system, 4; inclusion v. exclusion, 5, 8, 9; people's domain v. plural domain, 5, 8, 9, 23, 31, 38, 105, 139; superiority v. inferiority, 5, 8, 9

Tydings, Millard E., 117
Tydings-McDuffie Act of 1934, 114

United Nations, cooperation with, 130
U.S. Code: Section 801, 124; Section 1255, 165
U.S. v. Bhagat Singh Thind, 121
U.S. v. Curtiss-Wright Corporation, 75
U.S. v. Harris, 98
U.S. v. Hohri et al., 174
U.S. v. Jung Ah Lung, 72
U.S. v. Lee Yen Tai, 86
U.S. v. Sing Tuck, 89, 90

Van Reed, Eugene, 6, 52
Van Schaick, L. H., 95
Vetos: legislative, 167; legislative power of, 168; of one-house, 168; by President Arthur, 60; by President Hayes, 59; by President Hoover, 116; by President Taft, 104; by President Truman, 147
Vietnam War, 43, 163, 167
Vinson, Fred M., 125, 129
Virginia Company, 16, 17
Voluntary employer compliance, provisions for, 177
Voorhees, Donald, 173, 174

Wages and Hours Board, 145
Waite, Morrison R., 99
Wakamatsu Silk and Tea Colony, 6
Walsh, Richard J., 138
Walter, Francis E., 150
Wan Shing v. U.S., 75, 80
Wang Kan-chang, 153, 154
Wanghia Treaty, 1844, 44
War Relocation Authority, 134; appropriation made for, 138; leave procedure of, 137
Warren, Earl, 124, 156
Washburne, Elihu B., 51
Washington, George, 30, 31, 33, 36, 39
Webb, Ulysses S., 126, 127
Webb v. O'Brien, 127

ABOUT THE AUTHOR

HYUNG-CHAN KIM is Professor of Education and Asian American studies at Western Washington University in Bellingham. He is the author and editor of several books, including the *Dictionary of Asian American History* (Greenwood, 1986).